ROYAL INSTITUTE OF PHILOSOPHY LECTURES

VOLUME ELEVEN · 1976–77

HUMAN VALUES

ROYAL INSTITUTE OF PHILOSOPHY LECTURES

VOLUME ELEVEN · 1976-77

HUMAN
VALUES

Edited by

GODFREY VESEY

THE HARVESTER PRESS · SUSSEX

HUMANITIES PRESS INC. · NEW JERSEY

First published in 1978 by
THE HARVESTER PRESS LIMITED
Publisher: John Spiers
2 Stanford Terrace, Hassocks, Sussex

and in the USA by
HUMANITIES PRESS INC.
Atlantic Highlands, New Jersey 07716

British Library Cataloguing in Publication Data

Royal Institute of Philosophy
   Lectures.
   Vol. 11: 1976–77: Human values
   1. Philosophy, English—Addresses, essays,
   lectures
   I. Title II. Vesey, Godfrey III. Human
   values
   192'.08   BI111

   ISBN 0–85527–951–6

Library of Congress Cataloging in Publication Data

Main entry under title:

Human values.

   (Royal Institute of Philosophy lectures; v. 11,
1976–77)
   Includes bibliographical references and index.
   1. Ethics—Addresses, essays, lectures. 2. Social
ethics—Addresses, essays, lectures. I. Vesey, Godfrey
Norman Agmondisham. II. Series: Royal Institute of
Philosophy. Lectures; v. 11, 1976–77.
BJ1012.H84   1978   170   77–28237
ISBN 0–391–00746–7

Printed in Great Britain by
Latimer Trend & Company Ltd Plymouth

CONTENTS

FOREWORD

The subject-matter of ethics: In order to define Ethics, we must discover what is both common and peculiar to all undoubted ethical judgments; but this is not that they are concerned with human conduct, but that they are concerned with a certain predicate 'good' . . . This predicate is indefinable or simple . . . 'Good', then, denotes one unique simple object of thought among innumerable others; but this object has very commonly been identified with some other – a fallacy which may be called 'the naturalistic fallacy'.[1]

Thus G. E. Moore, seventy-five years ago, intentionally directed the thoughts of moral philosophers away from human conduct, and towards 'a certain predicate "good"'. He charged those who identified good with a *natural* object, such as happiness, of committing a fallacy, but yet provided no tenable answer to the question 'What is a *non*-natural object?'[2] So, unintentionally, he raised in other people's minds the prior question 'Does "good" denote an object at all?' His Cambridge colleague, C. D. Broad, spelt out the alternative: 'Or do sentences like "This is good", though grammatically similar to sentences like "This is yellow" which undoubtedly ascribe a certain characteristic to a subject, really need an entirely different kind of analysis? Is it not possible that the function of such sentences is to express or to stimulate certain kinds of emotion, or to command or forbid certain kinds of action, and not to state certain kinds of fact?'[3]

The theory that the function of sentences like 'This is good' is to express or to stimulate certain kinds of emotion is called 'emotivism'. The theory that their function is to command or forbid certain kinds of action is 'prescriptivism'. A substantial part of the recent history of moral philosophy has been the history of attempts to square various refinements of either emotivism or prescriptivism with our common-sense intuitions about the subject-matter of ethics.

In spite of having been involved in the making of an Open University television programme with the title 'What use is moral philosophy?',[4] a title which one would be unlikely to bestow if one thought the answer was 'Not much', I must confess to a certain disenchantment with the enterprise on which Moore launched us when he directed us away from human conduct and towards 'a certain predicate "good" '. It was in this mood of disenchantment with a major movement in moral philosophy that I planned a course of Royal Institute of Philosophy lectures in which the emphasis would not be on the abstract 'object of thought' goodness, or on some function that sentences containing the word 'good' are thought to perform, but on less abstract and linguistic matters. Moreover, I thought, the investigation should differ from Moore's in another way. Like Socrates, he sought what is 'common and peculiar' to the subject under discussion. But to consider only what is common and peculiar to humans is to ignore what is peculiar to a particular human. For certain purposes it is right to treat people as equals; but for others, such things as who they are in relation to ourselves (child, pupil, husband or wife), and what sort of people they are, with what past and what future planned, are the things that matter.

Dr. Elizabeth Newson, Joint Director of the Child Development Research Unit at the University of Nottingham, examines how 'a sense of personal worth' is established in a child by the child's parents exercising a degree of caring that goes beyond what could reasonably be expected if the child was not their own. In her account of what she calls 'the socialisation relationship' she says that even moments between parents and children which seem to isolate and crystallise issues 'are never based wholly in the present, but take account of the past and anti-

cipate the future'. I think this is true, and that she is right when
she says:

> What is typical and significant in the long-term relationship
> between parent and child is that every interchange, every
> minor or major conflict, has a *history of understandings (and
> misunderstandings)* which contribute to each partner's percep-
> tion of the incident. Thus no exchange between parent and
> child starts from scratch, as it were, but from the vantage
> point of their mutual negotiations up to this moment. In the
> protracted nature of the relationship is its potency.

The relationship's potency is for giving the child a belief in
'his own intrinsic worth, his own fundamental *considerability*'.
Children who have no sense and recognition of their own value,
Dr. Newson says, are defeated children. If a child does not have
a sense of intrinsic worth, she asks, 'how can he be motivated
to achieve his goals, or indeed to set himself goals at all?'

Because of the way it is established, a sense of one's own
worth cannot exist without a corresponding sense of the needs
of others. As someone like William McDougall might have said,
you cannot have a self-regarding sentiment without a complementary other-regarding sentiment. (Professor Findlay puts it
rather more strongly in his lecture in this volume.)

If Dr. Newson is right about this then I suppose that there is
some sort of psychological contradiction involved in the idea
of a person with a sense of his own intrinsic worth whose goals
are exclusively egoistic: the so-called 'rational egoist' is a
psychological impossibility. This provides a link with the paper
by Bernard Mayo, Professor of Philosophy at St. Andrews
University, for he attempts to show that personal integrity is
very much the same thing as moral integrity 'by taking as a test
case the rational egoist, for whom non-moral considerations are
supposed to be overriding, and showing that he is not merely
unacceptably, but inconceivably, defective'; and a stepping-
stone in his attempt is the thought that 'someone for whom
future situations are of no concern is radically "dissociated";
and someone for whom considerations for others are not considerations has also "come apart" in a bad way'.

Mayo's approach, of course, is not that of a research psychologist. It is that of a moral philosopher reflecting on the adequacy of Hare's proffered criteria for a judgement being a moral one. He is primarily concerned with the 'overridingness' criterion, that is, that moral principles cannot be overridden, they are superior to, or more authoritative than, other kinds of principle. After listing five difficulties with the view that overridingness, together with prescriptivity and universalisability, constitute sufficient conditions of morality, he suggests that we should stop asking what it is for one consideration to override another, and instead consider the agent *for whom* they are considerations. 'When we speak of certain considerations being dominant *for an individual*, the point is not that they dominate *other* considerations, but that they dominate *him*.' (A similar point is made in Susan Khin Zaw's paper, and is implicit in Hampshire's.) This means that we have to consider what it is for a person to be the one and only person he is. And here it is not just a person's past that matters. More importantly, Mayo says, he is constituted by what Bernard Williams calls his 'projects': 'A person's future is, in an important sense, *his* even more than his past is.' To a limited extent a person can disown his past, but he cannot disown his future. This is significant for consequentialist theories, such as utilitarianism:

> The Williams thesis claims that it would be glaringly unacceptable to require someone to abandon a 'project' of his at any moment, just in case the results coming in from the impersonal hedonic computer happen to swing that way. The project in question need not, of course, be a moral one; but it may be; and if it is, we have a *prima facie* case of lack of moral integrity required as a sacrifice at the utilitarian altar.

Mary Warnock, Senior Research Fellow of St. Hugh's College, Oxford, describes herself as 'a confessed perpetrator of the naturalistic fallacy', but she does not mean by it quite what Moore meant. Moore's use of the term was, in fact, a bit of an imposture. The fallacy in the naturalistic fallacy, he makes plain in Section 12 of *Principia Ethica*, is the fallacy of identifying the 'is' of predication with the 'is' of identity. It is the fallacy of inferring, from the proposition 'I am pleased', that 'I' am the same thing as 'having pleasure'. He calls it the naturalistic fallacy because he holds, *for other reasons*, that in all propositions like 'Pleasure is good', in which what comes before the 'is' is a natural object and what comes after it is an ethical one, the 'is' is not the 'is' of identity. It is a bit of an imposture because calling it 'the naturalistic fallacy' suggests to people who have not read *Principia Ethica* that the battle has been won on logical grounds, and that they need not consider the 'other reasons'.

Mrs. Warnock's naturalism is her allegiance to the view that 'feeling strongly about something, valuing it highly, is an inevitable consequence of the nature of human understanding'. Following Sartre, she argues that people would be incapable of deliberate action if they had not the power of conceiving possibilities, and of envisaging the unreal, this power being the faculty of imagination. It is imagination, also, which supplies the meaningfulness of experience. Hence the importance of a proper education of it.

There are contributors to this volume who would not dream of using words like 'eternal' and 'eternity'; there are others to whom the words seem to come quite naturally. P. Æ. Hutchings, Associate Professor of Philosophy at the University of Western Australia, is one of the latter. (Roy Holland is another.) Hutchings says that what distinguishes all love from lust is that 'it bears an impress of eternity'; and much of his paper is an explanation of what it is for it to do so. 'Love is at once *now* overwhelming, and with respect to subsequent "nows" essentially preemptive.' 'Faithfulness is the giving of that, due, time for love's unfolding.' The problem, of course, is what to say about the failing case. This is what Hutchings calls 'the sting in the paper's tail'.

Moore, I said, directed the thoughts of moral philosophers away from human conduct and towards 'a certain predicate "good" '. We saw how, in doing so, he unintentionally provoked a question about the *function* of sentences like 'This is good': 'Is it not possible that the function of such sentences is to express or to stimulate certain kinds of emotion, or to command or forbid certain kinds of action, and not to state certain kinds of fact?' I then remarked that a substantial part of the recent history of moral philosophy has been the history of attempts to square various refinements of either emotivism or prescriptivism with our common-sense intuitions about the subject-matter of ethics.

One of our common-sense intuitions is that there is a place for reasons and reasoning in practical matters. We talk of a person's reasons for doing something, and also of his reasons for thinking some action right or wrong. Does the functionalist approach to ethics lead us to give a distorted account of this? To talk of the functions of language is to talk of what is primarily inter-personal. Does the functionalist approach favour modelling our account of personal choice of action on inter-personal debate?

The emotivist might reply that the function of an ethical sentence is not merely to influence others, it is to express the speaker's emotion, his approval or disapproval of something. His reason for saying that some action is right is that he has a feeling of approval towards it; and feelings are personal, not inter-personal. Professor R. M. Hare, who is a prescriptivist and not an emotivist, has a short way with this: ' "I approve of A" is merely a more complicated and circumlocutory way of saying "A is right". It is not a statement, verifiable by observation, that I have a recognisable feeling or recurrent frame of mind; it is a value-judgement; if I ask "Do I approve of A?", my answer is a moral decision, not an observation of introspective fact.'[5] Hare himself, in his book *Freedom and Reason*, tries to show how a theory of moral reasoning can be founded on two logical properties of 'ought'-statements, their being prescriptive and their being universalisable. This puts the place of reasons and reasoning in practical matters firmly in the public domain. The question is: Is the inter-personal-debate model of personal choice true to what we find when our approach to human conduct is, so to speak, direct, and not inspired by a wish to defend a particular account of the function of ethical sentences?

In connection with this question it is interesting to compare the papers by Dr. Margaret Boden, Reader in Philosophy and Psychology at the University of Sussex, and Stuart Hampshire, Warden of Wadham College, Oxford. Dr. Boden remarks that 'the prescriptivist view of ethics characterises morality as a matter of proclaiming (and, preferably, following) specific priorities that should govern conduct', and argues that there are philosophically significant analogies between moral thinking so understood and the reasoning of sufficiently complicated computers. In saying this she is not arguing *against* the prescriptivist view of ethics, but *for* 'a basically mechanist view of the universe, and of human beings as creatures of it'.

Hampshire, on the other hand, argues against what he calls the 'computational morality' of the Cartesian or council-of-war model for the human act of choice. The computational moralists who pursue the ideal of an explicit weighing of arguments before moral decisions are made and opinions formed, he says, 'in fact arrive at a pretence and are deceived by their own abstractions'. They model the rationality of the act of choice on the rationality of a public debate. But the rationality of the ideally rational man is as much perceptiveness as power of argument. There is, he says, nothing exceptional or anomalous in the reasons for our conclusions, whether practical or theoretical, not being present to consciousness at the time, and not being accessible to consciousness afterwards. As Aristotle put it, the agent must have the virtues within him.

I think there is more to be said on this on both sides. It is not a purely academic issue, for much sometimes hangs on our understanding of what it is to be a rational human agent – for example, when someone's defence against a charge of murder is that of 'irresistible impulse'. In her paper ' "Irresistible Impulse" and Moral Responsibility' Susan Khin Zaw, Lecturer in Philosophy at the Open University, tries to discredit 'a picture of the rational human agent as not a subject but a helpless Newtonian object whirled along by his desires, powerful forces whose strength and direction determine his apparent actions'. It is not that an 'irresistible impulse' is irresistible in the way in which a physical impulse, such as a hearty shove in the back, is irresistible. The impulse does not come from outside the agent; it is his own impulse. Nor is its irresistibility a matter of its being strong or overwhelming. His desire is irresistible in that he has no reason for it, and hence there is no reasoning to be argued against: he merely acts in pursuit of the end, without attempting justification and impervious to deliberation about it as an end. The desire is irresistible because it does not express itself in the form of practical reasoning, and so there is nothing to resist it with. But this does not mean that it is not the agent's own impulse.

I suspect that Dr. Boden is resourceful enough to find an analogue in computational morality for the distinction between an impulse which is irresistible but the agent's own, and one which is irresistible but comes from outside the agent. But could even the most intelligent computer be programmed to recognise absolute goodness, that is, goodness which we recognise by the light it itself provides, and in connection with which it is natural to introduce the idea of that which is eternal in a human being, namely the soul? Roy Holland, Professor of Philosophy at the University of Leeds, affirms that in the absence of absolute conceptions there can be nothing profound in ethics. He mentions as one of a number of possible sources of scepticism about absolute conceptions the philosophical training which disposes people to look to the performative element of discourse for solutions to problems about absolute senses of words. People so trained, he says, will see the idea of the reality of absolute value as a shadow cast by prescriptiveness and universalisability.

Perhaps the capacity to recognise absolute values is too rare for us to speak of a common-sense intuition about it. And yet there is an intuitive feeling among the philosophically unaffected that is affronted when philosophers say that moral values are subjective. There was mention of this at the end of the television programme to which I referred earlier. The speakers are Professor Hare and Dr. Anthony Kenny.

HARE . . . If I tell you that I think that torturing is always wrong, you get some information about what I think about torturing. The second thing that happens, however, is different. What I have conveyed to you, and what, if you agree with me, you will think, will be that torturing is wrong, which is something prescriptive.

KENNY But I don't get any information about any objective moral values, and I think that this is what some of your critics have had in mind when they say that your view annihilates moral values. You denied that it does this but it seems to me that you do annihilate moral values in the same sense as somebody annihilates Santa Claus when he tells a child that Santa Claus doesn't exist.

HARE Of course, it would be an awful pity to annihilate Santa Claus if Santa Claus was doing any good, but if either he didn't exist or he wasn't doing any good, or if the belief in him might have been of positive harm, then it wouldn't be a bad thing that people should learn that he doesn't exist and learn to get on without him.

I am struck by this, and by the fact that J. L. Mackie devotes the first and longest chapter of his recent Penguin book, *Ethics*, to 'The subjectivity of values'. I am prompted to ask the Wittgensteinian question: What can it mean to say that people are wrong (or right, for that matter) about an entire realm of being or discourse (in this case, the realm of moral values)?

This is not an easy question. One way of approaching it is via a critique of the Lockean empiricist dogma that for ideas not to be fictitious or invented is for them to have 'a foundation in nature', the criterion of an idea's having a foundation in nature being that it is *causally produced* by something in nature.[7] Perhaps this dogma is somewhere at the back of Mackie's subjectivism. To judge from his book *Problems from Locke*, he is broadly in agreement with Locke on the language and reality issue.

Another way of approaching it is via the following consideration. One can settle, by the use of the appropriate criteria, whether or not something *within* a realm exists, is real, is objective, or whatever. But what can it mean, without any criteria, to say this of the entire realm? One can do so only by treating

another realm as a paradigm. Kenny comes close to treating
the realm of people as a paradigm when he accuses Hare of
annihilating moral values *in the same sense* as somebody annihilates Santa Claus when he says Santa Claus does not exist.
Of course moral values do not exist in the same sense as existing
people exist. If they did they would be people. The common-
sense intuition is not the positive one that moral values *are* anything (people, or anything else that someone may favour as a
paradigm of existence, reality, objectivity, or whatever) but the
negative one that they *are not* illusory, or matters of taste, or any
of the other things that the term 'subjective' means in various
realms of being or discourse. Being a negative intuition it
emerges only when confronted with subjectivism, and can find
expression only in the not-further-explicable complaint that the
subjectivist has somehow impoverished the world.

There are points of resemblance in the substance, though not
the style, of Holland's paper and that of J. N. Findlay, Professor of Philosophy at Boston University. Both men eschew
what I called the functionalist approach to moral values. (As
Findlay puts it: 'Imperatives are secondary structures in value-
constitution; the primary structures are the ultimate objects of
necessary, rational pursuit and avoidance.') Both acknowledge
a debt to Plato. But Findlay acknowledges a further debt – to
Meinong. And it is in Meinongian terms that he discusses the
'objectivity' of moral values:

> For there to be values or disvalues for someone . . . it is
> essential that his interests should *colour* the things in which he
> is interested, should somehow flow over from the attitudinal
> into the objective order. Values and disvalues must be pre-
> sent 'out there', just as facts and probabilities and hypo-
> thetical outcomes are given as 'out there': they must con-
> tribute to the total phenomenological scene. . . . The dry
> world of neutral fact exists only for certain sorts of philo-
> sophers.

This, however, is by the way. Findlay's main concern is to
provide a high-altitude survey of all in the constitution of
human values that can safely be generated by our universalising

zest along with our sympathising and empathising sense of affinity with our fellows.

Holland concludes his paper by contrasting the ethics of absolute conceptions with consequentialism. He shapes his discussion round an example provided by Bernard Williams: A visitor arrives at a South American town to find a firing squad about to shoot twenty Indians as a reprisal for acts of protest against the government. The captain of the militia offers the visitor a 'guest's privilege' of shooting one Indian on the understanding that if he does so the rest will be set free, but if he does not, all twenty will be shot. There is no chance of the visitor's overwhelming the captain by force, so what should he do?

Holland speaks of 'the sense of outrage at being asked to contemplate Williams' example and other examples of a similar kind' and says: 'It is a kind of *temptation*: that is what the revulsion is about and if anyone does not feel it I would suppose that for him the examples provide material to be ingested like data by a computer.'

The sort of consequentialist considerations which Holland finds abhorrent are to the fore in the paper 'Assessing the value of saving lives' by Jonathan Glover, Fellow and Tutor in Philosophy at New College, Oxford. Perhaps the main thing that emerges is that we have not established criteria to enable us to answer the sort of questions of priority that arise. Why not? Is it possible that there is an intuition, even in the least religious of us, that we ought not to take certain responsibilities upon ourselves?

GODFREY VESEY

Honorary Director
The Royal Institute of Philosophy

Professor of Philosophy
The Open University

NOTES

[1] G. E. Moore, *Principia Ethica*, Cambridge University Press, 1903, Table of Contents, Ch. 1, Sections 1, 2, 6, 7, 10.

² He provided an answer, but it was not tenable. In fact he later described it as 'utterly silly and preposterous'. (P. A. Schilpp (ed.), *The Philosophy of G. E. Moore*, Evanston and Chicago: Northwestern University, 1942, p. 582.)

³ Schilpp (ed.), *The Philosophy of G. E. Moore*, p. 58.

⁴ The script is in Godfrey Vesey (ed.), *Philosophy in the Open*, Milton Keynes: The Open University Press, 1974.

⁵ R. M. Hare, *The Language of Morals*, Oxford University Press, 1952, pp. 6–7.

⁶ Godfrey Vesey (ed.), *Philosophy in the Open*, pp. 52–3.

⁷ John Locke, *An Essay Concerning Human Understanding*, 1690, Bk 2, Ch. 30, Sections 1–2.

1

UNREASONABLE CARE: THE ESTABLISHMENT OF SELFHOOD

Elizabeth Newson

Out of my normal context, and separated from my usual reference groups, perhaps I need first of all to explain the background from which I speak. As a developmental psychologist whose main research interests are to do with child rearing in the various social environments in which it takes place,[1] I have been particularly concerned with the long-term dialogues (verbal and non-verbal) that go on between parents and children, in the course of which they commonly come to certain understandings about their mutual tolerances and intolerances, and learn to live together with some regard to these limits. I stress the intersubjective nature of these understandings because I take it as axiomatic that children bring up their parents in the course of parents bringing up their children, even though parents are more powerful in physical terms and marginally more powerful in psychological terms. Secondly, as a child psychologist working clinically with parents and handicapped or problem children, I am also interested in another kind of dialogue: that which takes place between parents and professionals *with the child as focus*. I am concerned to find ways of making this dialogue as effective as possible, in particular by recognising the differences that inform parental and professional approaches to our common focus, and then using these differences to enable a complementary partnership that builds upon the advantages of each.[2]

I have been asked to explore in this paper the concept of 'unreasonable care'; and this, too, needs explaining. The concept evolved out of a suggestion of mine[3] that the crucial characteristic of the parental role is its *partiality* for the individual child; and I went on to propose that a developing personality *needs* to perceive itself as especially valuable to somebody: 'needs to know that to someone it matters more than other children; that someone will go to unreasonable lengths, not just reasonable ones, for its sake'. Hence the notion of 'unreasonable care' as something which parents give to their children out of their emotional involvement with them, but which communities and institutions inevitably find it difficult to simulate. 'The best that community care can offer a child is *im*partiality – to be *fair* to every child in its care' (*ibid.*). Whether this is enough for a child is one question which we have to ask; to answer it effectively, we need to consider just what 'unreasonable care' is all about.

HANDICAPPED CHILDREN

Although in my research unit we have been following the rearing of 700 normal children from birth onward, it was not until we started to undertake comparative studies of the upbringing of handicapped children that we articulated the notion of unreasonable care. Indeed this is one of the major advantages of comparative studies: to turn to handicap, after being steeped in the normal, first makes one most conscious of the differences, but then brings one back much more sharply and productively to the parallels. It is worth following the same route here, while keeping in mind that we are focusing on parental roles generally rather than on handicap in particular.

Although services for handicapped children are improving rapidly, largely as a result of growing communication between parents and professionals, they are still far from perfect. Parents to whom a handicapped child is born can find themselves in an unknown world, in which the shock of what has happened to them is compounded by the shock of finding that, far from receiving full support from the community, they and their child are apparently seen as untidy nuisances. Rod Ballard, father of a child with Down's syndrome, writes: 'some of us are filled with a black despair which comes from the failure of professional people to be honest with us about our situation'.[4] Ballard is a university sociologist, and his contribution as a parent to a medical book on handicap is an indication of the new strength of parents as a vocal consumer group; but if he, as a high-status professional himself, is in despair about the dialogue between parents and professionals, how much more so will be those who are unused to making themselves heard in any role? This is the semi-literate unemployed father of an autistic girl arguing with me about whether he should keep her hospital appointments.

> You don't know what it's like for common people like us, you know, with those high-ups in the hospital and the education and places. They won't listen to you, you know. They look at you as if you was stupid. They got this little smile on their face and they don't listen. They don't reckon you've got anything to tell them about your child – they don't tell you anything, an' all. Couple of hours getting there and waiting around, then in and out in three minutes – there's always three or four nurses waiting to throw you out – get rid of you. So what I'm saying is, what's the use of going – what's the point?

Sheila Hewett, who studied the upbringing of 180 cerebral palsied children under eight years, talks about parents feeling that 'doctors (and other professional people) are opponents rather than allies, to be approached with a mixture of caution and militance rather than confidence';[5] and this was a feeling which had come from bitter experience.

Sometimes the major problems seem to arise in parents' contacts with administrators. Partly this is because local authorities work to budgets like the rest of us, and there is never quite as much money as one would wish to provide a really good service for all children in need of it: some inertia in the system may actually be necessary in order to balance the books, and though it will not be publicly admitted that full services are provided only grudgingly and to those who demand most loudly and persistently, this may well be the real situation. The father of a cerebral palsied girl sums it up like this:

> This is a lot of the trouble with children of this type. If the parent is like me, damned awkward, then you get what you want and your child gets somewhere. But if you're the normal run of people who accept the fact that authority is authority and 'this must be done in a certain way and we accept patiently that we must wait' – then they get nowhere fast. There's only one way to get anywhere if you've got kiddies like Maureen and that's to bang on the table. (*Ibid.*)

Administrative authority is particularly difficult for parents to deal with because it tends to be faceless, and may in fact deliberately shelter behind that facelessness when evading its responsibilities to individuals. Members of the so-called 'helping professions' are not faceless, and indeed we usually expect to develop some kind of personal relationship with our clients; none the less, we too may evolve defensive ways of escaping from personal and painful responsibility: rigid appointment systems, staff hierarchies, unexplained technical jargon. Parents are often the more bitter when they find that an apparent concern is not followed through. For example, if parents have gone through a stressful period of consultations and tests with their handicapped child, and the consultant finally delegates to his registrar the job of explaining the diagnosis, they are likely to feel snubbed and rejected: that a traumatic moment in their lives has been made little of. Similarly, once their child has been diagnosed, parents often feel that they have been abandoned and are of no further professional interest to anyone: in a limbo of knowing the name of their child's condition, but not knowing what to do about it, or *whether* there is anything they can do about it. Sometimes parents suspect a lack of really helpful knowledge behind the vaguely kind assurances, and sometimes they may well be right. 'He said to come back to him if we had any problems,' said the mother of an autistic five-year-old, speaking of the educational psychologist, 'and we did try, but we could never get past his secretary, so I don't know whether he meant it. But we asked him quite a few questions when he first told us she was autistic – how we should handle her and that – whether we should smack her – but he never really answered us.'

Some children have complicated handicaps or multiple handicaps in which one element may be more straightforward than another: but the clearest element to the professional may not be the most significant for the child's total condition. The parents of a three-year-old mentally handicapped boy who also had fits found that their paediatrician always focused on the medical management of the fits and never mentioned the question of his severe mental retardation and what might be the prognosis for him; unfortunately, they saw it as the paediatrician's role to initiate this discussion, and did not like to press the issue to someone who plainly seemed embarrassed about it. The ironic result of this failure to communicate was that the paediatrician believed them to be unrealistic parents who could not accept their child's retardation, which in fact they rightly understood as his and their central problem. Another child was originally referred to medical attention at two and a half because she was not developing speech; between the referral and her first appointment she had a convulsion, the first of what was to be a total of three. This changed the nature of the case in medical eyes: interest centred upon possible epilepsy, and her need to develop language, still seen as primary by the parents who were daily trying to communicate with her, was forgotten. The fits were easily controlled, but otherwise nothing further was done; and at five she entered a school for retarded children, still without speech, though she was beginning to use a private sign language to her father. From time to time she saw the psychologist who noted that she was 'a puzzle' and that her difficulties now seemed to have 'an emotional component'. She was not diagnosed as aphasic until she was eight, and was then rejected by the only available school for aphasic children on the grounds that (a) she had emotional problems, (b) she had had fits at one time, and (c) she had attended a school for retarded children, *therefore* her intellectual status was suspect.

What these examples (and so many others, unfortunately) have in common is that the professionals involved have an intermittent responsibility for a number of children – a responsibility which they can shelve between consultations – whereas the parents have a continuous responsibility for their own. Continuous responsibility has the effect of focusing parents on the question that most needs to be asked if anything useful is to be done for their child (and it is the question that professionals too should constantly ask themselves): *'so what?'*. 'My child is autistic . . . or spastic . . . or deaf . . . or retarded: so, what? What are the implications? What can we expect from him? What can we do to help him? Where do we go from here?'

Parents of handicapped children are faced every day of their lives with the whole child in all his complexity and have to cope with him as a person as best they may. The interminable crisis of handicap is their life; the question 'so what?' is reiterated in practical terms in all their dealings with the child. They do not have the luxury of dismissing the child as 'a puzzle' with 'emotional components', or giving him a tidy diagnostic label and forgetting about him until the next appointment; to them, quite rightly, an assessment of the child is not an end in itself, but a new piece of information that could underpin their effectiveness in helping the child, if only they knew how to use it. They expect to be shown how to use it properly, and to see professionals using it. Too often their expectations are frustrated.

It is also true that professionals, out of their experience of many different handicapped children, can come to work on the basis of what they often call 'reality' but which is actually a lowest common denominator. Having a lowest common denominator in mind can make them content with a wait-and-see policy that subjects the child to half-an-hour's scrutiny, a few notes added to his file and another appointment in three months' time. The child's parents, for very good reasons, are seldom content to wait and see. Their ideas of the possible best and worst of their child's potential are based, not on a lowest common denominator of many children, but on continuous and intimate experience of *this* child. Their faith in the half-hour sample of the child as perceived by the professional is not very great, even if it was in fact an average sample; because they know that the child has good days and bad days, and they correctly think that the professional ought to be aware of the whole range of the child's behaviour if he is to advise them effectively. They believe that they need help to cope with the worst behaviour, and counselling in order to build on the best behaviour, so that the child's best performance now may become his average as soon as possible; and they want that help now, not in several months' time. Just as they expect to take an active part in bringing up their normal children and meeting their problems as they arise, so they expect to tackle the problems of the handicapped child once they know what they are: they are interventionists by all the traditions of their parental role. We must remember, too, that parents are usually well ahead of professionals on the time scale, in that they are likely to have suspected and worried over the possible handicap for some time before they sought professional opinion.

Professionals themselves are becoming more aware, with recent research, that parents' instincts are right, that earlier intervention is helpful in most handicaps and essential for some: and that, while sometimes it may be necessary to wait and see before a firm prognosis can be made, it is almost always possible at least to say 'but meanwhile we can make a start here . . .'. Yet parents of handicapped children are still conscious of having to go to 'unreasonable lengths' for the child, not just in terms of extra time and trouble to meet the handicap, but in pushing against the advisers who only work to rule: to quote one more mother, of a cerebral palsied child:

> I speak my mind, I've learned that, all these years of struggling with her and seeing different doctors – you know – and having to fight for the child all the time, which you *do* have to do. Because she can't fight for herself, therefore you have to do it. (*Ibid.*)

INVOLVEMENT AND PERSPECTIVE

Handicapped children introduce dramatic stress into parenthood; but the fighting spirit that these parents find so necessary comes from their deeply personal involvement with their child –

bone of their bone, flesh of their flesh – and such involvement is typical of parents generally, whether or not their child needs to be fought for. Probably rather few young parents fully anticipate the power of this involvement before they come to feel it; but in it lies both their strength and their vulnerability. Parents are vulnerable in that the ability of the child to 'get under their skin' transcends anything they are likely to have experienced previously. 'I didn't know I'd *got* a temper until I had Lawrence,' said one mother; and many others echo her recognition that behaviour which she could cope with calmly in other people's children, in her own strikes directly at her personal self-esteem. The colicky baby, who cries untiringly and cannot be comforted, reiterates to his mother the message that she has failed him in her basic mothering role of comforter and protector as clearly as if he had actually said 'Look, I'm still crying, you're a bad mother.' The child who has a tantrum in a shop, refuses his dinner when on a family visit to acquaintances, or 'shows off', uses 'rude' words or behaves 'cheekily' in front of neighbours (by whatever the mother's criterion of *showing off, rude* or *cheeky* may be) proclaims to the world that his parents are ineffective at bringing up children: that they have (significant word) 'spoilt' him. Over seventeen years of talking to mothers and fathers about issues in child rearing, we have been constantly reminded that children are seen as living testimonials to their parents, by the words and phrases that continually recur in these conversations: 'she shows me up'; 'he lets me down'; 'making you look a fool'; 'do you credit'; 'feel proud of him'. The vulnerability that such total involvement of the ego brings is compounded by the fact that parents cannot easily escape, either from the individual situations which I have described, or from the long-term responsibility of continuing to cope with a series of such situations and with the lasting relationship that they both illustrate and determine.

The assumed permanence of the parental role brings a long-term perspective to issues of child-rearing which is of major importance both in defining parenthood and in distinguishing it from other adult contacts with children. The knowledge that they bear lasting responsibility for the child includes the imperative to look ahead, to take the long-term view, to think explicitly about the effects in future time of what they do now. Much sociological and psychological research of the sixties and seventies has shown that parents' styles and principles of child discipline vary widely, and that in particular middle-class parents' styles emphasise the child's *continued* responsibility for his actions while working-class parents transmit a more short-term 'pay for what you've done and get away with what you can' philosophy; and our own work has contributed towards these ideas. However, it is important to understand that parents of different class groups do *not* differ in their most basic aim: to socialise the child by means of their behaviour towards him. Parents of every social class have in common that their disciplinary attempts are *long-term intended*, even though the chosen techniques of some are characteristically short-term effective.

Parents in fact go about their parenthood on the assumption that the child is indeed father of the man; and this belief is a potent source of apprehensiveness. It is particularly striking in their approach to questions of control, where mothers are continually exercised by the problem 'If I let this go now, what will be the effect in time to come?'; but it is also very apparent in parents' anxiety about children's educational progress during the second and third years of primary school, an anxiety almost entirely derived from the belief that progress at this age has both prognostic and causative significance: if they felt that time lost now could be easily retrieved, nothing would matter beyond the child's happy adjustment. Parents on the whole work on a Kellyan basis: 'There is a continuing movement toward the anticipation of events, rather than a series of barters for temporal satisfactions, and this movement is the essence of life itself.'[6]

At the same time they find it difficult to believe in Kelly's reassurance that 'No-one needs to be the victim of his biography'. It is precisely because they fear that their children will become victims of their biographies that they try to write into the early chapters a scenario which they hope will build up to a successful *dénouement*.

The long-term perspective is so central to child rearing that it seems worth illustrating it by reference to parents' own words before going on to consider its consequences. The first example is a working-class mother worrying over her seven-year-old's progress at school:

> It's *not* a good school. I think they take far too long over teaching them to read; I mean, they're just playing, right up to the juniors. I had a word with the headmistress about it, I said 'Don't you think she should be able to read by now? All this playing about isn't doing her any good.' But she said 'Well, it's the new education, my dear – it's not like it was in *your* day!' Well, I'm a *nit* – I *hated* school – but I'm sure I could read at that age, and when I think that Carolyn might be a worse nit than I am . . . ! I mean, now the headmistress showed me a piece of embroidery; she said 'Now a child's done that, and this is what our methods do – every child has its own good points, and our methods *bring out* that good point.' Well, that frightened me all the more – I thought, what's the good of it if the only thing they can do is *sew*? I mean, I know she didn't mean it like that, but. . . .

The six mothers who follow are all talking about their attitudes to discipline and control. The first is referring to a four-year-old child, the others to seven-year-olds.

Foreman's wife:
(Do you think smacking does him any good?) Sometimes I begin to wonder. I think it does *later on*, if you know what I mean. At this age I don't think it's doing a lot of good. But I think that you're kind of moulding them now, and it's sinking in, so that a bit later on . . . I mean, if I thought that when he were about seven or eight he were going to back-chat me like he does now, and I thought smacking would stop that, I'd half-kill him *now*, you know what I mean?

Newsagent's wife:
He's got very much a mind of his own – but it's no good expecting an adult with a mind of his own if you have a wishy-washy child, you just can't. If he's going to grow up

with his 'yes' being 'yes' and his 'no' being 'no', he's going to have a mind of his own when he's young, isn't he?

Gardener's wife:
If I didn't stop them, they'd be the gaffers of me all the while . . . so you might as well give them a good hiding and done with it . . . Well, I think if they never have a good hiding they think they can get away with a lot when they get older, now they do. We had good hidings, yet we never did them things what's going off today, did we?

Executive's wife:
I think it's much better to try and reason with them, even if it takes much longer; because after all, when they've been smacked the smack is gone, and they are more likely to forget what it's even for; whereas things you *say* are likely to come back in their minds a little bit.

Painter's wife:
A smack now is better than prison later.

Machine operator's wife:
I don't try to smack 'em an awful lot. In a way it's a difficult age, seven – if you hit 'em too much you can turn them the wrong way, but if you *don't* hit 'em you can turn them the wrong way as well, you see – you've got to try in between. I have to try and use my intelligence, if I've got any, and try and work it out myself.

There appear to me to be three major consequences of the long-term perspective that characterises parental care, and I should like to explore each separately. The first is the possibility of evolutionary negotiation between parent and child. The second concerns assignment of responsibility for effectiveness. The third is the tolerance of inconvenient idiosyncrasy.

EVOLUTIONARY NEGOTIATION

In a socialisation relationship covering a time-span of something like sixteen or seventeen years, there is time to work subtly and slowly, building a complex structure of shared interpersonal experience upon a core of permanence. Parents' attempts to come to terms with their children and bring their children to terms with them are indeed very unlike the notion of 'a series of barters for temporal satisfactions' which Kelly rejects as a model for personality growth; for while there will be moments between parents and children which seem to isolate and crystallise issues, and in which bartering, explicit or implicit, certainly takes place, even these points of focus or crisis are never based wholly in the present, but take account of the past and anticipate the future.

Behaviour between people socialises the participants (of whatever age) to the extent that each person's actions are evaluated by the other and the evaluation is perceived by both. Because parents expect to have a socialising role towards their children, they tend to communicate rather more evaluative responses to their children's behaviour than other adults would do to the same children; but children also communicate evaluative responses to their parents, even though they are not necessarily conscious of a socialising role towards them. What is typical and significant in the long-term relationship between parent and child is that every interchange, every minor or major conflict, has a *history of understandings* (*and misunderstandings*) which contribute to each partner's perception of the incident. Thus no exchange between parent and child starts from scratch, as it were, but from the vantage point of their mutual negotiations up to this moment. In the protracted nature of the relationship is its potency.

Let me give just two illustrations of this from parents' transcripts; they contrast because the first incident described is dramatic and the second comparatively trifling, yet both seem to me to vibrate with the power of the relationship's history. The first mother, a mature student, is talking about her six-year-old daughter.

Recently I smacked Katharine, and she said 'How *dare* you!' – you just didn't *do* this. It's not a punishment, it's an indignity. I felt terrible. . . . I have felt this, as a matter of fact, for some time; but it was this recent occasion with

Katharine where she verbalised this, so indignantly and so precisely, that I felt, This is *right*.

On the face of it, it is the mother who at this moment is being socialised by her child's evaluation of her action; yet if we examine the child's statement it is clear that the sense of outrage which she expresses can only have come out of a history of having her dignity treated with greater respect than this. The negotiation of the present moment is thus informed and enabled by a long past. Other mothers have described similar experiences of being socialised into less violent behaviour by their child's reaction to a smack; but the child who flinches at his mother's approach and cries out 'not again, Mummy', though he shocks his mother equally effectively, does so from a very different shared understanding.

Superficially, the incident that follows seems trivial, although as a statement it is remarkable for the mother's ability to follow through and describe the subtly developing processes of reasoning that go to make up one deliberate socialising sequence. What is important here is the way in which this mother, a skilled manual worker's wife, takes up her seven-year-old's peccadillo and gives it significance by setting it in a moral framework for the child's consideration; but she is only able to do this because she already has a history of understanding with her daughter, and she only wishes to do it because of her sense of the growth of future understandings. Notice how the mother uses non-verbal messages – 'I just kept sewing' – 'I looked at her' – in conjunction with words, and how the potency of the exchange is emphasised by its low key.

This soft ice-cream van came round, and she was stood here – she'd just come home from school; and I said 'Ooh, a soft ice-cream', I said, 'Go and get two cornets quickly' – and off she went. She came back with a Zoom for herself and a choc-ice for me, and she said 'Here you are, I've brought you a choc-ice'. I said, 'No, I don't *want* that, Edwina, I would have sent you to the shop for that'; I said 'I just wanted this *soft* ice-cream'. I says 'Well, you've bought it, well you can eat it now'. I wasn't that upset, but I pretended, cause I thought, she's not gone for what she was *sent* for, you see. And I said 'I just *fancied* some of the soft ice-cream'. I says, 'Well, *you* have it now, Mum doesn't want it, so go and stick it in the fridge till you've eaten your own Zoom thing, and have that as well'. So she walked away, never said a word; and I thought Aye, and you don't care, Edwina, you don't – you know? So off she went; and she came back, ooh, a few minutes after, and she says, 'Well, it's ice-cream, isn't it?' I says 'Yes, but that's not the *point*, Edwina, Mum wanted the soft ice-cream'. I said, 'You could have gone across to the *shops* and got the other – and the point is, when I send you for a thing, you get what I say and not what you think you'll get'. Well, off she disappeared again, and I thought, well, not an 'I'm sorry, Mum' or anything: so I thought, *no*, I'm *not* going to say 'It's only ice-cream, never mind, Edwina' – I'm just going to see. So after a bit she came back – and I just kept sewing, you know, didn't take any notice – and she said 'Mummy, I'm sorry I didn't bring you that. . . .' I said 'Sorry doesn't always do, Edwina, you must try and do as you are told to do, as far as you possibly can'. She said, 'Well, are you going to eat it?' So I looked at her, and I thought, well, I really think she's learned a little lesson, you know, and maybe next time she *will* do as she's asked. So I said 'All right, go and fetch it' – and when she came back she nearly burst into tears, and she said 'I *am* sorry, Mum'. And she said, 'Never mind, we've ended up laughing, haven't we, Mum?' – and then she was all right. But I thought, well, I've carried it through just to see how she *would* react to this thing.

The fact that both participants know that the dialogue is a continuing one means that, although from time to time new demands will be made and new agreements or compromises reached, the urgency is seldom immediate. There is thus room for an adaptation and accommodation of one to another which takes some account of idiosyncratic priorities. Because the relationship stretches ahead, there is little need to state positions and principles too uncompromisingly at an early stage, and therefore far more opportunity for gradual negotiation to fit circumstance. Rather than having rules imposed upon him, the child can have some image of himself as a contributor to their evolution, even though they may not entirely please him.

RESPONSIBILITY FOR EFFECTIVENESS

On the other hand, however, the evolutionary opportunities given by a protracted time-scale are also limited by the permanence of responsibility for the child's socialisation: that is, for parents this responsibility will not be removed by time passing. It is characteristic of professionals' responsibilities for children that they are normally brought to a close within a relatively short and predictable time: the school year comes to an end, the child is referred on to a different professional specialism, perhaps one or other moves away from the area. Thus, although professionals may feel a strong sense of responsibility to devote their best efforts to their clients during professional contact with them, this contact will not actually extend to having to live with the results. If the teacher has tried hard to teach the child to read (within what can be reasonably expected of her during the working day); if the nurse has done her best to respond to the child's anxieties (again, within what can be reasonably expected of her during the working day): then their professional consciences are clear, and the fact that the child still cannot read at nine, or has had regular nightmares ever since he came out of hospital, need not perturb them. Parents, however, are much more highly committed to effectiveness in what they try to achieve with their children, for while they can tolerate delay and divergence, they know that in the end real failure (on whatever criterion) will rebound on themselves, both in terms of blame and in terms of having to cope with the consequences. Thus parents quite literally ask themselves, 'What if he gets to fifteen or sixteen, and he's *still* wetting his bed . . . or telling lies . . . or not washing . . . or hitting out in temper . . . or too shy to talk to people . . . or illiterate? He'll be in real trouble then, and it'll be our fault.' It is with this in mind that, when they feel that things are

B

going wrong for the child, parents go to unreasonable lengths to take action which they hope might be effective. In doing so, sometimes life is made uncomfortable and difficult for the family as a whole.

This brings up one aspect of the issue of 'impartiality' which I touched on at the beginning of this paper, when I suggested that the partiality of parents for their own children is a crucial benefit of parenthood, to be contrasted with the impartiality that community or institutional care strives for. Now I would not want to imply that parents do not value impartial behaviour towards groups of children. They certainly expect it of other adults who have dealings with their own children: that is to say, although parents might be only too glad to see their children given preferential treatment at school, they also realise that they would find it intolerable if other children were preferred to the exclusion of theirs. 'She has favourites' is regarded as a major criticism of a teacher, by parents, teachers and children alike. Favouritism is also, however, deplored within the family; parents make conscious efforts to avoid it, or to hide the feelings that might be interpreted this way by their other children.

The stretching of the principle of fairness becomes an issue, however, when one child is perceived to have special needs. Because teachers have the agreed role of being impartial in helping to the best of their ability *all* the children in their care, there are limits as to how far they can go in giving extra help to individuals for fear of being seen to favour one child at the expense of others. Parents, an intrinsic part of whose role is to seek the best that is possible, whatever they think that means, for their own child, are free to pursue this aim without reference to other children than their own; but they also have freedom to judge when one of their children has particular needs not shared by the other children in the family, and to make special provision for these. Thus, just as a child with an illness that involves special dietary needs will be somehow accommodated to in the family budget and in food preparation time, so will a child who is having particular difficulty with sums or reading, or feeling depressed about his friends, or waking up with nightmares, be given an additional share of the family's attention. Sometimes, of course, this care will be long-term, where the child has a permanent handicap, or where his personality is of a kind to make heavy weather over every difficulty; sometimes it will be in terms of meeting momentary crises; sometimes too, it will take the form of fostering a talent or an interest, where the child is given an enormous investment of parental time to help him follow his particular star as far as it goes. In each case, however, the parents are concerned to meet needs *effectively* at the time they arise, whether to forestall or cope with crisis or to nurture a dream.

THE TOLERANCE OF IDIOSYNCRASY

The willingness of parents to mobilise themselves to meet idiosyncratic needs urgently is, of course, partly based upon the fact that the family, while it is a group in itself, is individual-oriented; while the school, as a much larger group with more explicit organisational patterns, is more oriented to the require-ments of the group. The salient difference between socialisation within the home and socialisation to school expectations lies in *the degree of tolerance accorded to egocentricity.* In school, egocen-tricity must fairly quickly learn to accept subordination to group needs. Obviously the pre-school child *is* developmentally more egocentric than the school-age child: it is not just a question of age, however. Obviously too, as I have already suggested, parents themselves subscribe in general terms to the idea that one child cannot be allowed to dominate the whole group: it is their conscious intention that one member of the family should not ride roughshod over the others. Nonethe-less, children of any age, including adolescents, do dominate their families egocentrically for brief or longer periods accord-ing to their special problems or needs or preoccupations of the moment: a four-year-old needs to share her parents' bed for a while, an eight-year-old needs hours of home support to tolerate a stressful classroom, an adolescent wants to talk end-lessly through his problems in the middle of the night. My argument is that it is the family's special function to put up with such episodes of domination because they are necessary to the child's development at the time and because no other institution in society will tolerate them.[7]

The acceptance of idiosyncrasy goes much deeper than the response to moments of frank crisis, however; and I believe this is its importance. In many different ways, parents accept as valid, and worthy of their attention and respect, demands from the child which they might reasonably judge as irrational whims. Sometimes they themselves see this as trivial indulgence, and deprecate their own co-operation with the child as making them look foolish; nonetheless, they do co-operate. Let us briefly consider some examples.

One of the most striking is parents' connivance in the child's rituals. Many children like their day to be punctuated by events that not only happen at predictable times but are played out in predictable ways. Some insist on their clothes being put on in a particular order; some will only drink from one mug or eat from one special spoon; some must daily have a dollop of foam from their father's shaving. Parents who read or tell stories to their children often find that the child sets great store by the words, and even the expression, being precisely the same at each performance. It is common behaviour in parents that, when the child protests at some breaking of his ritual, they will accept their fault in making a 'mistake' – 'Oh, sorry, sorry . . .' – and will try to put it right rather than override what to the outsider might seem nonsensical demands. The rituals that surround bed-time are particularly powerful: of the 700 children in our study, at the age of four one child in three had a specific ritual which he insisted upon every night and which had compulsive force in that he would have objected vigorously or become upset if some part of it had been omitted; and all these children's parents were thus co-operating in situations of which these two descriptions are fairly representative:

Labourer's wife
She always asks you to kiss her – she'll say, 'I do love you, see you in the morning,' and you can't come out the room unless you kiss her goodnight and say that you love her and

you'll see her in the morning. You've got to tuck her in and let her say 'I love you a million *million*' – we get that every night; you've got to sort of wait for that – she'll say all that before she lets you come out of the room: 'I love you a million *million*', and then she'll squeeze you and give you a kiss. Well I say it back to her, 'I love *you*', and then she'll say, 'I love you a *million*', and I say, 'I love *you* a million', and so it goes on, every night – I don't think she'd go to sleep, really, without it. Everything the same, every night – nothing different, always the same thing.

Packer's wife:
Well, he's saying, and I'm always answering, 'Good night, see you in the morning, and a Happy New Year!' So I always have to say it back. It's been ever since New Year he's said it. He must insist on a Happy New Year *every* night. So of course I have to say it back, or you wouldn't get no peace until you said it.

It may be suggested that it is easy enough to go along with rituals like this, or even with those which insist that the mother has to 'do a little dance as far as the door and *then* say good night', or that a father on shiftwork gives back in a paper bag next morning the kiss that his son blew out of the window at bedtime. Other demands, however, run counter to parents' wishes. For instance, the use of a dummy or a cuddly blanket for comfort, encouraged by parents in the first year, becomes more and more an embarrassment to them as the growing child continues to carry around with him the loved but aesthetically unpleasing object – particularly when he brings it out in company. Nonetheless, although it is clearly open to parents to throw the object away or burn it, very few of them do so; it is typical that they regard it as a problem, worry about it and complain about it, but accord to the child the right to override their feelings. Parents' attitudes to wakefulness are another example. They generally believe that children *ought* to go to sleep when put to bed, sleep through the night, and remain quietly in their own beds if they do happen to wake in the night; however, a third of the mothers of one-year-olds were prepared to pick the baby up within five minutes if he cried after being put down, a quarter of mothers were prepared to chat to a four-year-old during the night if that was what he wanted, and two-thirds would take a four-year-old into bed with them – a practice which, until recently,[8] has not been encouraged by professional advisers of parents. When our children reached seven, we found many whose mothers very much wanted them to stay at school for dinner, but who in fact still came home at lunchtime because they preferred this.

Behaviour which is commonly tolerated although believed to be disapproved of by the cultural mores is of particular interest, because it is a recognised part of the parental role to socialise the child in order to fit him for the culture. Parents are very aware that they have a responsibility to prepare the child, in terms of self-help skills, social controls and basic social graces, for the group-oriented demands of school; this is why four years old is a crisis point for parents, in that socialisation has to be stepped up in order that the child shall be presented with confidence to the world. It is thus accepted that parents advocate and expound the culture to the child; at the same time, however, they also in part defend him from some of its expectations. Early on, in the privacy and seclusion of the home, they do this in the ways I have described, often in the guilty belief that they are far more indulgent than most parents. Once the child is actually spending much of his day in the wider world, they are forced to press cultural demands more strongly; but at this point they often strike a kind of unstated bargain with the child that he may bend the rules at home in exchange for complying with them elsewhere. The child himself, as an increasingly social animal, is obviously at this stage also responding to direct socialising pressure from the community; but it is perhaps made more possible for him to do so where home remains in some sense a refuge from these expectations.

There are many examples of the parents' joint role as agent of, yet protector from, cultural pressures. For instance, parents are likely to place heavy emphasis on the need for truthfulness in the child, either outside the home or when communication between home and outside world is involved; inside the home, however, there is much more tolerance of fantasy, joking and 'playing with' notions of truth and falsehood. Again, both children and parents have ideas of what level of emotionalism is appropriate for community display and for home indulgence: by seven, children on the whole reserve both their weepy moments and their demonstrations of love and affection for the privacy of the home. Temper tantrums, too, are subject to cultural control: a survey of seven-year-olds in five primary schools in a sample week produced a grand total of only one temper tantrum in school: at home, 22 per cent of seven-year-olds were reported as having tantrums once or more in a week. Some interesting findings concern differential expectations of children according to their sex. There is a cultural expectation that little boys engage in physical fighting but little girls do not; and parents certainly back this up in the comments they make to their children about disagreements with the peer group outside the family. Children reflect the sex differential in their actual behaviour in the neighbourhood group: 32 per cent of our seven-year-old boys were known by their parents to get involved in fights with their peers, compared with only half as many of the girls. However, within the home, while fighting increases for both boys and girls, for boys it goes up by 36 per cent, whereas for girls it goes up by 43 per cent, leaving a much smaller proportional difference between them. Parents do not exactly approve of girls fighting at home; but they do not disapprove with quite the same force as when they are on show outside. By the time our children were eleven, expected sex roles were determining their activities with still great pervasiveness; but again we found mothers willing to override outside expectations for the sake of the child's private interests. They would teach a boy knitting or embroidery or buy a girl football boots, while at the same time acceding to the child's own reluctance to betray such an interest to his friends. Here again, the mother defends the child's individuality against the undiscriminating urgency of cultural demands, while acting in the long term as the mediator of those demands. In the end, of course, the mother has to be aware of the power of the culture –

sometimes, especially in the case of sex roles, because the peer group is less protective of the child's individuality than she is.

THE DEVELOPMENT OF SELFHOOD

In drawing attention to the sanctuary that the family provides for the child's individuality, I am not by any means suggesting that group-oriented institutions such as the school have no positive role for the child's personality development. It is through extending his horizons from home and family to school, peers and other less intimate figures that his adaptation to the more formal systems within which he will have to live takes place. Elsewhere, we have tried to describe this process:

> In his first months in the infants school, the child's teacher will make considerable allowance for his individual quirks and foibles: less responsive than his mother to his ego-centricity, she is still a tolerant, nurturant figure, to whom he can ascribe a mothering image and who can offer him a protective transition from home to school expectations. Loving his teacher uncritically, yet also compelled to share her with a greater number of peers than he has been used to, he learns two massive adaptations: he identifies with his teacher, and thence with the school world which she represents; and he is introduced to a discovery for which he is now intellectually ready – the discovery that group co-operation brings its own rewards in greater achievement and more complex and satisfying play. These crucial lessons of the infants school, mediated chiefly by the teacher herself, allow him to become fully integrated with the peer group and with the school as social institution, and bring him under the powerful influence of both: and in this way he is enabled to wean himself from the protective nurturance of his teacher, and become an independent 'junior'. At this stage, while retaining a close and friendly relationship with his class teacher, he is also more able to look beyond her to other teachers with whom he enjoys more casual contact; and, detached from his personal dependency, he begins to

show the emergence of 'us and them' loyalties in relation to peer group *vis à vis* teachers, turning more frequently towards other children as a source of comfort and support in meeting difficulties at school. Socialisation takes on a new emphasis.[9]

But in order to make full and constructive use of these opportunities for growth, the child needs to have a very certain idea of himself as a person, and in particular as a person of value and substance. I confess that I do not know how this sense of self-hood is to be achieved if not through the long-term acknowledgement as someone to be reckoned with that ordinary parents ordinarily give their children. Simply by having shared the child's history, parents are in the first place uniquely enabled to act as a memory bank for the child: conversation with and around a child commonly contains many references to his own past life and to the family's joint past experience. The importance of these casual references (and also of small family traditions and family jokes) to the child's own image of himself as a person of permanence can be understood when we contrast the adolescent who has spent his childhood among the characteristically transient relationships of the 'reasonable care' of community institutions: a major problem for such children is the sense of rootlessness and lack of identity which comes from having no single person who remembers them at earlier stages of their lives. But of equal importance, I propose, is the fact that *because* parents know about their children's idiosyncrasies, and because their child is a person so adept at getting under their emotional skin (for better or worse), they show just those tolerances which make the child aware that, small though he is, he can still exert individual power in some areas. Perhaps it is even important that parents also enhance this sense of power in the child by occasionally demurring: that the child should know that they want him to give up the dummy, or that they don't like children fighting in the home, but nevertheless accept it in their own despite.

In short, I am suggesting that a successfully integrated personality structure requires that a sense of personal worth be dovetailed with a sense of the needs of others; and that the major sources of these understandings are, in the first case, the special partiality which parents have for their children, and, in the second case, the fairness and even-handedness which the child may hope to expect from other adults, and which will indeed be fully backed up by his parents.

There is a corollary to this. We all know that in fact some parents are more effective than others in helping the child to acquire a firm confidence in his own identity and his own capability. What we are still rather unsure of, perhaps, is what are the consequences to the child of such ineffectiveness. Bruner quotes an unpublished colleague, P. M. Greenfield, as questioning: 'If a mother believes her fate is controlled by external forces, that she does not control the means necessary to achieve her goals, what does this mean for her children?' It seems feasible to extend her question: if a child does not believe in his own intrinsic worth, in his own fundamental *considerability*, how can he be motivated to achieve his goals, or indeed to set himself goals at all?

Our own research findings cast a chill light on these questions. In particular, we have been able to evaluate for our 700 children how far each mother's behaviour is informed by child-centred attitudes, not in the sense of the warmth which she brings to the relationship, but in the respect and autonomy which she accords to the child as a person, in different areas of their interaction both at age four and at age seven. We also have recorded for each child his verbal reasoning scores at the age of eleven. Both of these measures are heavily correlated with the social class affiliation of the family: further up the social scale, both mothers' scores on child centredness and children's scores on verbal reasoning are higher; thus obviously they will correlate with each other overall. But if we look *within* our working-class population – that is, keeping the effects of social class constant – we still find a positive correlation between child-centredness in the mother and verbal reasoning in the child.

It is because I believe that children who have no sense and recognition of their own value are defeated children that I have placed such emphasis upon some of the characteristics of parenthood that can bring such understandings about. I have barely alluded to the structures in society that are so powerful in evolving life-styles hospitable or inimical to the growth of an effective self-understanding; we have documented them, and continue to document them, very fully elsewhere.[10] But I cannot do otherwise than accept Bruner's disquieting observation: that

> . . . in so far as a sub-culture represents a reaction to defeat and in so far as it is caught by a sense of powerlessness, it suppresses the potential of those who grow up under its sway by discouraging problem-solving. The source of powerlessness that such a subculture generates, no matter how moving its by-products, produces instability in the society and unfulfilled promise in human beings.[11]

NOTES

[1] Newson, John and Elizabeth, *Infant Care in an Urban Community*, 1963; *Four Years Old in an Urban Community*, 1968; *Seven Years Old in the Home Environment*, 1976; *Perspectives on School at Seven Years Old*, 1977; all Allen and Unwin, London.

[2] Newson, Elizabeth, 'Parents as a resource in diagnosis and assessment', in Oppé, T. and Woodford, P. (eds.), *Early Management of Handicapping Disorders*, Elsevier, Excerpta Medica, Amsterdam, 1976.

[3] Newson, Elizabeth, 'Towards an understanding of the parental role', conference papers, National Children's Bureau, 1972.

[4] Ballard, Rod, 'Early management of handicap: the parents' needs', in Oppé and Woodford, 1976, *op. cit.*

[5] Hewett, Sheila, *The Family and the Handicapped Child*, Allen and Unwin, 1970.

[6] This quotation and the following one both from Kelly, G., *The Psychology of Personal Constructs*: Vol. 1: *A theory of personality*. Norton, New York, 1955.

[7] Significantly, it is those voluntary organisations which have tried to respond like a caring family to 'unreasonable' expressions of need in individuals, who have shown most effectiveness: the Samaritans, for example.

[8] Hugh Jolly, the paediatrician whose *Book of Child Care* is probably the most comprehensive and practical guide for parents since Spock, initiated a crusade for 'taking family life into the bedroom'

by allowing children into the parental bed, in his column in *The Times*, 1.12.76.

[9] Newson, J. and E., 1977, *op. cit.*

[10] Newson, J. and E., 1963, 1968, 1976, 1977, *op. cit.*

[11] Bruner, J. S., *The relevance of education*, Allen and Unwin, London, 1972.

2

MORAL INTEGRITY

Bernard Mayo

'Moral Integrity' has struck me for some time as one of those things that is more a matter of name-dropping than of real acquaintance. But when I undertook to say something about it, I soon discovered that I had bitten off far more than I – or perhaps anyone – could chew within the hour. In this I find myself in good company: for Professor Winch also chose this title for his Inaugural Lecture[1] – I apologise for overlooking this when I chose my own title – and in his first paragraph he explains that he will be saying nothing about Moral Integrity, though he expresses the hope that what he has said will be found to have a bearing on it. I shall not be discussing his lecture, except incidentally; but I commend his wisdom in not trying, as rashly as I am, to say something directly about the topic.

If we ask the obvious sort of questions which spring to mind: 'What is Moral Integrity? Is it a good thing? If so, why?' we soon find that there are many different things it could be, and not all of them need be good, or if they are, for the same reasons. Is Moral Integrity, for instance, the same thing as Personal Integrity? What about the Integrity of the Artist? What we really need is a complete catalogue *raisonnée* of the varieties of Integrity; but this would far exceed the scope of a single lecture. What I shall try to do instead is to draw together certain distinct themes, and indeed certain distinctive and contrasting styles, in recent moral philosophy, an exercise which I hope will throw some light on the connecting link itself, the notion of integrity, and on the question whether personal integrity and moral integrity are the same notion.

The contrasting styles I have in mind are, first, the style of those who take, say, Hare's *Language of Morals* as a fairly good example of what moral philosophy should be like; and, on the other hand, what I shall call the style of the transcendental biographers, some specimens of which I shall be examining. It is in their writings that the notion of integrity is, I think, nearest the surface.

I shall start in the first style, by asking whether it is a necessary condition of something's being a moral consideration that it possess the character of *overridingness* (I). This will lead to difficulties calling for a new approach; and I shall suggest that 'overridingness' is better seen as a matter of personal identity, that is, personal integrity (II). Finally, I shall try to show that personal integrity, in turn, is very much the same thing as moral integrity, by taking as a test case the rational egoist, for whom non-moral considerations are supposed to be overriding, and showing that he is not merely unacceptably, but inconceivably, defective (III–VII).

I

Among those who seek to elicit the sufficient and necessary conditions for the correct application of the term 'moral', it is a familiar view (since Hare) that moral judgements and decisions must be prescriptive and universalisable. These two conditions need express no more than the truism that morality necessarily involves *practical considerations*: there must always be some question as to what is to be done (as opposed, say, to what should be believed); and there must always be reasons for or against doing something. The conditions are insufficient, however, because there are many kinds of practical considerations – legal, aesthetic, technical, etiquette, and so on – which are obviously not moral considerations. So a third condition is added, that of being *overriding*. As Hare says, 'it is characteristic of moral principles that they cannot be overridden . . . this characteristic . . . is connected with the fact that moral principles are . . . superior to or more authoritative than any other kind of principle'.[2] These three conditions seem to constitute a purely formal definition of the moral, without respect to content: moral judgements could be about anything whatever; though Hare, of course, claims that the formal conditions in fact constitute quite severe constraints on what can count as moral. The *definition* is, however, content-free. Now the view that over-ridingness constitutes (with the other conditions) a sufficient condition of morality – what I shall call, for short, the analytic thesis – leads to several difficulties, of which I shall list five.

1. Is a Satanic morality intelligible? – that is, a moral code which is the exact inverse of our conventional morality? One who thinks it is is the Australian philosopher D. H. Monro.[3] He adopts the analytic thesis: moral principles are those that 'come highest in the peck-order'. He thinks the Satanic morality *is* intelligible. G. F. Warnock,[4] on the other hand, thinks it is not. I think Warnock is right, but for rather different reasons from his.

2. Overridingness suggests a picture in which practical considerations are arranged in a serial order. But any considera-tion whatever, except the very lowest, could be an overriding one. This would make practically all considerations moral. To speak of the upper reaches of the hierarchy is not much help, since the boundary between upper and lower will be arbitrary.

3. The various types of non-moral considerations, some of which I have already listed, seem to be distinguished readily enough from one another by criteria which have nothing to do with overridingness. It is difficult to believe that we do not have a similarly distinct understanding of what moral considera-tions are, independent of the question of their standing in the peck-order.

4. The analytic thesis would make it impossible even to raise the question, whether for a particular individual morality might play a less than dominant part in his life, or whether some non-moral concern might not be for him of overriding importance. Examples like the (perhaps by now over familiar) Gauguin case can be multiplied indefinitely, of people for

whom morality has been of secondary importance. When Mrs. Erlynne (in *Lady Windermere's Fan*) said 'Manners before morals,' how could this be understood, even as a witticism, if there could not conceivably be people whose lives embodied the observance of her behest?

5. Finally, the analytic thesis would also seem to rule out, or fail to come to terms with, the case of people whose lives do not display, in the systematic way required for the thesis, any dominance-patterns whatever. It is unrealistic to suppose that peck-order tables can show what a person's morality actually is; yet someone whose decisions and judgements showed no consistent ordering of priorities could not be said for that reason to be an amoral person.

II

I now want to suggest, drawing on the work of the transcendental biographers, that we can make more sense, and less difficulty, with the notion of overridingness if we abandon the peck-order model and stop thinking of moral considerations in terms of a serial order of preference. It was a mistake to be asking what it is for one consideration to override another, without much considering the agent *for whom* they are considerations. Of course, there had to be an agent in the picture, but he did not occupy the centre of the picture, any more than the thinker usually does, when we discuss the question of conflicting evidence; evidence has to be, in the last resort, evidence *for* someone, but what it is for a human being to be weighing up the evidence is very seldom the question we are interested in. But practical considerations involve the agent as a person in a much deeper way than theoretical considerations involve the thinker as a person. The overridingness condition was selected to express what is common to the ideas of importance and seriousness, which go so closely with the idea of morality; but when we speak of certain considerations being dominant *for an individual*, the point is not that they dominate *other* considerations, but that they dominate *him*. What most deeply concerns a man is what is, in the deepest sense, a concern of *his*.

Another shortcoming of the 'overridingness' approach is that, in so far as it does acknowledge the presence of the agent for whom moral considerations are overriding, it does not acknowledge his attitude to the overriding considerations of *other* agents. At the most, it does so in a very weak and distorted way, by falling back on the universalisability condition. My respect for the overriding concerns of others would have to be an extension, mediated by the universalisability principle, from my own respect for myself as a centre of overriding concerns. As a second-order principle, this is both far too weak, and it reverses the proper order of things.

I come, then, to a view which takes integrity to be the object, rather than the subject, of moral concern: what ought to matter to a moralist, rather than what a moralist himself should be: though these considerations are not independent. I am thinking here of the kind of view put forward by Bernard Williams in *Critique of Utilitarianism*, which depends heavily on a strong view about personal identity; and clearly the notion of integrity has a great deal to do with the question of what it is for a person to be the one and only person that (pathological cases aside) he is.

A person is a continuant, something with a continuous temporal extension, in a much stronger sense than an ordinary material object (including his body) is. A material object is only causally linked with its past and future. But a person is constituted by his past and future: not *only* by his memories – which is familiar doctrine – but, more importantly, by what Williams calls his 'projects'. These are more important, because memories themselves are largely, and indeed essentially, a matter of projects initiated, continued, completed or abandoned; a duplicate set of merely passive presentations could not constitute the memory of a person. (By contrast, a project certainly cannot be anticipation of future memories.)

I am speaking here of an internal sense of identity, of a person who is conscious of himself as a centre of agency in a world of change. This is not the only way, not even the only morally relevant way, of seeing a person as the person he is. There is also an external way – not wholly external, since it is also accessible to the agent himself – according to which a person is constituted by the sum of his behavioural dispositions. (Manners makyth man.) But it is the internal kind of identity that we are most concerned with here.

Now since only the future person (including, of course, the immediate future person) can be affected by either his own, or other people's actions, it will be important to consider whether there is a – so to say – falling off of moral relevance in the more distant reaches of the future state of the person who is at the receiving end of moral acts and judgements. The answer must be No; just as it would be if we were to ask, looking to the past, whether an offence committed a long time ago is for that reason alone less serious than one committed yesterday. Actually I am inclined to go further and say that the answer is not *just* as firmly No, but even more so, in that a person's future is, in an important sense, *his* even more than his past is.

This may seem implausible at first. Certainly a pain I am going to suffer is in one sense not a real pain, just as a pain I did suffer is not a real pain – if this only means that a future pain is *not yet* a pain, just as the past pain is *no longer* a pain. But I think it is arguable that future pains, and future experiences and doings in general, are *mine* in a stronger sense than past ones are. Legal responsibility aside, I can to a greater or lesser extent *disown* parts of (what is normally taken to be) 'my' past. A minor and rather trivial example of this – necessarily so since I am fortunate in having no reasons to do any more drastic disowning – is the fact that I am occasionally irked by being expected to defend a thesis which I may have published twenty years before.[5]

If I am right that, to a limited extent, we can disown our past, then an asymmetry appears because there is no way that I can think of by which I can disown, as it were, a future pain as not being *mine*, so that I needn't worry about it. (Of course there *could* be all sorts of reasons, of a familiar kind, why I shouldn't worry about it, but this could not be one of them.)

Even if I am wrong, and a person's future is no more important a constituent of him than his past, it still remains true that a person is very largely a construct of his own future; and since a person's future, just to be a *person's* future, has to have some minimal coherence, just as his past does (even allowing for some disowning), the central importance of projects is clear.

Developed as an anti-Utilitarian argument, the Williams thesis claims that it would be glaringly unacceptable to require someone to abandon a 'project' of his at any moment, just in case the results coming in from the impersonal hedonic computer happen to swing that way.[6] The project in question need not, of course, be a moral one; but it may be; and if it is, we have a *prima facie* case of lack of moral integrity required as a sacrifice at the utilitarian altar. This is not quite the point Williams actually makes, which is rather that *any* project so sacrificed would evoke a sense of moral outrage. Of course there are standard defensive moves to safeguard Utilitarianism against this kind of objection; and one actual critic of Williams has already retorted with an *ad hominem* argument, appealing to another outbreak of moral indignation at so callous a disregard of the general welfare.[7] For my purposes it is sufficient to note that if there is even a *prima facie* moral case against inroads on integrity of this kind – what we might call the unity of the person – there must be a stronger case still for the preservation of moral integrity. But we still lack a clear concept – as Williams admits: 'To reach a grounded decision . . . should not be regarded as a matter of just discounting one's reactions, impulses and deeply held projects in the face of the pattern of utilities, nor yet merely adding them in – but . . . of trying to understand them.'[8]

III

I now come to what I take to be much the most central case of Moral Integrity. It is one of those models that trails a long history of philosophical perplexity. I must first segregate him from two other familiar models. He is not the single-minded villain (though he has his problems); nor is he the akrates or backslider (though he, too, or his numerous varieties, have even worse problems). He is the *rational egoist*. Is *this* character exhibiting lack of integrity, and, if so, must he be suffering from it? The conflict between rational egoism and morality has a philosophical history going back to Plato's Glaucon's Gyges, and there are a lot of beaten tracks in this area, including one of the more recently trampled ones, the primrose path of dalliance with the transcendental, which I will remark on in due course. My excuse for thrashing about in this area is, first, that there are some areas of philosophy where perplexity is so endemic that even continual restatement is of value; and second, that several writers have in fact said (or re-said) something of value, two in particular in connexion with Moral Integrity, though neither has actually used the term. I refer to a recent article by Michael Stocker revealingly entitled 'The Schizophrenia of Modern Ethical Theories',[9] and one by Charles Whiteley called 'Morality and Egoism',[10] where the characteristic of the egoist's way of life is identified as *hypocrisy*.

Philosophers do tend to talk in terms of idealised models, rather than real-life examples, but this is not an avoidable fault. We can only describe and evaluate our real-life examples in terms of some limited set of concepts, and it is not a profitless exercise to see whether some one key concept or conjunction of concepts can be fully and consistently instantiated; and to do this is to construct a model. We can see this in the cases I have just excluded: Satan is a traditional model for the single-minded villain, and the coherence or incoherence of this model is of relevance when we are tempted to ascribe wholly un-mitigated evil to, say, a Hitler. Similarly Medea, or rather Ovid's portrayal of her, is a test case for the akrates.

Now in the case of the rational egoist, both Plato and Whiteley have their models, and so does John Hospers, whom I come to in a moment. Plato's Gyges model fails because the brilliance of its science fiction is tarnished by the improbability of its psychological fantasy: the offences that the 'keep it dark' operators are supposed to get up to are simply not on: such things as raping the Queen and taking over the government (Plato's own examples) can hardly be kept dark. But plenty of quite serious crime can, of course, be kept dark; this is where John Hospers' celebrated bank clerk comes in.[11] He represents an appropriate scaling down of the extravagant Gyges model to occupy an apparently impregnable position on the rational egoist front. (The bank clerk is a young man who commits a single perfect crime, in the detective-story sense, and lives happily on the proceeds ever after.)[12]

Now when I myself first grappled with the bank clerk problem, I tried an *ad hominem* argument to the effect that he had not, after all, satisfied the conditions of rational egoism. Hospers has indeed written in some obviously necessary stipulations, such as that the bank clerk is not a man of worrisome disposition, or nagging conscience. (And even if he is, we could easily add a bit of science fiction, the invention of a new drug, to be called a conscience-killer or moral tranquilliser. If anyone thinks, as I should like to, that such an invention is conceptually, not just biochemically, impossible, he is trying an interesting alternative route to the same conclusion.) But I thought I had detected a gap in the defences. Even though no one knows of the crime, this is only true if by 'no one' we mean 'no one *else*'. For he has not kept dark from himself this one and only, but very positive, step in the direction of depravity and corruption; and it is not in his interest to become (more) corrupt and depraved. But I soon realised, of course, that this is no answer at all, because such terms as 'depraved' and 'corrupt' will effect no purchase on a man of his sensibilities; we should have to fall back on a remoter question, whether it was in his interest to have, or to have acquired, those sensibilities. And this points in the direction of incoherent babble: how can it either be, or fail to be, in a man's interest to be, or not to be, the man he is? I say this points in the direction of babble, not that it actually lands us there, because I still hope to salvage something of this idea.

Whiteley, however, has done a more thorough job by constructing a model of the rational egoist who does seem to have all the necessary qualifications, and who, in addition, actually conducts his whole life, and not just one short, unique and uncharacteristic episode of it, on pure rational egoist principles. He is the one who does not suffer from, but positively glories in, lack of moral integrity. Whiteley calls this dominant feature of his life *hypocrisy*, because it is characteristic of his way of life that, being a rational egoist who, quite rationally, desires not to live in a society of other rational egoists, he has to endorse, and actively propagate, a morality of altruism and concern for others which he himself does not adopt. There is an awkwardness in choosing terms here, which will turn out to be symptomatic of a fundamental weakness in the rational egoist model. We need a pair of terms (here I have used 'endorse' and 'adopt') of which the first indicates what the agent appears, deceptively, to be doing, the other what he actually does. Whiteley himself says that the egoist's hypocrisy consists in the fact that he *subscribes* to a principle which he does not *keep*. I shall come back to this later.

IV

First, let me give an example of the transcendental kind of argument. The example is Thomas Nagel's, and it involves a return to the notion of a person and his projects. First, the challenge. Whiteley says that what the rational egoist does is a matter of 'hypocrisy. But it is not inconsistency'. The critic must show that the egoist is not just hypocritical, but inconsistent; or, rather, that the *concept* of a total rational egoist is incoherent. Again, Whiteley says that a discrepancy *must* exist 'between the principles which determine his own actions and those which he wants other people to be induced to follow'. The critic will have to show such a discrepancy *cannot* exist.

Nagel's view[13] is that, just as it is a necessary condition of the intelligibility of the language of prudence that one must acknowledge the force of reasons that *will* obtain, so it is a necessary condition of the intelligibility of the language of morals that one must acknowledge the force of reasons applying to other people. Prudence (even by etymology) requires a point of view from which all times in one's life are equally real; *now* is just *some* time, one time among many. Just so, ethics requires a point of view from which all persons are equally real: *I* am just *some* one, one person among many. Moral language depends on the ability to adopt the impersonal point of view, and this is part of a deep structure of thought and action which it is hardly in our power to renounce. For example, as Nagel observes, 'when they are wronged, people suddenly understand objective reasons, for they require such concepts to express their resentment'. And, continuing the analogy with prudence: someone for whom future situations are of no concern is radically 'dissociated'; and someone for whom considerations for others are not considerations has also 'come apart' in a bad way.

A transcendental argument I take to be one that seeks to establish the preconditions of intelligibility of a pervasive mode of discourse. However, it need not (and Nagel does not) claim that the discourse itself is absolutely indispensable. Dissociated people might still exist, and the badness of their coming apart might be merely a function of our own non-egoistic values. It remains to be argued that a rational egoist would find himself so severely incapacitated that it could not be in his interest to be a rational egoist: in other words, that rational egoism is an incoherent notion.

V

I come now to a set of five related arguments designed to show that Whiteley's rational egoist cannot exist, at any rate in any recognisably human form; so that total non-integrity, dissociation, moral schizophrenia, or whatever, cannot be coherently modelled. Whether these arguments should be called transcendental is a terminological point of no importance.

1. *Can* a person subscribe to, or advocate, principles he does not keep, has never kept, and has no intention of keeping? We must be careful here about expressions like 'he keeps the principle only when it suits his advantage to do so'. If this means that it pays him to do the same thing as he would be required to do if he were acting on the principle, then this can hardly be called *keeping* the principle. (I do not *keep* to a compass bearing if my otherwise directed steps just happen to land me at a certain map reference.) It could, however, mean something more. It could mean that it pays him, not merely to perform a certain act, but to perform it *as if* he were acting on principle. But the difficulty is to explicate that 'as if'; it is the difficulty I

have already noted (at the end of section III), the difficulty of selecting a pair of terms for the pretence and the genuine article; and this is *not* a merely terminological point. It will be the substance of my last argument (5 below).

2. Most rational-egoist model-builders endow their models with a range of human interests which is either absurdly narrow – confined to such things as wealth and power, as in the Gyges case – or so indeterminate that the question is left open, and, when we try to close it, the same things tend to get left out. Consider the group of attitudes, interests and values associated with such things as love, respect, esteem – and consider what it is both to bestow, and to receive, such attentions. (Some of my remarks may be contentious with regard to one or other of these different, but related, attitudes: love, in particular, is far too complex and varied to satisfy any simple set of conditions; but I would claim that, even in departing here and there from the paradigm, the essential connexions remain.) First, then, is it possible for the rational egoist to bestow these attentions, or even their opposites? It seems pretty clear that the thorough-going rational egoist cannot recognise any objects of respect or esteem, or even contempt, since the system of impersonal values in terms of which alone people can be so regarded, is one to which he gives a purely fictitious assent – if, indeed, even ficti-tious assent is possible (to be discussed later). It might seem, however, that he can at least offer friendship or love. But his love too must be a sham: for, first, he cannot love anyone *for* anything, beyond, perhaps, the merely sensual; and, second (a point I owe to Michael Stocker's article),[9] even in the course of dwelling on the *ex hypothesi* beloved, in her very presence, he should, to be consistent, be asking himself if there isn't someone else he would be doing better out of by loving *her* instead.

True, there is a superficially plausible answer to both points. To the first, it could be objected that we do not love people *for* their qualities. To this I must, to avoid a lengthy discussion, simply retort: take away everything in your love that relates to what you can think or say about your beloved, and, if there is anything left, you may remove it from the group of values I am here concerned with. To the second point, it could be objected that this love-destroying feature of the rational egoist's policy is one which a truly enlightened egoist will already have taken into account; part of his policy will be to avoid having such thoughts in the presence of the beloved. But the 'policy' of switching on spontaneity at predetermined points is clearly a necessarily self-defeating one.

3. If the rational egoist cannot bestow these attitudes, still less can he receive them. Of course, if his deception is successful, he may *be* the object of respect, esteem, and even love; but can he obtain any (even egoistic) satisfaction from affections based on what he knows to be perfectly false? Or – worse still – from affections that he cannot even understand – if my concluding argument is correct?

4. Perhaps he can do without love and respect. This reminds me of a character in a novel who said 'I can do without happiness'. Such sweeping renunciations invite the question, what can he *not* do without. How severely truncated a personality will survive the lopping off of love, respect, and this general dimension of value? It seems clear that it is not in the interest of any *human* being to be deprived of these; and even if the deprived being were still ostensibly human, it becomes increasingly doubtful whether even his – or its – remaining interests can be a source of satisfaction. Even wealth and power can be conceived of as sources of satisfaction only to a being who has wider interests than these.

VI

5. But the most telling kind of argument against the coherence of the rational egoist position is probably the appeal to the nature of the moral understanding, and the way in which moral concepts enter into a whole corpus of thought and language. Julius Kovesi summed this up with his Heraclitean remark that moral situations are not puddles into which we step.[14] What makes a situation a situation of any kind, including a moral kind, is itself a function of a language. Professor Winch, in the lecture I referred to,[15] argues against Hare, that morality could not have the action-guiding function which, according to Hare,

is its central feature, unless there were already practical perplexities which *call for* guidance; but to identify those practical
perplexities must itself require the language of moral concepts.
Now all this will be unavailable to the thoroughgoing rational
egoist, who will thus, by a fine irony, find himself cut off from
the very community which he is supposed to prefer to the
society of other rational egoists like himself. He cannot even
speak the language of the natives.

This is the line, then, along which we must look for an
answer to the earlier question; can anyone subscribe to, and
advocate, a principle which he does not keep? The answer
must be that he cannot, since the principle is of a type which he
is *ex hypothesi* debarred from understanding. He is supposed to
know what it is to act on (a non-egoistic) principle, but in fact
he always acts only *as if* he were acting on principle. If the 'as
if' here means merely that the act appears to others to be done
on principle, because it does in fact conform to the principle,
this is uninteresting, and says nothing about the egoist's life-
style. It has to be that the 'as if' refers to the intention of the
agent: he *intends* his act to appear to others that way. But the
way he intends it to appear – what it is for an act to be done on
principle – is something that must itself form part of his intention; and this something must itself include an intention *really*
to act on principle. For it would be quite insufficient to the
egoist's purpose if he intended that his act should appear to be
done on principle but should also appear to be done by someone
who did not intend really to do it on principle. This is indeed an
instance of something that is a necessary feature of all forms of
human communication: every communicative act involves an
infinite series of encapsulated reciprocal expectations. I have
expounded this at some length in an earlier address to this
Institute.[16]

The pretence of the egoist, then, must involve a full understanding of what a genuine case of acting on principle would be.
Can the egoist understand this? There is some problem even in
the idea that our egoist can understand principles of any kind,
even an egoistic kind. For if he were rational (and well-
informed) enough, wouldn't he be able to conduct his life with-

out having any use for rules? However, let us concede that the rational egoist can understand rules of prudence. No question of pretence arises there. But how can he understand the moral ones which he (wholly and solely) pretends to act on? The ways in which he sees other people acting will not be intelligible to him, since he lacks the concepts which give consistency and forms of description to such behaviour. Only purely negative verdicts will be available to him, such as that they are acting foolishly or sheepishly in so unaccountably neglecting their own interests.

But does perhaps this introduction of negative values show that the egoist need not lack the entire repertoire of value concepts? To condemn someone as foolish or slavish is to exercise capacities for appraisal which must also allow for praising the wise and the masterly. We might go on from there to think of our egoist's attitude to other egoists who may happen to be around. Even if he would rather be the only egoist around, because the others interfere, can't he nevertheless admire their wisdom, clear-headedness, technical excellence? And these are indeed values. Can't he also admire their powers of duplicity, their ruthlessness and insensitivity? These are not values, but couldn't they be *his* values – and even a perverted set of values would enable our egoist to maintain a foothold in a possible world? But all this is an illusion. The terms from which we started – foolish/wise, slavish/masterly – belong to our actual evaluative discourse, and this is a network within which they are essentially connected with other values. For instance, we can only condemn or pity someone for foolish neglect of his own welfare if *we*, and not just he, set a value on his welfare. But the rationalist egoist does not set any value, except a purely instrumental one, on someone else's welfare. As we have seen, he cannot even understand what it is for A to be (non-egoistically) concerned for B. If, *per impossibile*, the fact could be brought home to him, he could only see it as a case of A having a most serious identity problem.

VII

I conclude that total hypocrisy, complete non-integrity, is an impossible concept. This conclusion could perhaps have been reached more quickly by way of the analogical (or perhaps subsumed) case of total mendacity. And veracity does play a central part in the notion of a moral agent. But it plays this central part not just in relation to moral agency, but in relation to the notion of what it is for someone to be characteristically a human agent, speaking the language of his community.

But can anything useful be concluded about lack of moral integrity in real life, as opposed to our theoretical models? Or can we say only that the real life cases cannot approximate very closely to the ideal of the perfect rational egoist, because the ideal itself is incoherent? This would be better than nothing; it is perhaps some comfort to the vast majority of us who are not much drawn to a policy of ruthless exploitation of our fellows, to realise that the self-denying habits and principles which have been produced in us not only are not, but could not be, the results of manipulation by the Rational Egoist. Perhaps it is also some warning to those who might be tempted in the direction of a little more secret self-concern, that further (even if very much further) along that road there comes an unimaginable breakdown.

NOTES

[1] Reprinted in Peter Winch, *Ethics and Action*, pp. 171–92.

[2] *Freedom and Reason*, p. 169.

[3] *Empiricism and Ethics*, p. 129.

[4] *Contemporary Moral Philosophy*, p. 59.

[5] In this, too, I found myself in good company: when the first volume of the *Synoptic Index* of the Aristotelian Society's *Proceedings* was published, I found that G. E. Moore, when duly synopsising a fifty-year-old paper, had filled his entry with disclaimers like 'purports'.

[6] 'A Critique of Utilitarianism', §§4–5, in Smart and Williams, *Utilitarianism For and Against*.

[7] John Harris, 'Williams on Negative Responsibility and In-

tegrity', *Philosophical Quarterly*, 24, pp. 270–3.

⁸ 'Critique', p. 118.

⁹ *Journal of Philosophy*, 73, pp. 453–66.

¹⁰ *Mind*, 85, pp. 90–6.

¹¹ *Human Conduct*, pp. 181–2.

¹² Russell Grice, in *Grounds of Moral Judgment*, 101ff., has constructed a rather more robust character called the Master Criminal.

¹³ *The Possibility of Altruism*: see especially pp. 144–5.

¹⁴ *Moral Notions*, p. 119.

¹⁵ *Ethics and Action*, p. 172.

¹⁶ 'The Moral Agent', in *The Human Agent* (Royal Institute of Philosophy Lectures, vol. I (1966–7), pp. 55–8).

3

EDUCATING THE IMAGINATION

Mary Warnock

My topic may seem a bizarre mixture of epistemology and value theory; and perhaps it is best to acknowledge this oddity at once. I should also, perhaps, confess that such a mixture has always seemed something to aspire to. Any philosopher who has made it seem that feeling strongly about something, valuing it highly, is an inevitable consequence of the *nature of human understanding*, that from the facts of knowledge or perception one can derive the inescapable facts of emotion or desire, any such philosopher has always deeply appealed to me. I am therefore a confessed perpetrator of the naturalistic fallacy. Indeed I go further, and say that I love the fallacy. So Spinoza, Hume (however much people say that he first discovered naturalism to be fallacious) and Sartre all seem to me to be *real* philosophers, on the grounds that for them this connexion between knowing and wanting seemed inevitable. My aim is to illustrate this kind of connexion by suggesting that the human imagination is such that we ought to value it and respect it more highly than anything else; and that therefore, if it can be educated and improved, it is to this education that we should give priority, if we are concerned with education at all. It may seem on the face of it absurd to say that we ought to value any particular human faculty or capacity. It may be thought that this is not the *kind* of object or evaluation with which at any rate philosophers should be concerned. But the fact is, of course, that we *do* value very highly indeed all kinds of capacities that we have,

44

such as sight, and hearing and understanding. And being un-ashamedly naturalistic, I have no hesitation in saying not only that we do value them, but that we ought to; they are, in every sense, valuable.

I am using the name 'imagination' for a collection of human capacities and abilities which seem to cluster together, but which need not, of course, be thought to constitute a faculty or power totally separate from others in the human range. Elements in this collection are perceptual, classificatory, linguistic (or connected with meaning) and emotional. Mental imagery, memory, insight and understanding are all linked in the collection. It is with the exploration of these links that the philosophy of the imagination would be concerned. I want to start by giving a few illustrations of the manner in which I believe these functions I have mentioned are connected, by way of justifying the use of the single term 'imagination' for what may seem a somewhat random and extensive range of phenomena.

First, then, we should consider perception, and with it inevitably the classification or ordering of the perceptual experiences we have, as well as the interpretation which is an essential part of what we ordinarily take to be our direct perceptual experiences. For it is scarcely necessary to illustrate the intricate way in which what we see and hear is dependent upon a particular, albeit very ordinary and unexciting, interpretation of it. Perhaps to be more accurate one should say that it is what we *say* we see and hear which is so dependent. For it is impossible to separate the language we use to report or describe our experiences from the interpretation of these experiences. The interpretation is already contained in the language itself (hence the notorious difficulty of supplying examples of impressions as distinct from ideas, of sense data, or of objects of immediate as opposed to mediated perception). Thus, if I say that I heard the sound of horses' hooves on the road outside, I am already committed to a series of assumptions about space and time (the sound was relatively distant, and it lasted over a period of time, getting gradually louder as the horses passed the window, and fading as they went down the hill to the paddock). I am committed to interpretation, moreover, in the light of *knowledge* (for instance that the road is tarmac, and the horses shod). Perhaps I may know by experience or calculation that one single four-footed animal could not have made these sounds, so there was more than one, and I may know by experience whether the sound was of walking or of trotting horses. No one, I think, would deny that within the simple example of such a reported experience, there is contained not only evidence of the ability to hear, but also of the ability to remember, and learn by past experience, and to fit what we hear into a regular and expected pattern. If the actual sounds did not fit into some such pattern, we should be at a loss to report what we actually heard. But even if I were not sure that what I heard was horses, in order to report that I heard a sound which wanted an explanation I should have to hear it as displaying a shape or pattern of some kind or other, though not, now, a familiar or expected one. The sound would have to have some cadence or other, if so musical a term may be used here. Now one of the functions of imagination on which I suppose everyone would agree is the function of forming mental images, of reproducing non-actual sounds and sights, of creating a non-physical world out of, as Kant says, the materials of the real world. This function is the first thing one thinks of in connexion with imagining. But Kant argues, it seems to me rightly, that *unless* an experience is experienced in such a way as to be reproduceable by the imagination, then it cannot be reported on or classified or understood. We might say that if I can report that I heard horses' hooves, or if I can even report that I heard a strange sound a bit like horses' hooves, then I must be able, or have been able at the time, to rehear the sound in my mind's ear, to reproduce it, that is, in my imagination, to re-present it to myself. But of course how accurately I reproduce, how exactly I can recreate *this* experience, as opposed to other similar experiences, may well be something that varies. Suppose for instance that you question my report. *Could* it have been horses? Are you sure? I may try to think whether my report was accurate by rehearsing in my mind exactly what I heard. Perhaps doing this will convince me. Perhaps in my imagination I can now recapture and reinterpret the sound, and say, 'No, I suppose it could have been something else.' But to do this is very difficult, because in rehearing one is rehearing not the sound itself but the sound *as originally heard*. The interpretation may already be inextricably *in* the image. To take another example: Suppose you say, 'I heard someone calling my name,' and you are questioned. 'Are you *sure* it was your name?' How can you possibly reproduce either actually with your voice, or potentially in your mind *the very sound you heard*, without articulating it as your name? (This is an example derived from Brentano.) If you heard the seagulls calling 'Ann' how can you rehear them without still hearing 'Ann' in what they cry? It *can* be done no doubt, but only with an effort. The connexion between hearing, rehearing and interpreting is extremely close. The close connexion is illustrated perhaps most clearly of all in the hearing of sounds as constituting a melody. Wittgenstein uses examples of this kind (hearing a melody, hearing it as a variation on a theme and so on, in speaking of the role of imagination in perception, or perceiving something *as* something, perceiving *an aspect*). It is surely only in hearing something as a melody that one can go over it, rethinking it, hear it again and reproduce it. This may be said to be an accident of the human voice. Given a keyboard one could produce and reproduce harmonies, not mere single line melodies and one would reproduce collections of notes which constituted neither harmonies nor melodies; but nevertheless there is a point in the example. For recognising, rehearing, having on the brain, all these are connected with a kind of interpretation or understanding, a perception, not only of the sounds, but of the *shape* of the sounds, their direction or purport, which is the very connexion I want to emphasise.

It is not a long step from this point to move to the affective nature of such images and reproductions. Hume had no doubt of the connexion between images and feelings. Indeed, though feelings were, in his vocabulary, part of the class of impressions (direct and immediate experiences), and images were ideas (faint copies of impressions, used in thinking and reasoning), yet he was quite prepared to assert that sometimes impressions and ideas were capable of being confused; and not only so, but that one of the functions of imagination was precisely to *convert*

c

ideas into impressions, to turn *mere* thought into feelings. The
more powerful the imagination, the more akin to genius the
imaginative gift, he argued, the greater this ability to convert
would be. So the function of what is usually called the creative
imagination was to create in other people ideas so powerful
that they were, or were indistinguishable from, impressions.
Thus you could perhaps by a powerful poet be made to feel the
sufferings of the dead in Hades, a mere idea if ever there was
one, as if it were *real suffering*, your own.

Later on, the connexion between imagining and feeling was
a commonplace, but nowhere so explicitly worked out as in
Wordsworth's theory of poetry and of images. The *Forms*, that
is the actual visual images of the hills and the phenomena perceived in childhood were, when he called them up and reflected
on them, inescapably bound up with the feelings, were indeed
creative of those feelings of love and fear which he felt bound to
express. So that the recollection of emotion, which meant
literally the *recalling* of the visible shapes, become for him the
essence of poetry. And it seems to me that this theory of poetry,
or theory, if you prefer it, of emotion, is not a mere romantic
fashion. It is of the greatest general importance.

Aesthetically, at least, it seems that a divorce between images
and feelings is productive of nothing but the false, vulgar and
sentimental. Mechanically produced images without feelings
are matched in the other direction by an assault on the feelings,
gratuitously carried out with no felt images to support it. But
this is perhaps a side issue. I hope I have said enough, by way
of example, to suggest the inextricable connexion between the
various aspects of the mental and perceptual life which I have
designated imaginative. The fact that many of our readings of
our perceptual world are thoroughly humdrum, that we share
them with our neighbours and never call them in question,
that they inspire us with no more profound emotion than a
feeling of familiarity, or even of tedium, this should not blind
us to the fact that our interpretations *can* be eccentric or idiosyncratic, and that the world can sometimes look and feel to us
threatening or sinister or wildly exciting. There is no sharp line
to be drawn between the imaginings of nightmare, of dream, of

daydream and of ordinary, daily, non-dreaming life, which itself is compounded, as I hope to have suggested, of sensory stimulus and the interpretation of this with the help of memory and common-sense knowledge.

Having thus established, as I hope, a fairly coherent cluster of phenomena, to be called imagination, there are three other points I want to make about it. The first two can be very briefly made. Imagination in this sense is a universal, shared capacity which everyone has. Though some children may be described as imaginative, others not, the fact is that if they can see and hear and recognise things, if they can talk and understand the significance of the familiar or the unfamiliar, then they have imagination, however limited. Secondly, besides being in this sense universal, imagination is highly individual. If it is true that only I can see with my eyes and hear with my ears, even though what I see and hear is the same as what you see and hear, it follows that my perception of the world is my own; and though, for the most part, we shall interpret the world alike according to our common needs and necessities and capabilities, though we shall for the most part even like the same things and dislike the same things, yet it is possible that any one of the stages of my interpretation of the world, or reaction to it, may be unique, peculiar to me, and capable of being shared only with effort and difficulty. (But of course to try to find out how someone else sees the world, how it strikes them, is of absorbing interest.)

The third point is more complicated and probably more controversial. Sartre, in his various writings about imagination, stressed, perhaps to the irritation of some of his readers, the point that imagining is to do with the unreal. In some ways this is such an obvious point that it seems hardly worth making. We all know that 'imaginary' wealth is different from real hard cash. Imaginary threats are different from actual threats, and to fear the one kind is sensible, to fear the other is paranoiac. Imaginary illnesses are not the illnesses which actually kill us; and so on. But it must be remembered that Sartre, following Brentano and Husserl, wanted to eliminate from the description of the imagination anything which could be called an image, that is, any representation like a picture in the mind. Thus he had to explain *how* it was that imagining a chair could be so different from perceiving a chair, if the difference, the mode of unreality, could not be explained in terms of an image of the chair in the mind. The unreality of the imagined chair came to be something greatly in need of explanation, and hence perhaps his insistence on it. I do not intend to follow his unsuccessful attempts to deal with this descriptive aspect of the matter now.

But in concentrating on the unreality of the imagined, Sartre also had it in mind to establish that imagination had an essentially *negative* function; that in thinking imaginatively one was always distancing oneself from the real world and thinking, not how things *actually are* but how they *are not*. *Le Néant*, indifferently for Sartre Nothingness, the negative, the unreal or the non-existent, is crucial to the analysis of imagination. And for him this has important consequences. For it is the distinctive feature of human consciousness to be capable of experiencing that dimension of awareness called *le Néant*. Consciousness (the-for-itself) is conscious (human beings, I would prefer to say, are conscious) because they can detach themselves from experience, and be aware of two things at once; of the sensations or perceptions they are having, and of themselves having them. They must be aware that their experience does not absorb everything; it is not everything in the world. They, the perceivers, are not identical with the object of perception, nor is the object identical with them. They can adopt a detached and exploratory attitude both with regard to themselves and with regard to the objects of their perception. They can expect things to be of a certain kind and find that they are not; they can remember that they used to be different, or predict that they will be different in the future, or simply grasp that they might have been otherwise than they are. All these are aspects of the negative mode of thought, of which imagination is a crucial part. Now I have rehearsed all this somewhat over-familiar theory not in order to criticise it, nor to trace it to its sources nor even to consider it in any detail, but only because there seems to me to be an interesting trace of truth in this sort of view of imagination.

In the first place, to say that imagination, and indeed consciousness as a whole, is in this respect negative, connected as much with possibilities as with actualities is surely to connect it with language. For as soon as you describe something you necessarily draw attention, indirectly, to the qualities the thing has *not*. Language, notoriously, enables you to say things truly or falsely. Choosing your words is choosing them from a range of possibilities. If your hat is indeed green, and you so describe it, it would have made sense to say it was red, though that would have been a lie. None would dispute this. And it seems that Sartre was virtually identifying consciousness with language-using (or potential language-using) when he made the power of envisaging unrealised possibilities, the awareness of non-actual features of things, into the defining characteristic of the conscious. Why he did not come out into the open and say that this was what he was doing can, I think, be fairly easily understood. In the first place, though this may seem trivial, such an identification of consciousness with linguistic competence creates difficulties with regard to infants, brain-damaged or aphasic people and animals (Sartre more than once suggests a ruthless Cartesianism about animals, that they are machines). Perhaps more seriously, he always had an extraordinarily ambivalent view of language, which can be detected in many different parts of his writing. This point is admirably made and illustrated by Joseph Halpern in his recent book *Critical Fictions*. On the one hand, Sartre half-recognised that language gave to its users precisely the ability to detach themselves from the actual, to 'surpass' the world, to stand back and become aware of the difference between themselves, the percipients, and the objects which they both perceived and described; and thus he half-recognised that any refinement and perfection of language would be a refinement and perfection of consciousness itself. On the other hand, he also hankered for the *massif*, for a plain uncomplicated world of actions, of doing, not saying. And in this mood, language seemed to him a distortion of reality, an obfuscating and necessarily falsifying fog, getting disastrously *between* humanity and the world. Words, on this view, represented the ultimate limit of Bad Faith, since they pretend to an accuracy and exactitude which in fact they insidiously destroy, more dangerously the more sophisticated their use. However, if we can discount this emotional attitude, I think we can say with some confidence that Sartre *did* recognise the close inevitable connexion between language and consciousness; and hence, in particular, between language and that mode of consciousness peculiarly devoted to the non-real, the imagination. And this is the first element of truth in the theory.

But, you may say, even if this is true, even if there is such a connexion, why should we particularly *value* this faculty to conceive of what is not the case? Why not just say that this is something that people can do, a characteristic human feat, not to be wondered at, still less to be greatly admired? What possible place has a statement of fact, that humans talk, in a lecture supposed to be about values? The consideration of this objection leads to the second respect in which I believe that Sartre's theory is true, or at any rate broadly true. For he makes a further connexion, between the ability to comprehend the *Néant*, to conceive of what is not the case, and the power to *act*. After all, action, when it is not mere reflex or bodily movement can be considered as intervention in the real world *with a view to changing it*. The argument is that if one could not in any way envisage the potential as well as the actual, if one could not grasp the possibility of things being otherwise than they are, then the notion of deliberately setting out to change the world would be inconceivable as well. If for example I am thirsty, I do not merely suffer this discomfort passively. In normal circumstances I envisage the possibility of slaking my thirst. I can imagine a cold drink and wonder whether it is in the refrigerator. I can imagine various possible drinks and in comparing them decide which one it is that I most want. And so I finally take action and change my condition to one of satisfaction. Of course this simple example shows, among other things, how our freedom may be limited, by lack of resources or lack of executive efficiency; but it also shows that the notion of a changeable future, of non-actual circumstances, is essential to what freedom we have.

If we go on to consider a more complicated example than this, then obviously the playing with possibilities, the attempt to think what it would be like if this or that were brought about, has a yet more important part in deliberate action, which may itself become a complicated chain of means and ends. It would probably be agreed, at a common sense level, that an *imaginative* person is more capable than another who is less imaginative of thinking of new, hitherto unrealised possibilities, and of entering with feeling into a non-actual future. It is thus generally agreed that it is the imaginative who are innovators and experimenters in the real world. But the point that I, following Sartre, would make is that *everybody* has this power of conceiving possibilities, and of envisaging the unreal which is imagination; and that if they did not have it, they would be incapable of deliberate action, that is they would not be free. And so we come at last to a reason for valuing the imagination above all faculties. Not only is it nice that we have it; not only does it give rise to pleasant fancies and agreeable dreams; not only is it connected with all the emotions both nice and nasty from love to jealousy and fear; but it is also at the heart of individual freedom, the defence of which, as a respectable value, need hardly be undertaken.

So now it is time to raise a further question. Granted that imagination is universal . . . that we all have it; granted even, that without it we could not be free agents, even in principle, can this faculty be educated? I shall argue that it can. I shall suggest that educating the imagination is more like teaching someone to read than it is like teaching a child to walk . . . that is to say someone not taught will not just pick it up, but may be permanently deprived by his lack of education. I must then first try to show why I believe that the imagination is educable and then consequentially to show what kind of education will nourish or benefit it. It should then follow, if the evaluative part of my argument already presented is accepted that *that* sort of education is what we should attempt to provide.

So what is the basis for the assertion that the imagination is educable? I think it is necessary, in order to discover the grounds, to go back to the beginning and consider again the way in which, I have argued, imagination is interwoven with perception. I have argued, and I will not repeat the arguments, that imagination enters into our perception of the ordinary world and enables us to interpret it in one way rather than another. It is what prevents our perceptions from being totally random, unfamiliar, confusing or unpredictable. But it is also that which, being individual and peculiar to each of us, enables each to find his own interpretation . . . to see pictures in the flames, to make melodies out of birdsong, to see a landscape as sad or as sublime. We may use the word 'vision' perhaps, as shorthand for what it is that the imagination creates, though I would be the last to wish to confine imagination literally to the visual. But 'vision' will do, because a vision is significant to the person who has it. It is something which he does not passively receive but which he grasps, and understands or tries to understand. At least he feels sure that in some way it has meaning; and I am suggesting that it is precisely the *meaningfulness* of experience which is supplied by imagination. Thus if a man makes a film, he may make it of the most ordinary ingredients, but may make it in such a way that those ingredients are presented as sinister or happy or absurd. Again a picture may make one see a kind of landscape as romantic or beautiful or threatening, which one had not thought of in that light before. When this happens the film-maker or the painter has imaginatively 'seen' the landscape or the slice of life and has passed on his vision to his audience. His interpretation of meaning need not be explicit in order for this to be a true account of what has happened. But of course it may be explicit or he may try very hard to make it so. Wordsworth provides many statements or attempted statements of what he has *seen in* the objects of his sight and memory. Coleridge, too, often seems to hunt for the exact significance which eludes him but which he nevertheless feels certain *is* contained in what he actually saw. 'O that I could but explain these concentric wrinkles in my spectra' he cries. (This of a mildly opium-induced vision on the night of November 23rd 1803.) The explanation he wants is an explanation of the *meaning* or *significance* of the wrinkles. He knows that in some sense what he sees is symbolic. If only he looked harder he could see *through* it to something valuable and powerfully felt. A poet, he says, must have eyes as sharp as the eyes of an Arab in the desert or an Indian tracker in order to see the significance of the world.

Such visions can be shared. And to share them is itself to educate, even if the visions are not worth very much in themselves. For it is educative to discover that there are different ways of seeing things. It enlarges the understanding, provides new possibilities of enjoyment, and awakes the power to see and interpret for oneself. In this way education is what sharpens the eye, and so the imagination begins to be active and free. One can, manifestly, be taught to look and listen even if one cannot be taught to see and hear. And to be taught this is to have one's imagination educated. It is not only a vision which can be shared, but, obviously, ideas as well. And, as J. S. Mill said 'the imaginative emotion which an idea when vividly conceived excites in us' is a fact, an experience which actually occurs.

In the end I believe it is the possibility of such an imaginative emotion which is the point of education. Such an emotion, such excitement, interest, pleasure, whatever it is called, is of value in itself. One does not have to ask what is it valuable *for*, or to what does it lead, it is simply good in itself, the best thing there is. Prosaically, one cannot teach children to feel. But one can teach them to see enough *in* the things before them to become excited rather than bored at the thought of them, and this is the education of the imagination.

I doubt if anything more in the way of proof is possible to show that the imaginative faculty is educable. We *know* that it is so from experience, because it happens. We can think of actual cases where an absorbing interest was aroused in something through education, an interest which without education could never have been more than transitory or fleeting. It is a familiar phenomenon. But what sort of education does this entail? It is now time at last to turn to the final part of the question: What sort of education am I saying is so good? Well, to use the imagination, I have argued, is to see more in what is before us than bare perception (if such a thing could be conceived) would allow us to see. And so the education of this capacity is such as to open one's eyes to the further possibilities, to the meaning, significance or point of whatever presents itself. This may be partly a matter of *actual* seeing. Children can be taught to notice their surroundings, and even from an extremely early age there is a difference between the child who is constantly with someone who finds things interesting, worth commenting on and pointing out, and the child who has no such stimulus. So much is an educational cliché. So one of the lasting demands of the kind of education I claim to be valuable is that it should be undertaken by people who themselves find things exciting, interesting, funny, significant, worth at any rate going on about. And this, though it sounds straightforward enough is actually quite a dfficult demand to meet. (One of the lunacies of some current educational theory, incidentally, is that in its eagerness to insist that the teacher is not set above the pupil, it derides those teachers who teach particular subjects because they like them. It is the role of the teacher, according to this theory, to guide and organise the interests of the pupils, not to display his own, still less to impart what learning he has himself acquired.) My own view is that without a teacher who is capable of intense interest in what he is teaching, or at least an absolute certainty that there is a point in it, no education is really possible; and that with such a teacher, though results cannot be guaranteed, they may be both surprising and lasting. The depressing thing about this view is that you can teach or train teachers to avoid some gross mistakes in teaching; you can instruct them in what signs to look out for in their pupils which should alert them to possible needs or troubles; you can, and should, teach them to think about what they are doing, and to become theorists as well as practitioners, but you cannot easily teach them to be imaginative. By the time they come to be teachers it is often too late. But perhaps this is an unduly pessimistic conclusion, and there is no need to elaborate it here.

Now it may seem that my theory of the imagination and its functions is hopelessly romantic; that what I am urging as supremely valuable is an education in sensibility which could have no practical use and which might be positively at odds with the more basic demands of the educational curriculum, and at best should be relegated to the general studies, un-examinable, unimportant part of education at school. But I should like to make two points. First, and most important, the kind of education of the imagination that I am talking about, though it includes education in 'arts' subjects, is not exclusively such; and secondly, even if it were, it is doubtful whether it should be so relegated in the school time-table. To deal with the first point: What I am urging is that the goal of education should be to understand and interpret a whole range of phenomena, natural and man-made, objects of mathematical, mechanical, aesthetic interest alike, so that within the parti-cular field of study, whatever it is, the feeling of there being *more*, more to learn, more to think about, more to try or do, is the predominant feeling. Such an interest is by no means to be confined to 'arts' subjects, though it may arise here as else-where. The only thing it seems to me which makes such a goal even partly attainable is that the subject in question should be introduced in sufficient detail, sufficient time should be allotted to it, for the pupil to begin to understand what is really in-volved. And this is the real objection, in my view, to the almost universal demand for *breadth* in education, for a decrease in specialisation. For I do not see how anyone can, except by the merest chance or on account of some personal dynamic demand for knowledge, quite rare in children, come to feel the infinite possibilities of any subject, its intricacies, its own demands, if what he gets of it is a prepackaged example, a chosen bit pre-digested and designed especially to show him how the subject links with other subjects. This is not the appropriate time or place to enter in detail into the risks of the prepackaged; nor into the kind of compromise between breadth and depth, be-tween the narrow and the broad which I believe all curricula have to attempt. But I should just say that I am not, of course, advocating that anyone, whether at school or even university should be plunged straight into the intricacies of a subject with-out selection; nor do I believe in a kind of sacred barrier be-tween one subject and another. But the best education allows the pupil constantly to see that there *are* further details, that there is more to do if he chooses to do it, and that if he understands *this* bit thoroughly he may be able to go on by himself and make connexions for himself which no one else has thought of. To be told in advance that there are such connexions, which are to be illustrated, to be educated entirely in someone else's bright idea of what is the most important little bit of the subject, this is death not only to true learning but to any conceivable free imaginative journeyings into the subject on the part of the pupil. So one of the first demands of education is that there should be a fair degree of specialisation whether the subject matter be arts or science.

But there is a further related point. I do not believe that nearly enough emphasis is laid, in educational philosophy, on the obvious function of education in enabling people to live better, after they have finished being educated, than they would have lived without education. Too often the point is obscured by arguments about the nature or definition of education, which turn out to show that education goes on all the time, and that therefore life after education is life after death. But there is a sense in which we all know that education for most people doesn't go on for ever. And I would argue that, to put it briefly, education is largely a preparation for work, since without work no life is complete. Now if it is true that the imagination is, as I have argued, the power to think of what is *not* the case, to envisage things as they are not yet but may become, and if this is the essence of human freedom to act, then work is itself a way of exercising imagination, and the most important way. The satisfaction of work is the satisfaction of doing, making, changing, controlling. It is our normal intervention in the world, whatever the nature of the work, or the bounds of our particular bit of the world. To get on, to complete something, to get things under way, these are all things which we want, and if we have them we are on the way to being happy. All these things are the exercise of the human power to master, control, dominate and change the immediate or more remote world; and they are all dependent upon the imagination in my account of it, for such powers *could* not exist without the capacity to think of the future, to plan, and to envisage possible change. So for education to concentrate on imaginative growth does not in the least entail that such education should be concerned only with the peripheral, non-essential aspects of the preparation for life. But it is probably also true to say that even if the education of imagination were mainly a matter of educating people to enjoy literature and the arts, it should not be dismissed as a mere froth on the surface of education as a whole. For learning to feel the imaginative emotions may well come more easily through the arts than in any other way. And this does not, incidentally, mean always *doing*, always improvising on the glockenspiel, painting with the poster paints, writing one's own poems, or acting out a drama in spontaneous action on the stage. Just as much, it means learning what other people have done, listening to music someone else has written, looking at other people's paintings and reading. Both the sensibility and the intelligence can be educated in this way, and certainly the imaginative emotion which follows on ideas can be experienced. And such emotions, as I have already said, are in my opinion, of *intrinsic* value, such that to live without them is to live in the universe of death.

There is one further, somewhat practical, point to be made. I do not believe that it is possible to educate the imagination without ensuring for every pupil a certain degree of solitude. Though everyone has imagination, and though it is a faculty as common as sight and hearing, yet each has his own vision, his own conception of the world. And since imagination is not merely perceptual but also emotional and interpretational, its exercise takes time, and a degree of contemplation. I believe that perpetual society destroys the imaginative faculty, and that children who fear solitude and are bored immediately they are alone are becoming deprived in this very respect. It is the duty of education, it seems to me, to counteract the very strong pressures of current fashion to make solitude seem a disgrace or a disaster. Every move in the direction of working in groups, or team activity, of joint projects and communal discussion, is a move in the wrong direction. Even the insistence that everyone must participate in everything is damaging. Corporate activity may be a fine thing from time to time. But independence is perhaps finer. Now the imagination is above all else that in virtue of which we can be independent. Whatever our situation we can think as we please, interpret as we please, and feel as we are led to by our own interpretations. In the last resort, the education of the imagination is to be valued because it is the only possible education for freedom. And freedom or *in-dependence* is a goal for each person separately. It is of course a romantic ideal, just as the view of imagination which I have expressed is a romantic view. But I do not believe that for that reason it can be shown to be false. And the ideal follows, it seems to me, inevitably from the notion of imagination itself. What we value arises from the nature of things.

4

CONJUGAL FAITHFULNESS

P. Æ. Hutchings

'Faithfulness' is defined in *The Oxford English Dictionary* of 1901 in a way that leaves out what one might take as a central paradigm. The *OED* entry reads, in part

Faithfulness . . . the quality of being faithful.
A. Fidelity, loyalty (to a superior or friend) . . .
B. Strict adherence to one's pledged word; honesty, sincerity. . . .

The feudal system, the army, and the rest of such things are provided for in (A) 'loyalty to a superior . . .', and so are friends – after superiors. In (B), commercial interests are satisfactorily covered: 'strict adherence to one's pledged word, honesty. . . .' It is a nice piece of social history: from William the Conqueror to the latter phases of the Industrial Revolution, in two definitions. But a very odd piece of social history, in that conjugal faithfulness, the most existential one that there is, does not rate a mention.

I shall take conjugal faithfulness as a paradigm of Faithfulness, principally because it is an existential faithfulness. However, while we still recall the terms of the *OED* definition, it is useful to notice how conjugal faithfulness bridges part (A) and part (B) of the definition. Conjugal faithfulness is faithfulness (a) to a person, and it involves (b) pledged words, and one's putative adherence to them.

The pledged word is crucial to faithfulness most notably in

delimiting as it sets up, the matter of the faithfulness; but it
delimits rather than sets up. The matter is prior to the pledge.

When the faithfulness of God is praised in the Psalms, it is
faithfulness to a covenant which has been spelled out, and made
with a person – or in this case a people, Israel:

> He shall defend thee under his wings, and thou shalt be safe
> under his feathers; his faithfulness and truth shall be thy
> shield and buckler.
>
> (*Book of Common Prayer*: Psalm xci, 3)

And we may extract a pattern from the Old Testament: two
convenantors, and a covenant delimiting a matter and binding
both the wills and the expectations of each party. Thus the
covenant, as a promise, sets up obligations with respect to the
matter promised – the covenant itself requiring the faithfulness
or steadfastness of the parties should the occasional wills some
time after the covenant not be as well disposed to the matter as
they were at the time of the covenant. This overall pattern is
to be extracted, and it is an important one; but if that were *all*
that one got out of the Psalm or out of real examples of faithfulness, one would deliver a paper on promising, and one
would merely gloss it with remarks about faithfulness: 'faithfulness is something which is exhibited *to* promises, or is steadfastness *in* them', and so forth.

However, there is more to faithfulness than its being a noun
derived from the adverb 'faithfully'. And it is Søren Kierkegaard's account of conjugal faithfulness that takes us to the
heart of what more there is.

For Søren Kierkegaard's Judge William in *Either/Or*[1] it is not
the legalistic pattern of covenant and steadfast observance
which is interesting, but the Psalmists 'claim' in another place:

> for I claim that love is built to last for ever and your faith-
> fulness founded firmly in the heavens.
>
> *The Jerusalem Bible*, Psalm 89[2]

This is splendidly poetic; and it may be soundly ontological,
or at any rate soundly existential. Judge William thinks so:

and if the matter is as Judge William thinks it, the ambition of the present paper may be secured.

The Ambition of the Present Paper

The aim of this paper is to advance the claims of a *substantialist* account of faithfulness: 'substantialist' having been chosen because it echoes an item from the vocabulary of Judge William's letter and because it engages with the central notions of the letter. Conjugal faithfulness is taken as a pattern,[3] a paradigm, because it, at least on Judge William's account of it, illustrates the substantialist view. What is this view? It is the view that not the promise, delimiting, and binding on the will, is the subject of faithfulness, in the classic case; rather it is the matter, itself, of the promise which binds. Not all cases, alas, are classic ones, but we shall come to this point only at the very end of the present paper: and the point will be the sting in the paper's tail.

Before we consider Judge William's text it may be useful to make a short conceptual detour by way of a clarification of notions.

What would be the Point that a Substantialist Doctrine of Faithfulness tried to make?

If one were to ask 'Why be faithful?' one might get two answers: (i) 'If faithfulness is to covenants, agreements, promises, etc., then that you have *made* one is reason enough for keeping it'; (ii) 'You are faithful because of the very *reasons for making* the covenant, promise or agreement.' Promises are made not just for the sake of making promises; they are made, and necessarily made, for other reasons; and they may in the end be kept for these other reasons. Faithfulness is properly to these reasons. One is not, I maintain, faithful to the *promise*, although idiom seems to allow this.

Perhaps in fact, as well as in idiom, one can be, as it is put, (1) 'faithful to *a* promise'; but, idiom and its doubtful guidance aside, one can *certainly* be (2) faithful *to the matter* of a promise;

and (3) faithful to persons, (3.1) *under* delimiting *designations* (such as 'wife', 'husband', 'friend', 'pastor', 'advocate'), (3.2) *in the matter* of a promise or promises (e.g. to forsake all others).

Promises and the Flagging Will

The business of delimitation touched upon though not, unfortunately, analysed as fully as it need be, we may pass to another, linked aspect of promises. One might say that the purpose of a promise is to keep alive – in some way – the reasons underlying it, as well as to set *out* the obligations which the promise sets *up*. How does a promise keep alive the will with respect to what is promised? Does it? Is it always the promise that does it? Or is this vivification properly the work of something other than a promise? Certainly Judge William thinks that it is the matter, and not a promise about it, that can permanently sustain the will.

Judge William is prepared to offer an account of love such that conjugal faithfulness is *of the matter*, and is not an affair of promises respecting the matter; and he is prepared to justify – if indirectly because he never quite cites them – two of the most difficult clauses of the marriage service. On his account, the marriage may, in some sense, need the promises, but the will never seems to be going to need to fall back on them alone. 'Never seems,' I said, but at the end we must reconsider this 'seems'.

You will recall that in the Church of England service[4] the curate says – or said – to the man, at the second 'Wilt Thou':

Wilt thou love[5] her, comfort her, honour her and keep her in sickness and in health; and, forsaking all other, keep thee only unto her, so long as ye both shall live?
(Marriage Service of the Church of England:
Book of Common Prayer)

It is notable that conjugal faithfulness begins as 'forsaking all other' and is supposed to go on as a 'keeping only unto her, so long as ye both shall live'. Reading the marriage service we might be inclined to argue: 'If such promises are not needed, surely we would not make them; if they are needed, they must, presumably, be difficult to keep. And if difficult, they can possibly become so difficult that, if they do get kept, faithfulness in hard cases is to them and simply to them.' A not implausible, but a rather bleak account.

Judge William invests less than we might expect a Judge to, in an argument from the difficulty of keeping the promises to a conclusion that, if kept so in travail, promises become the object of the faithfulness. And 'the effort as such' to keep the marriage vows does not impress Judge William. When this effort is made – and successfully – it is the matter of the marriage which is the object of it, not the vows, and not even – though this is a trickier point – the matter mediated through the vows. Actual faithfulnesses are due to an ontological and will-sustaining somewhat, and not to promises, even promises about the somewhat.

The material, substantial, somewhat is defined by Judge William from the outset as 'Aesthetic'. The so-called 'letter' to '*A*' is on 'the Aesthetic Validity of Marriage', and we must take seriously the notion of the aesthetic if we are to understand the ontology of love and of marriage, and so of faithfulness, that we are offered by Judge William.

What 'properly constitutes' marriage, 'gives it its *substantial content*', is 'love',[6] and 'love itself is the aesthetic'; it is this love, and not just promises about it, which can sustain the will.

What can be meant by 'Aesthetic' in a Context where it is an Aesthetic Somewhat that can sustain the Will?

There are at least four[7] main senses in which love may be said, in terms of Judge William's use of the expression 'aesthetic', to be aesthetic; we have time this afternoon to look at length at only one of them, at what we might call the *eternal-as-aesthetic/ aesthetic-as-eternal*, sense. This answers to a somewhat Kantian idea, though it is given a very Existential turn indeed by Kierkegaard. At the very end of the paper we will touch briefly on love as 'uniting', as does the Hegelian aesthetic, 'the universal and the particular', the Idea and the instance. This union of universal and particular cashes out eventually as a barbed notion; but what we call 'the sting in the tail' of the paper can wait till the end of it.

Developing his thesis of *The-aesthetic-as-eternal* Judge William uses the expressions 'eternal' and 'infinite' concerning love some seventy[8] times, and there is a subtle interplay of contextual usages. Let us begin with the first occurrence of 'eternal'. Judge William is writing of Romantic Love:

> In spite of the fact that this love is essentially based on the sensuous, it is noble nevertheless, by reason of the consciousness of *eternity* which it embodies; for what distinguishes all love from lust is that it bears an impress of *eternity*. *E/O*, p. 18/p. 21 (italics mine).

Let us take the Romantic Love here as the classic *coup de foudre*: how does this 'embody' any 'eternity'? Judge William's model, though it is never acknowledged explicitly, seems to be something like Kant's aesthetic idea:

> . . . the aesthetic idea is a representation of the imagination, annexed to a given concept, with which, in the free employment of imagination, such a multiplicity of partial representations are bound up, that no expression indicating a definite concept can be found for it – one which on that account allows a concept to be supplemented in thought by much that is indefinable in words, and the feeling of which quickens the cognitive faculties, and with language, as a mere thing of the letter, binds up the spirit (soul) also.
>
> *Critique of Judgement*, trans. J. C. Meredith,
> Oxford, Clarendon Press, 1928, Part I, Book II,
> p. 179

The aesthetic idea 'binding so much up' can be taken, all at once, in one; taken, it has then to be unpacked, exfoliated. And it is this dialectic between (1) and 'all at once'-ness of *le coup de foudre*/the aesthetic idea as presented, and, (2) the need, then, to express in time what has been compressed into an instant, that makes up Judge William's ontology or phenomenology of love. Notice that Judge William does not simply want to maintain that a moment in which one falls in love merely resembles an aesthetic idea in this 'eternal' aspect: he wants to say that love *is* the aesthetic, and that it is structured as an aesthetic idea is structured. Judge William wants to have a whole ontology, not a mere analogy.

Behind the 'eternity', the given-in-one-ness, which Judge William ascribes to love, there hovers the notion of a *totum simul*, and the classic Boethian definition of eternity ('Eternity is the simultaneous and complete possession of infinite life': *Consolation of Philosophy*, Book V, Prose VI). The sense of a *totum simul* – 'simultaneous and complete' – is part of the sense of the sentence with which Judge William continues the passage already quoted:

> The lovers are sincerely convinced that their relationship is in itself a *complete whole* which never can be altered. *E/O*, p. 18/p. 21 (italics mine).

The relationship of love is all given, all at once. But it needs to be 'developed'. Judge William has first love, *le coup de foudre* as, for those whom he calls 'fortunate individuals',[9] essentially a something needing to be lived out: and lived out so for a life time:

> 'The first' is simply the present, but the present for [the fortunate] is the constantly unfolding and rejuvenating 'first'. *E/O*, p. 34/p. 40.

Love is, in other, and later, words of Judge William's, 'historical'; and *so* it makes claims 'as long as ye both shall live'.

Kant refers to the aesthetic idea as 'inexponible', and so is love-as-aesthetic inexponible. This means that, though you will never get out of it all that is, eternally, in it, you must devote all the time you have to this uncompletable task of exfoliation. A *mere* aesthetic idea is inexponible, but does not preempt all your time in its reading. Love, as the particular pragmatic and aesthetic given that it is, lays a more absolute claim on your time, as love; and as inexponible it lays claim on all of your time.

Mildly critical of certain recent analyses of time-transcendence and some related phenomena in the arts,[10] Professor

R. W. Hepburn of Edinburgh insists on the 'temporal adventure' of the aesthetic. The aesthetic artifact may be characterised by something about it which is *all given at once* but the processes both of complex givings, and of readings (simple readings, repeated simple readings, and critical readings), all take, and otherwise involve, time. Even so, the 'eternal' aesthetic is given, in some sense, temporally. Time is an inescapable dimension for the time bound. And it is a dimension even of eternal moments, and the 'eternities' of aesthetic ideas.

Judge William, altogether a precursor of Professor Hepburn, is so insistent on the pre-emption of time by the eternal in love that he redefines the aesthetic to take account of it, to make sure that the second phase of the eternal in the aesthetic is treated as properly as the first phase; that the unfolding is treated as seriously as the infoldedness of the aesthetic. Judge William writes:

> When one follows, either dialectically or historically, the development of the aesthetically beautiful, one will find that the direction of this movement is always away from spatial determinants to those of time, and that the perfection of art depends upon the successive possibility of detaching oneself from space and orienting oneself towards time. *E/O*, p. 114/ p. 139.[11]

The aesthetic ceases, with Judge William, to be defined in the tradition simply of *ut pictura poesis*,[12] or in terms of the 'all together and all at once-ness of the Kantian aesthetic idea. The aesthetic becomes redefined as a kind of tension between, and a resolution of, (1) the simultaneous-*cum*-spatial of the moment of the aesthetic idea's *being given* in a moment, and therefore *giving* in this moment a *totum simul*, and: (2) the exfoliating in time of the 'all' that is so given. This redefinition of the aesthetic by Judge William is insisted on in the interests of the 'historical' aspect of love, and in the interest of the 'protracted character of marriage'. But it might be taken as a proper redefinition of the aesthetic on its own, aesthetic, grounds: this we cannot go into here. But notice that Professor Hepburn, whose article was cited above, would undoubtedly applaud Judge William's revision. Hepburn quotes, in his paper, Poulet, who writes:

All the elements [of, as it were, a certain aesthetic ideal] are so closely intertwined that the effect can register only as *one*. It is all there, gathered up, not as yet unfolded (*ramassé . . . non encore déroulé*). If complex, then at the same time simple, because unified . . . (article cited, p. 154).[13]

But it is the *déroulement*, as much as 'all-at-once'-ness that the aesthetician must attend to.

Marvell's injunction 'To His Coy Mistress':

> Let us roll our strength and all
> Our sweetness up into one ball,
> And tear our pleasures with rough strife
> Through the iron gates of life.

is, on the aesthetic analysis of love, unnecessary. Love, on Judge William's account of it, comes already *ramassé*. And it simply awaits a *déroulement* – something calmer, in Judge William's experience, and altogether more domestic, than Marvell's projected passion. But, differences in 'tone' apart, the unrolling of something already rolled up into a unity is what 'historical' love is.

Love-as-aesthetic must unfold in time; for, Judge William writes,

> This is simply the significance of time, and it is the lot of mankind and individual men to live in it. *E/O*, p. 107/p. 130.

What is real for him is what Judge William calls time as 'internal history' which, he writes,

> . . . has the *idea*[14] in itself and precisely for this reason is aesthetic. *E/O*, p. 115/p. 140 (italic mine).

This puts it the other way round, but the point is dialectical: one might as well say, as Judge William has already said often enough if less directly, that 'the *idea* has its history in itself'.* Judge William does, a few lines later, say:

---

* Judge William does call marriage, in a particularly difficult and dialectical passage, among other things: 'The eternal which has the temporal in itself.' *E/O*, p. 79/p. 96.

It [this internal history] is an eternity in which the temporal has not vanished like an ideal moment, but in which it is constantly present as a real moment. *E/O*, pp. 115–16/ p. 140.

And this is why Judge William says, absolutely to the point of our present paper, of conjugal love, that:

it is faithful, *E/O*, p. 116/p. 140 (italics mine). (Cross refer, p. 47/p. 56.)

For faithfulness is *to* something in which the temporal 'is constantly present as a real moment'. One might put it that: faithfulness[15] is not just *to* love, it is *of the matter of love*. It is of the matter of love in so far as love is 'historical' and so consumes human time. Faithfulness is the giving of that, due, time for love's unfolding.

To put the issue at its most minimal: faithfulness guarantees existentially, as the marriage promises simply hedge with contractual guarantees, the lived, the human time, which love has pre-empted as due to its historicity. To be faithful to love is to continue to take it as it is given, because, as given, love is at once *now* overwhelming, and with respect to subsequent '*nows*' essentially pre-emptive. Faithfulness is simply openness to the large claims which love makes on time. Marriage, Judge William admits, is 'based upon resignation' ('as love is not'); on 'resolute purpose and sense of obligation'; and he says that 'purpose is resignation in its richest form'; but '*enthusiasm to will*' aroused by love, is primitive to all the rest. The contractual, covenanted, 'determinants' which 'season' first love into marriage are simply added to the 'natural determinant'. Though this 'natural determinant', as merely 'natural' needs something superadded, it is the first and the substantial condition of marriage. And 'enthusiasm to will' is generated by an 'eternal' matter.

So it is that the marriage vow 'till death do us part' could easily enough be got by Judge William from the nature of love-as-given. Early on in his letter he writes:

like everything eternal/[first love] has the double propensity of presupposing itself back into all eternity and forward into all eternity. *E/O*, p. 36/p. 43.

Judge William would approve of what Donne said:

> I wonder by my troth, what thou, and I
> Did, till we lov'd?
>   ['The Good Morrow']

Love projects itself back, and so into all eternity. And it must go on for all the future time that the lovers have:

> . . . one can inerrantly observe in every man whether he truly has been in love. Love involves a transfiguration, a spiritualisation, *which lasts his whole life long. E/O*, p. 37/p. 44 (italics mine).

His whole life long being all the human time that the eternal in love can have at its disposal. The 'protracted character of marriage' is simply *due* to the 'eternal' nature of true love whose unfolding must, essentially, be protracted for a lifetime.

'Forsaking all Other . . .'

Enough has been said to show how Judge William might persuade us that love, as eternal, pre-empts time forwards from *le premier coup, le coup de foudre*; but how does its eternity account for love's exclusiveness? How is the clause in the marriage service 'forsaking all other' due to the ontology of love? Why not a plurality of loves and a plurality of eternities?

The notion of a plurality is perhaps ruled out by the passage which has already been cited in relation to the idea of a *totum simul*:

> The lovers are sincerely convinced that their relationship is in itself a *complete whole. . . . E/O*, p. 18/p. 21 (italics mine).

But complete wholes, whilst they exclude one another, are not incompatible with one another, so this will hardly do. Complete wholes rule out what is heterogeneous with respect to themselves: they can, however, and do – and must – coexist with other complete wholes. What else can Judge William offer in favour of the absolute necessity *in the case* of our 'forsaking all other'? He wants a whole which is not simply a totality; he wants one that is – nasty word, but needed here – in some ways a 'totalitarian' totality.

There is a nice, and perhaps persuasive, piece of phenomenology, offered in Judge William's account of first love:

> ... first love is an absolute alertness, an absolute beholding. It is directed towards a single, definite and actual object, which alone has existence for it, everything else being non-existent. This one object does not exist in vague outline but as a definite living being. *E/O*, p. 36/p. 43.[16]

So 'definite' indeed is she or he that everyone else is 'non-existent'. It is not, then, very difficult to forsake those who no longer are.

But Judge William would like to get this exclusiveness of love, 'forsaking all other', somehow out of the 'eternity' of love, taking the piece of phenomenology just cited as a mere supporting argument. He says, rather often in the 'letter', that 'one loves only once'. This is the case, if it is, presumably because the eternity of one love is sufficient to occupy the whole of any given life time. If one sees historical time as a line, then this will do, for the horizontal: but why are there not a number of such lines in one person's life time, like the lines ruled in an exercise book?

It may take a life time to be faithful 'horizontally' to one love. But does it take, does it require, one love, *all* of the time at any time? Can I not love, plurally? Judge William (though remarkably broadminded about 'little amorous affairs', given the year of his letter, 1843), wants to say, as is traditionally said: you cannot love in the proto-conjugal or conjugal sense, plurally. To do so would be unfaithfulness to the matter of love.

Judge William argues the issue in this way:

> [conjugal love] feels no need of loving more than one, but senses the blissfulness of this restriction, for it *senses an eternity in this once*. *E/O*, p. 94/p. 114.

Even given that 'eternity' can be cashed in Judge William's

language as 'once', can we allow this punning move from 'this *once*' to '*one – and only one*'? 'Eternity', here, one supposes, must be linked to a notion of completeness, as in the earlier citation – 'their relationship is in itself a *complete* whole' – where completeness, however, carries the further notion that more than one of these completenesses is not only unnecessary but, rather, that two such completenesses would damage one another. But exactly how Judge William gets this out of his proffered argument is not clear.

Judge William wants the notion of two loves, or two spouses had at once, to be absurd because of the logic of the notion of love or spouse; or, since SK was not a modern conceptual analyst, he wants it to be absurd because of the ontological structure of these relationships of love. And perhaps the best he can do, to underwrite sexual faithfulness in marriage, is to appeal to his supporting argument, as we have called it, as a spelling out of the notion that an *eternity* pre-empts not only future time but also, by virtue of its 'completeness', *all* the time that is at any time available. And it might be allowed that eternity has this sense, or can have it, too; a spouse or love is not entitled to all the time of a day, but is entitled to all that is available for *that* kind of relationship, i.e. precisely *that* kind. One does feel, however, that 'eternity' does less for the principle of 'forsaking all other' than would some more psychological account of the inner nature of the relationship of love. This account, though Judge William talks of his own conjugal relationship in fairly intimate terms, we do not get in the letter. Judge William reproaches 'A', 'for after all you had found' – (unlike Judge William himself) – 'no single individual to whom you could wish to be everything'. And Judge William remarks later, 'he who loves has lost himself and forgotten himself in the other'. But less is made of all this than might be; perhaps just because in reality it is 'A', that is Søren Kierkegaard himself, who is the puppet master of Judge William. And, notoriously, SK never married.

How Substantial is *Judge William's Substantialism?*

For our present purposes the importance of Judge William's argument lies not simply in its persuasiveness or otherwise with respect to love, but in its attempting to show the *necessity in the matter* in the case of the marriage vows. These do not establish the marital relation, they simply hedge it: 'The gist of the matter is to preserve love in time.' And:

> . . . so long as there is no alteration in first love (and this we have agreed is contained in conjugal love), there can be no question of the strict necessity of duty . . . *E/O*, p. 122/p. 148.

Furthermore to anyone who sees the duty of observing the marriage vows as a duty and so irksome, Judge William remarks, as he does to the first reader of his letter, the ever present 'A',

> . . . the fact is you do not believe in the *eternity* of love. *E/O*, p. 122/p. 48 (italic mine).

A belief in the eternity of love would render vows at once appropriate – to make; and easy – to keep. This may strike us as a merely convenient doctrine of eternity, orthodox and convenient, that is, for Kierkegaard the possible candidate for ordination. But under his Judge William persona, Søren Kierkegaard faces those implications of his substantialism that would set him at odds with the orthodox at least in the nineteenth-century church. Judge William takes his aesthetic 'eternity' very seriously, so seriously that he is prepared to acknowledge the possibly radical consequences of his notions. He writes:

> . . . for it it were true that one loves several times, marriage would be a questionable institution; it might seem that the erotic suffered harm from the arbitrary exaction of the religious which required as a rule that one should love only once, and disposes of the business of the erotic as cavalierly as though it were to say 'you can marry once, and that's the end of it'. *E/O*, p. 51/p. 61.

Radical enough! And this passage might seem to play right into the hands of, for example, Shelley and the notes on marriage appended to 'Queen Mab'. If love could, itself, fail, so too could marriage whose substance it is. Judge William is certainly frank; he is also dialectical. And he sees the exactions of the religious, as, at bottom, something simply due to the case.

He reproaches 'A' in these terms:

> for you . . . love is obviously not the highest thing, for otherwise you would be glad there was a power capable of compelling you to remain in it. *E/O*, p. 122/p. 148.[17]

And a little later he writes:

> . . . when he [=Duty] says 'It [love] shall be preserved' there is in it an authority which answers to the heartfelt desire of love. . . . 'Fear not, you shall conquer' speaking not futuristically, for that only suggests hope, but imperatively, and in this lies an assurance which nothing can shake. *E/O*, p. 123/ p. 149.

True or untrue, the analysis of love and conjugal love which Judge William gives is crucial to *a* notion of faithfulness: faithfulness is to the matter of the promises, which the promises merely hedge, and not simply to the promises themselves. Faithfulness is, to pun deliberately, to the ineluctable *promise* of the matter as it was once, and first, and forever given.[18] Faithfulness is not to promises about the matter. Though marriage is a 'covenant', and one established by God, it is to love that the faithful are to be faithful, and not, at bottom, to the covenant.

This may all be so ideally; but the world can seem less than ideal. Love seems not always to be eternal, but sometimes to die. One seems to oneself to be able to love more than once, and more than one person at one time. Well, if the world seems to fall short of Judge William's 'aesthetic' conception in these matters, can it not be treated exactly as it *seems*? Judge William appears to let us take this way; he appears to let us treat the world as it seems to be and not as he says it is, when he makes his candid remarks on marriage as a religious institution, and when, for a moment, he sounds like Shelley in the 'Queen Mab' notes. But, in the last resort, since Judge William is really Søren Kierkegaard, we can suppose that he wants conduct always to be regulated by the ideal, however the contingent instance may turn out to be. But can he reasonably want this, now?

Conclusion (1)

Stendhal records of the admirable Duchess Sanseverina:[19]

> There were two outstanding traits in the duchess' character: once she had willed something, she willed it forever, and never reconsidered anything after she had made up her mind about it. In this connexion, she would sometimes quote a saying of her first husband, the charming General Pietranera: 'What insolence to myself! Why should I think myself more intelligent today than when I made that decision?'
>
> (*The Charterhouse of Parma*, trans. by
> Lowell Bair, N.Y., Bantam Books, 1960,
> p. 318; Chapter 21)

Strong will here is connected to strong, and steadfast, intelligence. Whenever Sanseverina does something steadfastly she is faithful to the matter of it rather than to a promise about it, because her will does not vacillate; and promises are, for her, otiose in so far as they might be taken as supports for a flagging will. As delimiting an expectation, e.g. Mosca's expectation of eventually making her Countess Mosca, promises precisely delimit. And they are kept. But they are kept because of what they are about, not simply because they are made. Having always been intelligent, Sanserverina allows herself to will only . . . Only what? The answer would have to be: only those things that can be, at some later time, as intelligently willed, as they were at the initial moment of willing. The implication of this, then, is that intelligent people will only things that abide at least as well as does their will. Are there such things? Love as 'eternal' in Judge William's sense ought to be one such thing, and ought to be classically one such. But equally, and notoriously, love ordinarily and quite often seems not to be like this.

What religion, the marriage service, exacts or seeks to exact may appear (to some) an extraordinary confidence in the matter of love which the matter in fact betrays: or the marriage service may seem to exact the observance of promises which the matter, by its failure, renders hollow.

Faithfulness under these circumstances of a failing matter can be taken in three ways: (1) as quite transcendent, i.e. as transcending the matter in such a fashion that faithfulness can be conveniently related, or relegated, to the sphere of the religious which, as is well known, deals with such things. Or (2) one can simply refuse to see faithfulness as any kind of virtue, and view it as a curious stubbornness on the part of the agent, and as a pernicious exaction on the part of the church, society, the institution of marriage, or whatever. Or (3) faithfulness can be seen under these circumstances as . . .

There ought to be a third way: and there ought to be one simply because we admire rather than reprove or laugh at faithfulness – notably conjugal faithfulness – which transcends or seems to transcend the present matter of the marriage.

Substantialism as a doctrine grounds faithfulness on the matter of the promises, not on the promises. The promises simply 'hedge' the matter, guarantee it the human time needed for its unfolding. This seems a rational doctrine in that the *ratio* of the promises, and not mere promises, is and remains the *ratio* of the faithfulness. However such a doctrine must allow that when the matter fails, the promises are void, and *the* marriage in question becomes – to particularise Judge William's words – 'A questionable institution.' Or it must somehow be maintained that the matter cannot fail: the notion of 'eternity' central to the *aesthetic validity* of marriage may seem to guarantee this unfailingness. Love as 'eternal' might be taken not only to pre-empt time, but to sustain itself in it, be able to last out the time so pre-empted. Or, on the other hand, Judge William's language of 'infinity' and 'eternity' may seem, simply, to introduce the necessary 'unfailingness' by subreption, and by a transparent subreption at that. One might go as far as Judge

William in one's phenomenology of love in a 'good' case: and refuse to go as far in a bad one. To be compelled to go along with the equation 'eternity' = 'unfailingness' in all cases, regardless of the contingent story about *a* case, would be – it suddenly seems – legalistic. To admit that love as 'eternal' is necessarily unfailing, comes to much the same as admitting everything in the 'principle' embodied in the tag, 'hard cases make bad law'. And, bound by this principle, one is in a legalistic system, not in an aesthetic or existential one. Judge William is suddenly seen in his gown of office. Or, to change the metaphor, we now feel the barbed and uncomfortable doctrine, muffled in the bland forensic eloquence.

One can find it altogether too Hegelian, this aesthetic notion of love-as-'eternal'; too Hegelian and requiring altogether too much of a 'union of the universal and the particular'.

It seems, on some occasions at least, too much to expect each particular to be taken as a perfect exemplar of its universal. An aesthetic particular is, of course, like, or rather like, this, a beautiful case of its idea; but then, seeing *that*, one might allow oneself, in the marital situation as one does in the museum director's case, to enter the *caveats* that: not all particulars are aesthetic, not all exhibits are classic, or worth the cost of their preservation.

But it is unlikely that Judge William could accept these *caveats*. His doctrine of love as aesthetic asserts that love is 'eternal', and so by implication unfailing. His notably Hegelian notion of the aesthetic as a union of particular and universal, instance and idea, asserts that all cases *are* up to the ideal, the eternal standard. If one is disposed to reject the doctrine of love-as-aesthetic – since this double pronged assertion is what it seems full blown to come to – and if, further one does not wish either to give faithfulness up entirely as an illusion, or to see it simply as a function of tough will, what is *now* open to one?

It would seem that all one can do is adopt an heuristic of 'as if' and acknowledge that one has to treat even *prima facie* bad cases *as if* they were good ones, and ideal, and so 'eternal' in the required senses of lasting the time pre-empted at their first moments. The sting in the tail of the doctrine that love is aesthetic now pricks us: The heuristic blunts the barb a little. This heuristic of the ideal is an alternative to a pure doctrine of will, or to a bald dogma of 'eternity'. One must choose, it seems, between two possibilities: (1) that the will alone, with its promises and covenants, sustains the will when the matter of the promises fails. This is in one way an attractive doctrine since the will is under our control, and the failing or not failing of the matter is not. We can be more steadfast than the world can be. But it is unattractive in that it seems formalistic.[20] *Or* we can (2) maintain, very contestably indeed, that the will need never be left with its promises alone to sustain it, because the matter never does and can never change. Judge William's talk of the aesthetic-as-'eternal' makes this kind of claim, but need anyone allow him the full cash value of his talk? If we are willing neither to grant Judge William full value, nor to make faithfulness faithfulness to promises and not to the matter of them, we can only invoke a moral-cum-aesthetic heuristic of the sort just sketched, an heuristic that would require us to treat very apparently failing matters *as if* 'eternal' in the sense of 'unfailing'. We grasp the barb – with kidgloves on.

Conclusion (2) – Conclusion to the Conclusion

This heuristic would not make faithfulness irrational; but it would make it very like its cognate, faith.[21] It would make it like faith in that faithfulness would go 'beyond'. Faith, e.g. religious faith, goes beyond the evidence to assent: faithfulness would go beyond the observed structure of the matter to an assent, an assent of the will, that the less than ideal matter must be treated *as though* it were not less than ideal.

Here, will, rather than the substance of a matter, seems to dominate: not now as will faithful to promises, but as will faithful to an ideals of the matter of the promise. A distinction: and perhaps a real one?

One of the senses of 'faithfulness' that the *OED* did not list – and one noted the omission almost with relief – was faithfulness to ideals. Ideals are so vague, so hopelessly general; but,

D

curiously, the notion comes in right at the end, in the extreme
case, in the extreme but by no means uncommon situation of a
love that seems as matter of the will to fail, we are not faced
with the issue of ideas as such, but with the concept of: the
idealisation of the failing case. And this concept presents itself
as a regulative principle of conduct. Substantialism necessitates
a very particular 'idealism': love-as-aesthetic necessitates
certain idealisations.

Faithfulness as simply due to matter recognisably apt to
evoke it, is non-problematic. But faithfulness can sometimes be
perforce – its matter failing – an idealising, a transcending
virtue. Ordinary human conjugal faithfulness may, that is, end
in our taking seriously the Psalmist's 'claim': 'That love is built
to last forever', and taking this claim seriously in a, possibly,
purely human context.

Faithfulness then can simply become faith; and as faith it
may or it may not be religious. It would be odd, though, to call
it 'aesthetic' – or to call it, simply, 'aesthetic'.

NOTES

¹ *Either/Or*, there are two readily available editions of this work:
(i) translated by Walter Lowrie, London, O.U.P. 1946 (Princeton,
Princeton U.P. 1946); (ii) translated by Walter Lowrie with revision
and a foreword by Howard A. Johnson, N.Y., Doubleday, Anchor
Books, 1959. The latter edition has been used in the preparation of
this paper: page references are given to (i) O.U.P./Princeton first,
and to (ii) Doubleday second, as *E/O*, p. 18/p. 21.
² 'Love and faithfulness': the note to Psalm 89 in *The Jerusalem
Bible* reads, in part, 'The pairing of "love" with "faithfulness" is a
feature of this Psalm'. *The Jerusalem Bible*, London, Darton Long-
man, Todd, 1966.
³ Though Søren Kierkegaard's Judge William would seem, in
making a case for love, to make such a unique case for so unique a
thing, he nevertheless wants to take conjugal faithfulness as a
paradigm for *faithfulness* in other contexts too. The Judge William
letter discussed in the body of this paper, mentions three kinds of
faithfulness: (1) conjugal (romantic), 'historic fidelity'; (2) knightly
fidelity, and; (3) faithfulness to a vocation or profession. On this last
Judge William writes that *impressa vestigia* of love are what 'I have
. . . before me, even in the universal sphere which is duty'. *E/O*,

p. 128/p. 155. Having defined the love relationship in the erotic context as one of uniqueness and exclusivity, Judge William will have to explain how *impressa vestigia* of something so unique relate to the 'universally valid sphere' or to the Principle of Universalisability. We get hints, in the letter, of Judge William's solution, but it is not worked out in detail. He writes 'the defect of earthly love is the same thing as its advantageous quality, i.e., its partiality': 'spiritual love' however, 'is constantly opening itself more and more, ever extending its circle of love . . . &c. p. 52/p. 63. How the earthly-erotic and the spiritual are to be reconciled, even by *impressa vestigia* is not at once clear to Judge William's/SK's reader.

⁴ In the Danish Marriage Service, revised version 1912, the phrase 'until death do you part' occurs [*indtil døden skiller jer ad*], but there is no phrase equivalent to the Anglican 'forsaking all other'. [I am indebted to Mr. Peter Holsig for a copy and a translation of the Service.]

⁵ 'Wilt thou love her . . . ?'; it has sometimes been remarked that a promise to love, i.e. to go on loving, is absurd, since love is not to be commanded by will. Judge William would see this *promise to love* as merely an affirmation of a present 'eternity'; an eternity capable of itself, with certain care and certain 'determinations' hedging it, going on into future time. Love *is* now, so its future can be safe-guarded, though not commanded, because, if it *is* now, its future 'eternally *is*' and need not be commanded.

⁶ Love is the substance of marriage: virtually the only syllogistic argument in Judge William's otherwise highly dialectical letter is the one:

> Love is the substance of marriage,
> *Love is eternal*
> Marriage is eternal

Judge William allows himself to equate first and Romantic love with conjugal, or temporarily to distinguish them from conjugal love, as the exigencies of his complex dialetic require. His central principle, however is that 'marriage is the transfiguration of first love', *E/O*, p. 28/p. 33.

⁷ The senses in which love/marriage are said by Judge William to be AESTHETIC seem to be:

(1) marriage has an *immanent teleology* (and an apriority), and so is analogous in structure to Kant's beautiful which is '*purposiveness* of an object, so far as this is perceived in it *without any representation of a purpose*' (J. H. Bernard's trans. *Critique of Judgment*, N.Y., Haffner Publishing Co., 1966, p. 73). Reference to '*representation* of a purpose' may be dropped in Judge William's context, since he distinguishes explicitly between *an aesthetic as representation* and *an aesthetic as lived* [Consider also, in its context, the phrase 'it must bear the stamp of

the accidental, and yet one must remotely sense an art', E/O, p. 90/ p. 103, cross refer Kant's remark in *C.J.*: 'A product of fine art . . . must appear just as free from the restraint of arbitrary rules as if it were a product of mere nature', 45, Bk II, Meredith's trans. pp. 166–7.]

(2) love/marriage is 'eternal', and in this is like, isomorphic with, an aesthetic idea, as: §(2.1) given, all, all in one, and; (2.2) needing to be, in time, exfoliated.

(3) love/marriage achieve a *unity of opposites*, see pages p. 51/ pp. 61–2; p. 81/p. 98; perhaps the most striking *unity* which the aesthetic of love achieves is that of 'freedom and necessity', see pp. 37ff/pp. 44ff.

(4) 'love is a *unity of the universal and the particular*', pp. 75–6/pp. 91–2; it is the role, classically, in post Hegelian thought, for the aesthetic to achieve this union, though the notion is, of course, older then Hegel. [See also: *Conclusion* to this paper: and in relation to the 'conclusion' note, 'one would not treat the particular individual merely as a moment in a process, but as the definitive reality', p. 58/p. 70.]

8 'Eternal' and 'infinite' used of love:

Eternal, eternity (approx. 60 occurrences): p. 18/p. 21; the 'little eternity' of p. 19/p. 22 would be Marvell's; p. 20/p. 23; p. 23/p. 27; p. 24/p. 28; p. 26/p. 30; p. 28/p. 33; p. 32/p. 38; 'the constantly unfolding . . .'; p. 34/p. 40; p. 34/p. 41; p. 35/p. 42; p. 36/p. 43; p. 49/pp. 58–9; Marvell's too 'the seductive eternity of the instant', p. 49/p. 59; p. 50/p. 60; p. 51/p. 61 ['a moment out of time', p. 81/ p. 97]; p. 94/p. 114; p. 99/p. 120: (p. 106/p. 128); 'naive eternity', p. 106/p. 129; pp. 115–16/p. 140; p. 116/p. 141; p. 117/p. 142; p. 118/p. 143; 'the hope of eternity which fills the moment to the brim', p. 120/p. 145; p. 122/p. 148; p. 125/p. 152.

Infinite, infinity (approx. 10 occurrences): 'bad infinity', p. 23/p. 27; p. 26/p. 31; *p. 49/p. 59*; 'infinity of energy', p. 54/p. 65 [finite, p. 60/p. 73]: 'that infinity which is your element', p. 70/p. 85: 'first love is discovered as an immediate infinity', p. 79/p. 95: 'the infinity which has finiteness in itself', p. 79/p. 96; 'the infinite moment of love', p. 94/p. 113; ('the most of infinite significance', p. 112/p. 135); 'an infinite reality in eternity', p. 118/p. 143. For the relationship between 'infinite' and the universal-particular nexus, see p. 76/p. 92.

9 Judge William presents himself as one of those 'fortunate individuals' who found, was found by, 'eternal' love: Søren Kierkegaard who wrote the whole book, in which Judge William is a mere persona it would seem did not find love; his treatment of Regina Olsen suggests this. By putting in this, unobtrusive, reference to 'fortunate individuals', 'A', who otherwise cuts a rather poor figure in Judge William's letter, has his revenge. For if it is not the case

that all cases of love are the same as they are to the fortunate, the large claims of Judge William's analysis of love as eternal, are much weakened. Again the phrase 'whether he has *truly* been in love', p. 37/p. 44, inserts another tiny, but possibly deadly, qualification.

[10] 'Time-Transcendence and Some Related Phenomena in the Arts', by R. W. Hepburn, in *Contemporary British Philosophy*, fourth series, edited by H. D. Lewis, London, George Allen & Unwin, 1976, p. 158.

[11] There is a subtle argument behind the redefinition of the aesthetic which turns upon Judge William's distinction between 'what *is* aesthetically beautiful' and 'the representation of aesthetic beauty', *E/O*, p. 111/p. 135. This is too complex to go into here.

[12] *Ut pictura poesis*; see, for an interesting historical account of this notion, Rensselaer W. Lee's *Ut Pictura Poesis: The Humanistic Theory of Painting*, N.Y., W. W. Norton Co. Inc., 1967.

[13] 'Ramassé non encore déroulé', Professor Hepburn is quoting from the essay on Maurice Scève's poetry in vol. IV of *Études sur le temps humain* (pp. 9–15).

There is an interesting footnote to E. Vinaver's 'Action and Poetry in Racine's Tragedies' in which he refers to 'the presence of each moment at every other': M. Vinaver expresses his indebtedness, for this notion, to M. Merleau-Ponty's *La Structure du comportement*, nouvelle edition, Paris 1949, p. 153, & 147ff.: the notion represents a rather condensed precis of the ideas of these pages of *La structure du comportement*, and the phrase is M. Vinaver's, not M. Merleau-Ponty's. See *Racine*, ed. R. K. Knight, Macmillan (*Modern Judgments* series), 1969, p. 160. 'The presence of each moment at every other' would match nicely Judge William's talk of 'the first' as 'simply the present, but the present is . . . the constantly unfolding and rejuvenating "first" ', *E/O*, p. 33/p. 40 and talk of 'the continuity with which the whole is posited by the first', p. 35/p. 41; 'the eternal which has the temporal in itself', p. 79/p. 96, &c.

[14] 'has the *idea* in itself'. This is the closest, perhaps, that Judge William comes to acknowledging quite explicitly an indebtedness to Kant's notion of the aesthetic idea: *E/O*, p. 15/p. 140. Perhaps Judge William's 'remark' to 'A': 'at such moments you are transfigured . . . your whole soul is *concentrated upon* [a] *sole point* . . .', *E/O*, p. 10/p. 11 and the whole context of it, represents 'A' as subject to an aesthetic-on-the-pattern-of-an-aesthetic-idea. Again, of 'A's 'polemic' Judge William writes: 'when I think of the multifarious expressions of it which I possess in their dispersion, and imagine them *gathered into a unity*, your polemic is so talented and inventive that it is a good guide for one who would defend the other side', *E/O*, p. 25/p. 29.

[15] Unfaithfulness of course in the marital-sexual context is classically defined in terms of *not* forsaking all other, and not going

on 'as long as ye both shall live'. To fail to comfort, to honour, to cherish, to 'keep her in sickness and in health' does not, in common parlance, amount to 'unfaithfulness'. So much for 'what we ordinarily say'.

¹⁶ The belovèd 'alone has existence', *E/O*, p. 36/p. 43. This phenomenology has of course been, in its general form criticised: see: 'Freud's reference (*Group Psychology and the Analysis of the Ego*, IXX) to "Bernard Shaw's malicious aphorism to the effect that being in love means greatly exaggerating the difference between one woman and another".' Freud perhaps had in mind Undershaft's remark to Cusins (*Major Barbara*, Act III), 'like all young men, you greatly exaggerate the difference between one young woman and another'. This quotation is from a footnote on p. 194 of Brigid Brophy's *The Adventures of God in His Search for the Black Girl*, London, Macmillan, 1973, q.v.

¹⁷ 'A power compelling you to remain in love', does smack a little of J-J. Rousseau's notion of the citizen who is 'forced to be free'. SK occasionally resorts, as does J-J. Rousseau so often and so notoriously, to a two-will model, see the remarks on Duty. But his real move is ontological: the will can and must, in love, remain steadfast because love is, as eternal, itself steadfast. (See *The Social Contract*, Book I, Ch. VII.)

¹⁸ George Santayana writes, somewhere, of love: 'Love is very penetrating, it penetrates to possibilities rather than facts.' Faithfulness as to the *promise* of a matter seems to be rather like Santayana's 'love'. (Quoted in *Keats*, by Walter Jackson Bate, Harvard U.P./ Oxford U.P., 1963, p. 123.)

¹⁹ Søren Kierkegaard would have found Sanseverina admirable in her freedom from the bane of *The Present Age*, reflection. Mosca, while still courting her, as yet only the widowed Countess Pietranera, says of her (to himself), '. . . where else can you find a soul like hers, a soul that is always sincere, that never acts "with prudence", that abandons itself entirely to the impression of the moment, that asks only to be carried away by some new object?' (Ed. cit., p. 85; chapter six.) Søren Kierkegaard's book begins: 'Our age is essentially one of understanding and reflection, without passion, momentarily bursting into enthusiasm, and shrewdly lapsing into repose,' *The Present Age*, trans. Alexander Dru, Collins, 1962, p. 33.

²⁰ 'Formalistic' here is a mild enough expression. It would be too coolly arrogant, in some interpersonal relations – and in the case of love or marriage it would be offensive to the other person – to be faithful *just* to one's pledged word: or, it would be offensive to let it be felt that it was *only* to one's pledged word that one would be being faithful.

Faithfulness in love involves, in extreme cases, an idealisation of

the bad 'now' on the matrix of the good 'then'/ 'once-upon-a-time',
whatever that idealisation may come to. Love which 'penetrates to
possibilities' must go on looking for them, even when everything has
turned out badly. This is what the heuristic, and its idealisations,
perhaps comes to.

   [21] If faithfulness becomes faith, then perhaps for Judge William
it has to become not 'ethical' but full religious faith: see his remark,
that 'marriage belongs essentially to Christianity', p. 24/p. 29. The
substance may be love, when love does not fail; when it does, a kind
of 'faith' takes over. But might this faith not be in some sense ethical
without being religious? or Christian? Judge William's constant
identification of the aesthetic, the moral, and the religious, as well as
seeming premature, can, too, at the end of our argument, seem
dangerous to his case. Or has he foreseen the dangers?

5

ON HAVING A REASON

Stuart Hampshire

The prescription that lays down how one ought to reason in moral matters is normally supported by a more general account of reasoning, which suggests limits upon what can be counted as reasoning of any kind, whether practical or theoretical. If, for example, one accepts, or presupposes, a Cartesian theory of reasoning, the normal case of reasoning is apt to be represented as conscious and explicit inference from one more or less clear idea to another in a set of distinguishable steps. The distinguishable steps are the feature that I wish to stress now. Given this Cartesian account, the normal case of rational deliberation before decision will also be represented as more or less explicit inference from one idea, or proposition, to another in successive, distinct steps.

Aristotle notoriously employed this model of deliberation at one point in his discussion of Weakness of the Will, which he illustrated by the practical syllogism. But the practical syllogism was probably intended as no more than an abstract model, and not as an account of the normal form which practical reasoning, ending in practical choice, should actually take in most cases. Reasoning about practical choices does sometimes take this fully explicit, step by step, propositional form, marked by the practical syllogism: particularly, publicly revealed reasoning takes this form. But the Nicomachean Ethics as a whole implies that very commonly, even normally, practical reasoning does not take this form. I am thinking of the doctrine of experience (ἐμπειρια), and of the performance of the man of experience, and of the part played by perception in moral matters and particularly by the perception of the mean, and also of Aristotle's remarks on the relation between knowing that something is right and knowing why it is right, and on the absence of a necessary connexion between them. Whatever may be the correct interpretation of Aristotle, the fact is that one can extract a non-Cartesian account of practical reasoning from him, and I shall build upon such an account a defence of inexplicit and condensed reasoning in ethics; and this type of reasoning is often called intuition.

A further point must be taken from Aristotle which applies both to reasoning in general, and more specifically and definitely, to practical reason. Homer described a council of war in which several leaders proposed competing plans and the final choice of a plan of action is the supreme leader's choice. This social institution and public occasion provide a clear, external model for the act of choice, for προαίρεσις, which can also be the private inner act of an individual; and this type of public occasion provides a vocabulary in which also an individual's silent choice, and its silent antecedents, can be described. The subsidiary leaders correspond to the individual's principal beliefs, not all of which can be reconciled in the actual situation: the supreme leader corresponds to the co-ordinating power of rational choice in the individual. Taking the model very literally, one may think of a man's thinking, when a difficult decision is to be made, as an inner debate in the forum of his soul, with the options all deployed in orderly inner speech; and this may sometimes, if rarely, happen. But it can scarcely be the normal and typical case, if only because 'persuasion' cannot be taken too literally in this context unless the speaker and the hearer persuaded are different persons; therefore the debate is not to be taken too literally either.

It is plausible to claim that conclusions about actions and reasoning on practical issues are best understood through their origins as social and public activities, of which a clear narrative account can always be given. In public discussion pros and cons are reviewed, one after the other, in a definite order and a conclusion of some observable kind occurs at the end. There is a verifiable order in which considerations are raised, and a verifiable answer to the question 'Did considerations X and Y play any part in your argument?' An actual speech is an event, and it is divisible into a set of events, such as the utterance of that particular sentence, and the making of this or that point. By contrast the order of events in an inner 'debate', when nothing was said, is often so unclear and so uncertain that one may doubt whether there was a definite order of events at all.

The presence of an argument to a man's mind (as opposed to the hearing of it) does not by itself constitute an event, nor is it necessarily sub-divisible into a set of events, which were steps in the argument. The reconstruction of the arguments present to a man's mind before a decision is not normally the true story of a psychological process, nor any kind of story at all. It is not like the minutes of a meeting with every substantial intervention summarised; if it is like the report of any meeting, it is more like the minutes of a British Cabinet meeting, which summarise the outcome of the discussion and which very roughly summarise the heads of discussion, but not necessarily in a historically accurate order.

There is a Cartesian error, which was not consistently Descartes', and which consists of assuming a necessary connexion between thought on the one side and consciousness and explicitness on the other. I claim that when we reflect on this assumption, we recognise that it is not accepted as true in our ordinary speech and thought and I argue also that it ought not to be accepted. There is nothing exceptional or anomalous in the reasons for our conclusions, whether practical or theoretical, not being present to consciousness at the time, and not being accessible to consciousness afterwards. Under conditions of difficulty or strain we may sometimes rehearse reasons to ourselves step by step, even numbering them, and we may recall the steps. But this is not the normal case to which all other cases of thinking should approximate. It is the exception, and the natural advantage of the species has depended upon it remaining the exception. For some purposes some kind of thinking is most efficient when the reasoning is internalised and condensed, and when it does not need to be rehearsed or to be brought into consciousness and made fully explicit, step by step.

The confusion behind the Cartesian error is between full consciousness, and step by step explicitness, on the one side and the power of reflection on the other. They are not the same, and a model of rationality that depends on developing and stressing one of them turns out to be very different from a model of rationality based upon the other. By the power of reflection I mean the power to review and to evaluate any movement of thought of one's own and, by reflection, to correct it. This is the power that one uses on occasions of uncertainty and difficulty, and when one does not know what to think. The model of rationality that stresses the desirability or necessity of explicitness in practical reasoning is that which I have called 'computational morality'. The claim is that it is desirable, or even necessary, that policy makers should set out the reasons for and against a range of possible policies, called options, and attach numbers to them; and their procedure then carries the implication that they have brought to full consciousness, and that they have made fully explicit, all the reasons that will determine their decision one way or the other. Then, and only then, their decision will be a fully rational one.

The other model of rationality, stressing only the power of reflection, allows that the trained and experienced thinker, coping with problems of a type with which he is familiar, immediately recognises complexities and shades of difference, and judges accordingly, often relying on his experience of the subject matter and making a judgement for reasons which he cannot state clearly and exhaustively. The ideally rational man, in this model of practical reason, notices, and responds to the immense variety of particular circumstances with which he is confronted. His conduct is not governed, in a mechanical way, by explicit formulae or rules which he imposes on the facts; his reasoning is as much perceptiveness as power of argument. He avoids a too rigid and abstract framework of moral principle in making his personal and political decisions. But he has the power to reflect on his reasoning retrospectively, a power that he will exercise when his decisions turn out badly. Then he will naturally ask himself what the factors were which led him to decide as he did; and confronting cases of uncertainty and difficulty, he will reflect on the factors influencing him before he acts, and try to spell out the salient factors. In these cases of difficulty, and of the breakdown of dispositions, reflection involves explicitness. But these cases *ought* to be the exception in the experience of a rational man making practical decisions.

The epistemological theory behind this second model of rationality is that we can never completely specify the vast amount of collateral knowledge which we bring to bear in responding to an ordinarily complex situation. Secondly, this failure to specify, and to make explicit, does not impair the rationality either of the agent or of his actions, provided that his actions are in fact reliably varied with varying features of the situations confronting him. If we, or the agent himself, can in retrospect see that there is a reliable method, or machinery, of discrimination and calculation at work, we do not require that the steps and stages of the thought should be explicit and clearly itemised.

There are kinds and domains of reasoning in which explicitness, and clear itemisation of steps, are either necessary, or, at the least, highly desirable: the obvious case is mathematical reasoning. Proof is the procedure which carries step-by-step explicitness to the limit as a procedure of justification. For well-known reasons mathematical reasoning, and its typical procedures, have often in the past been taken as the ideal of rationality, to which all other reasoning should be made to approximate as nearly as possible. But in the modern period a stronger influence on the model of rationality in practical thought has probably been legal reasoning; either as natural law, or as Kantian legislation for humanity, or as some watered-down version of Kantian moral law.

Legal reasoning is inadequate as reasoning if it is inexplicit and if the distinct grounds determining the conclusion are not clearly identified. As a model of rationality for practical reason, legal reasoning is precisely the contrary of the model of reasoning about substantial moral problems which I am suggesting. Many Protestants have been brought up with strong prejudice against casuistry, and they use the word 'casuistry' as the name of corrupt thinking on moral issues; and casuistry is a form of the application of legal reasoning to morality, and gives the impression of a false rationality, just as the quantitative computations of utilitarians do. With casuistry as with computation, the form of morality is observed, and the substance lost, because the reasoning is in both cases excessively abstract and removed by a deliberate abstraction from the concrete, and highly particularised, realities of actual situations. If the model of rationality in practical reasoning is not explicitness but reflectiveness, then a reasonable man is one who examines the causes of his mistakes, when his condensed reasoning has led him astray. He is the man who asks himself what led him to the wrong decision and what he failed to notice.

To be contrasted with law and utility theory, there is a sphere of practical reasoning and choice, which is obviously close to moral reasoning, and immensely different in the model of rationality suggested: this is the sphere of social manners.

Consider the rules, conventions, and habits of behaviour which fall under the broad heading of manners, that is, the social manners prevailing in any society and social group. The rules and conventions are apt to be:

(1) Learnt both by precept and by example.

(2) To become habitual, unconsidered, and wholly internalised.

(3) To be applied in particular situations which are immediately recognised as falling under a certain convention-invoking description; and this recognition, and the choice of behaviour to which it leads, both involve condensed reasoning. But there is a fourth characteristic of the choice of behaviour to be noted.

(4) In difficult situations of conflict of conventions, or of rules, of good manners, situations that are normally not too common, the subject has to make his choice of behaviour explicit to himself, and he also has to make explicit the reasoning which supports his conclusion.

Consider a case in which a very junior officer in the R.A.F. in wartime found himself next to an air marshal at the bar of a very famous hotel. The air marshal might have found it difficult to fit together the requirement of good manners, not to seem to listen to private conversations in a bar, and even less to interfere in them, with the requirement of a senior officer to ensure respect for the service, which the junior officer was very effectively holding up to ridicule: near to a moral conflict, it may be objected, rather than to a conflict of social conventions. Perhaps so, but the air marshal's feeling was in fact one of social embarrassment. He was concerned with the surface of the social situation, because he was concerned with how his behaviour accorded with the conventions and rules and with the conventional expectations of others in the bar. He wished to act conventionally; but in the face of this breakdown of conventions, he was driven to ask himself 'What is one expected to do in this situation?' His condensed thinking, backing his habitual responses, was inadequate in the situation of conflict. He hesitated, pondering the alternatives, which was itself a mistake. An immediate, assured, unquestioning response was required.

When he does decide what to do, he will be able to say what considerations influenced his decision. His apparent reasons will under these circumstances have been consciously rehearsed reasons. He may have deceived himself, and his apparent reasons may be rationalisations. But at least he will know that these particular considerations were present to his mind, and that they played some part in his decision. They may not be the effective cause of his decision, and there may have been powerful reasons for his decision which he did not make explicit to himself; for example, the fear of ridicule may have helped to make him do what he otherwise would not have done. He needs to reflect on the workings of his mind before he acts.

Aristotle allowed very little difference in this respect between morality and good manners. Both should be fully internalised as stable dispositions which in normal circumstances lead, effortlessly and immediately, to good conduct and to reasonable assessments of situations demanding action, and to making the assessments without too much brooding and effort. You need to have grammaticality in you, and therefore to perform in the same unhesitating way as the grammatical man.

So also for the virtues of justice and of self-control, which are the corner-stones of moral virtue as a whole. We have to act in the same confident style as the just and temperate man does, and that requires full knowledge of what one is doing; and one must choose to do it and do it for its own sake. And this can only happen if the virtues are fully internalised, or, as Aristotle puts it, if the agent has the virtues within him.

The three conditions of the agent having the virtues within him are intended to be necessary and jointly sufficient; and they constitute a proposed analysis of the Aristotelian notion of acting from a disposition and of acting as the man of good character acts: the three conditions are:

(1) Knowing what one is doing.

(2) Choosing to do it.

(3) Doing it for its own sake.

To take them in reverse order: the just man acts as he does for the sake of being just and not from other motives, such as earning favours. He is in this respect like the well-mannered man, who acts as he does for the sake of good manners, and not for some ulterior benefit. The second condition requires that his conduct is in no way forced or unwilled and that there are live options and that he knows that there are. The first condition requires that he knows that his conduct satisfies the relevant description in the rule; the rule is his reason for so acting. So the well-mannered man, who is so well brought up that good manners are second nature to him, has a reason for behaving as he does. His reason is the internalised rule, or rules, of conduct which determine his conduct, in the same sense that the propositions of arithmetic determine my calculations, also without my needing to rehearse them to myself. Aristotle's theory entails that there is no very significant difference between manners and morals in this respect, and this is part of the reason, within the theory, why there is no ultimate divergence in the normal run of things between a morally admirable life and a satisfying one; for the man who is rational in practical matters it has become second nature to act rightly and he does so more or less effortlessly and as a matter of course. He would be unhappy if he acted in a contrary way. The most significant advantages of knowing reasons are that (a) explicit knowledge of the reasons why is in itself an intellectual virtue and source of satisfaction and (b) explicit knowledge of the reasons why is necessary for the man who takes a leading part in public life and in affairs of state.

In so far as social ease is the desirable end of manners, and in so far as good manners are defined by explicit conventions of behaviour, it is plainly desirable that the conventions should be internalised and the right behaviour should be spontaneous and not carefully calculated. In so far as social ease is a subordinate end, taking human ends as a whole, and in so far as moral problems are not primarily problems of applying social conventions, the same argument for spontaneity in behaviour and the absence of calculation does not hold. The Aristotelian conclusion will need to be supported by another argument, if it is to be tenable. Otherwise one may conclude, against Aristotle, that right conduct, judged from a serious moral point of view, constantly requires explicit thought, and the careful weighing of arguments and making of explicit calculations. One may even follow those utilitarian moralists who will say that rationality in practical reasoning, where serious moral issues are concerned, is incompatible with habitual responses and internalised dispositions. They argue that in the context of practical reason on moral issues, rationality entails perpetual calculation, and specifically explicit calculation of consequences. This calculation may be performed rapidly and habitually, but the calculation ought normally to be reconstructed, and made explicit. This is the rival position that must be examined.

There is a clear, partial contrast that will help to explain what is meant by 'giving an account of one's reasons' for a decision. Judges give their reasons for arriving at a certain decision, and the reasons are published with the conclusion. If doubt is cast upon some part of the reasoning, doubt is cast on the conclusion. If the reasoning contains false steps, then the conclusion has at least to be re-considered. A reason here is a justification, and it is not cited as a cause; not only this, but it is also true that the judgement, which is the conclusion drawn from the supporting reasons, is not to be considered acceptable if the supporting reasons are not made explicit and are not acceptable. The judgement is normally to be evaluated as acceptable or unacceptable as a whole, consisting of both reasons and conclusion.

This is in contrast with moral and prudential deliberation outside the context of law. Suppose an agent who reviews the pros and cons of a policy of action alone and without publication or interpersonal discussion. A conclusion emerges, and he can truthfully call it the outcome of his deliberations. If he recalls his thought at the time, he recalls some of the explicit reasons for his decision. If his reasons were later shown to be mistaken, he would re-consider his decision; and if in fact this proves to be a false supposition, and he does not re-consider, then, in the absence of further explanation, his alleged reasons were not his reasons, but rather rationalisations. His decision may still be the right one.

The account of a man's reasons for a decision, whether given by himself or by another, amounts to a causal judgement. It picks out a special kind or category of cause: namely, a cause which is a thought. Unlike the report of reasons for a judical decision, the account of reasons for a personal decision, and for any ordinary practical decision, may not be intended as a justification, and the account may be combined with the admission that the actual, historical reasons were bad reasons. This admission only becomes impossible, or at least becomes paradoxical, if the account of reasons is a contemporaneous one, and not retrospective and historical.

I will not be expected to enter into the special difficulties of these singular causal judgements, the much discussed difficulties of confirmation and testing. The fact is that there are such statements as 'What made me, or led me, or caused me, to choose course of action X rather than course Y was so-and-so', where 'so-and-so' was the thought that so-and-so. If a man is unable to give an account of this kind about one of his decisions, unable even under the most favourable conditions, then he does not know what his reasons are or were.

A man might be unable at a particular time to give an account of his reasons and yet it might not be true, or not true without qualification, that he does not know what his reasons are or were. He might have difficulty in *saying* what his reasons were for a variety of reasons: for example, that he could not find the precise words, or that he needed time to disentangle a multiplicity of reasons: and so on. There is often a special difficulty in giving a complete account of one's reasons; and one may know that one has fallen short of a complete account and of a clear account. Being able to say adequately and knowing do not coincide in this type of case, as they do not in many others also. He may still not unreasonably think his conclusion is right, even though he cannot give his reasons.

'He had a reason for his choice or decision' is equivalent to 'His choice or decision was not an unthinking one'. 'I just chose X rather than Y, but for no particular reason' entails that the choice involved no thought or calculation, implicit or explicit. The cause, however it may be identified, was not of a kind that can be called a reason, or set of reasons. No beliefs and desires can be picked out from the totality of my desires and beliefs as determining my choice on this occasion, other than the desire to make this particular choice, or to do this particular thing. To the question 'Why did you want to do this? – What was your reason?', there is no answer in terms of a belief and desire which were picked out from the system of my desires and beliefs, and associated with this choice as determining it. If the choice was an unthinking one, though deliberate, the cause was not of a kind to justify it being called a reason.

What kind is this? The first condition is that the reasons must form an intelligible sequence of thought, when taken together with the conclusion which was an intentional action: an intelligible sequence, but not necessarily a logical one: the sequence is not necessarily a valid argument, but there must be some intelligible connexion, as a sequence of thought, between the reason and what it is a reason for. But suppose that a child's behaviour can be explained by a set of images and mental pictures, present in his mind, which are disclosed in his play and perhaps in drawings and to some degree also in speech. The images might provide an intelligible reason for his behaviour, for example, if they were frightening and if his behaviour expressed fear. But they still would not normally be said to constitute his reason for acting as he did, except in so far as the images do by themselves constitute a thought, which had his action as its consequence; and a thought may be an unconscious or pre-conscious thought.

This second condition upon an explanation being by reason makes the very same point as is made by philosophers who have written on intentions in relation to action. Observing animal behaviour, we may speak of the purposes and strategies of an animal, and we may naturally talk of them as trying to do so-and-so and as waiting for so-and-so and as failing to achieve so-and-so; that is, we may speak of animals' beliefs and desires, expectations, plans, attempts and frustrations, in the same way that we impute such psychological states and dispositions to human beings. But in the imputation of beliefs and desires to animals, and in attributing purposes and plans to them, one does not introduce contexts which have all the features of opaque contexts. One may intelligibly say of an animal that it is pursuing an object which is in fact non-existent but which it expects to see in a certain place. But the object of its pursuit and of its expectation is to be identified through the evidences of its behaviour on this, and on other, occasions and not in a radically different way. Therefore we cannot say of the animal that its pursuit of the object is the pursuit of it as satisfying a certain description, or set of descriptions, or that its expectation is only correctly specified if a certain description is used in the identification of the object; its behaviour does not by itself indicate in what specific terms the object of its pursuit and expectation should be identified.

Speaking of men, and of their desires and beliefs and purposes, we specify what a man wants, believes, and plans with necessary attention to privileged descriptions of the objects of his desires, beliefs and plans. If he desires to do something under a certain description, or set of descriptions, he desires it for a reason. The privileged description or set of descriptions, is the one that he would acknowledge as expressing his thought at the time, if he had the necessary skill to say what his thought was. This acknowledgement is the radically different way, distinct from evidences from behaviour, in which we can arrive at the object of his pursuit or of his expectation. The possibility of his acknowledgement of one description, or set of descriptions, as expressing his thought opens the way to the oblique contexts, which are a feature of statements about human beliefs and desires, but not about animal's beliefs and desires. But the governing desires are not in the normal case explicitly formulated.

The notion of my having a reason for my action is probably best explained through the related concept of intention; for the latter has been more fully examined recently by philosophers. It is well recognised that most of a man's intentions for the future have not been consciously and explicitly entertained or formulated. But they can normally be elicited by the questions 'Do you intend?' and 'Did you intend?', even though there has been no previous consideration; they can become the objects of reflection. The subject can put his previously unformulated intentions into words, either as historical fact, or in sharpening his intentions for the present or future. This existence of a thought, independent of the subject's awareness of it, is duplicated in the existence of a reason which a man has for his action; the mode of existence is exactly the same, and the method of recognition and acknowledgement or disclaimer is the same.

A man's intentions, which are a function of his desires and beliefs, are at any time multifarious, largely unformulated, and uncountable: as also are his desires, plans, his beliefs about his situation and about the means that will serve his ends. Why therefore should one think that he normally is capable, or normally should be capable, of rehearsing or reviewing the uncountable variety of noticed features of situations which determine his decisions? The degree of explicitness implied is not to be expected for intentions and cannot consistently be part of the model of rationality for practical reasoning.

We ought not therefore to pursue an unattainable ideal of rationality in practical matters as requiring an explicit weighing of arguments before moral decisions are made and opinions formed. The computational moralists who pursue this ideal in fact arrive at a pretence and are deceived by their own abstractions.

6

'IRRESISTIBLE IMPULSE' AND MORAL RESPONSIBILITY[1]

Susan Khin Zaw

Should the insane and the mentally ill be held morally responsible for their actions? To answer 'No' to this question is to classify the mentally abnormal as not fully human: and indeed legal tradition has generally oscillated between assimilating the insane to brutes and assimilating them to children below the age of discretion, neither of these two categories being accountable in law for what they do. In what respect relevant to moral responsibility were the insane held to resemble brutes and children? In the case of brutes, the answer seems to have been that the doings of the insane appeared to lack whatever it is that marks out human actions as distinctively *human*. What the insane did could not be thought of as issuing from deliberation, or as capable of having issued from deliberation, but seemed rather to be the result of the unbridled operation of nature – if a diseased nature. The natural comparison with insane killings seemed to be, for example, the killing of birds by cats. This distinction between animal doings and human actions does not depend on Cartesian views about the workings of animals; the operation of nature need not be thought of as mechanical. The thought is simply that where there is no room for deliberation there is no room for moral appraisal. Children, on the other hand, though capable of distinctively human action – i.e. of deliberating about what they do – were held not to be capable of the relevant kind of deliberation: for they were held 'not to know the difference between right and wrong'.[2]

Both these limbs of legal tradition are perceptible in the McNaughten Rules, which stated that in order to be acquitted of murder the insane killer must be shown not to have known the nature and quality of his act, or if he did know this, not to have known that what he was doing was wrong. This formulation allows an escape from a difficulty created by seeing the problem as one of global classification: if the basis of the exemption from moral responsibility is the kind of creature the madman is held to be, what to make of the madman who rages like Nebuchadnezzar only intermittently but between whiles is much like the rest of us? (That such a case was seen as a difficulty is an argument for interpreting the exemption as one based on classification by what one might call unnatural kinds.) The McNaughten Rules shift attention from the nature and quality of the madman, in the form of a judgement about the nature and quality of the whole range of his actions, to the nature and quality only of the particular wrongful act for which he is arraigned. His lucid intervals at other times thus become irrelevant (except in so far as they may cast doubt on the madness of the relevant act) and need no longer be an embarrassment. But if the reasoning goes: 'This man is like a brute, therefore his doings do not count as fully human actions, therefore he cannot be morally responsible for what he does', the lucid intervals undercut the conclusion by casting doubt on the initial premise. On the other hand, assimilating the insane to brutes spares us more subtle and complex difficulties by removing the need to discover the precise nature and quality of individual actions, in particular of that action which is the potential *actus reus* (the criminal act), since its nature follows from the nature we attribute to the man. That he is brutish may appear evident from quite gross observation of his behaviour, provided this is bizarre enough and in the right kind of way: and the early madmen in legal history do indeed appear mainly as frenzied and ferocious. That he is too childish to know the difference between right and wrong may be, and was, considered susceptible of proof by simple tests of the same kind as those used to establish whether he was fit to take charge of property. In both cases the question of his moral responsibility is seen as taking the form: What are the capacities of this individual? rather than: What exactly was going on in him at the time, what exactly was the nature and quality of the act which was taken as the *actus reus*? And if the capacities were conceived of as deriving from the intrinsic nature of the individual, it would not be possible to ask the question in a temporally indexed form – 'What were the capacities of the individual *at the relevant time*?' – which would prevent the variation of capacities over time from being an embarrassment. The view expresses a suitably crude conception of the kinds of thing a madman might be (suitable, that is, for early, ignorant and presumably unenlightened times): either spectacularly insane, or feeble-minded. And one might plausibly suggest that such madmen, being the most clearly visible forms of what we now recognise as madness, would very likely be the first whose existence would have to be acknowledged and taken account of by the law. However that may be: the kind of argument I have sketched is at least a possible, though crude and variously unsatisfactory, justification for exempting the insane from moral responsibility. Apart from the difficulty caused by the temporal variability of the characteristics of the insane, its chief drawback is the restriction of those who may count as insane to the frenzied and the childish. To later eyes, acquainted with greater varieties of insanity, both difficulties are bound to appear the direct results of a naïve and limited conception of madness. It is, moreover, a view of madness as a category, not an illness: hence the difficulty with *fits* of madness. Illness is something all flesh is heir to: one is born into a category.

Contrast now what is required for exemption under the McNaughten Rules. Pressure on the old ground of exemption came largely from *periodic* frenzy (lunacy); other forms of pressure may be imagined to arise with the perception of other forms of madness than frenzy – for instance, delusions leading to infringements of the law, which, while not performed in an obvious frenzy, were attributable to the madness in that they were not infringements under the description provided by the delusion. The McNaughten Rules allow for both the old and the new types of case. But to do so they have to change the rationale of the defence. Madmen are no longer exempted from moral responsibility because their doings simply are not up for moral appraisal: the possibility is now conceded that their doings may be actions in the relevant sense, but requirements are made of their moral appraisal which consist essentially of ascertaining *what* actions the actions of the madman are. The defence is not that the actions of the madman fail to be distinctively human, but that they are not that action prohibited by law. The new defence subsumes the old one, in that if the doings of the frenzied madman are not actions of the required general kind, they will not, *a fortiori*, be those actions of that kind prohibited by law, and if the whole range of actions of the childish madman is not up for moral appraisal because done in ignorance of moral categories, so of course the action for which he is being tried will have been done in ignorance. Nevertheless, the basis of the defence is no longer the nature of the person except in so far as it bears on the nature of the individual action. Lucid intervals may still be a difficulty, if the argument for the nature of the individual action rests on the nature of the whole range of the person's actions, but need not be if other evidence is available relating just to the action under consideration: madness may now be temporally indexed. It has become possible to think of it as a visitation: there is room now for mental *illness*. And lucid intervals can still cast doubt on the madness itself; for instance, they may suggest it is just faked. But more is required to show this than just that lucid intervals occur, once the possibility of temporal indexing is admitted.

What sorts of evidence could there be which would bear on just the individual action? Well, since what is at issue is whether the action can properly be described as that action prohibited by law, and what has to be proved to prove that a crime has been committed is that an intentional action of the relevant kind has been committed, beliefs will be relevant. Hence the admissibility of delusions. But what is relevant is the content of the beliefs, and not merely that they are the beliefs of a madman. For what has to be shown for conviction is that the madman intended to commit the crime of murder. The McNaughten Rules can be seen as formulating part of the doctrine of *mens rea* as it applies in the case of crimes committed by madmen. Thus, a madman so deranged that he thought, when chopping off someone's head, that he was actually cutting down a tree, would not know the nature and quality of his act, and his ignorance is such that he lacks the element of knowledge required for the *mens rea* for murder: for '*actus non facit reum nisi mens sit rea*' (an act does not make a man guilty of a crime unless his mind also be guilty). In contrast, a madman who intentionally kills his wife because of a false belief attributable to a network of delusions that she is the disguised killer of his mother, though he also could be said not to know the nature and quality of his act, cannot avail himself of this defence: what he did, though done under the influence of a delusion, was still murder. That an alternative description of the action attributable to the madness is available ('I killed the disguised killer of my mother' as opposed to 'He killed his wife') is irrelevant, even if the madman sincerely denies having done what he is accused of ('I did not kill my wife – the person I killed was not my wife'). However, someone who kills knowing that he is killing, and knowing whom, but thinking under the influence of a delusion that he has no alternative but to kill in self-defence, would be mistaking the nature and quality of his act in such a way as to save him from committing the wrong action, murder, by virtue of his not intending to commit it. Evidence of concealment still counts against the contention that the madman did not know that what he was doing was wrong; but the concealment is now of interest only in relation to the individual action concealed, and not as an indication of capacity to tell the difference between right and wrong.

The McNaughten Rules, in thus allowing the defence of insanity to be brought under the doctrine of *mens rea*, permit the exemption of madmen from moral responsibility to be assimilated to other forms of exemption from criminal responsibility. Madmen are not given special treatment because of their condition: they are acquitted on exactly those grounds which would lead to an acquittal of the sane. It is merely the instantiations of those grounds which, being attributable to their madness, are unusual. Now this, though it affords the satisfaction of providing a clear answer to the question 'In what does the exemption of madmen from moral responsibility consist?', thereby making possible clear criteria for the assignment of criminal responsibility, may leave us with a certain unease. One manifestation of this unease is the fact that the acquittal of insane murderers under failure of *mens rea* is effectively a technicality: their acquittal does not prevent them from being confined, though the ground of their confinement is not their guilt but their possible future doings under *any* description. Of course these grounds relate to the effects on others; but can the fact that the madman is such that he is liable to produce such effects be totally irrelevant to the propriety of attributing moral responsibility to him? Does not our different treatment of him spring from or imply a difference in the status we do or can attribute to him as a moral agent? Moral responsibility is a wider notion than criminal responsibility: if it is bound up with our concept of a person *qua* rational agent, its application to the madman, who is at best a dubious or special case of a rational agent, must be problematic. Ought not such considerations to bear on his relation to the law? Is it *right* to assimilate the treatment of madmen by the law to the treatment of the sane? Do the McNaughten Rules really capture all that there is to be said about the moral responsibility of the insane?

Unease manifested itself further in pressure to recognise yet more varieties of insanity. It was made an objection to the McNaughten Rules that there are many more ways of being mad than those implied by the purely cognitive tests of the Rules, and it was urged that the possibility of failure of *mens rea* in the case of madmen should be extended beyond lack of knowledge to lack of control. The claim was that the McNaughten Rules embodied too archaic and narrow a conception of madness as purely a defect of *reason*, of the cognitive faculty: but the advance of psychological understanding had shown the existence of forms of madness in which a man might know perfectly well both what he was doing and that it was wrong, and yet be quite unable, because of his mental abnormality, to prevent himself from doing it. A man who cannot prevent his own action cannot be held responsible for it: so in that sense at least, he must lack the appropriate *mens rea*. This is the defence of diminished responsibility nicknamed 'irresistible impulse'; and liberal espousals of it have prevailed. English law, while not specifically mentioning irresistible impulse in the statute, now allows room for it via the defence of diminished responsibility; the Homicide Act, 1957, section 2, enacts:

> sub-section (1) Where a person kills or is a party to the killing of another, he shall not be convicted of murder if he was suffering from such abnormality of mind (whether arising from a condition of arrested or retarded development of mind or any inherent causes or induced by disease or injury) as substantially impaired his mental responsibility for his acts and omissions in doing or being a party to the killing.
> (2) . . .
> (3) A person who, but for this section would be liable whether as principal or as accessory, to be convicted of murder shall be liable instead to be convicted of manslaughter.

The wording of the act, it will be noted, gives no guidance at all about what shall constitute substantial impairment of mental responsibility due to abnormality of mind: it merely says that where such exists, the crime will count not as murder but as manslaughter. What these grounds might be was left to the courts to determine: and an Appeal Court decision in due course laid down that this section covered irresistible impulse. This judgement is worth giving in detail; I quote the description of the case given by Nigel Walker:[3]

> Patrick Byrne was a 27 year-old Irish labourer. In December 1959 one of the girls in a YWCA hostel at Birmingham discovered him peeping in at her window. He burst into her room, strangled her, and indulged in perverted sexual behaviour with her body, which he also mutilated. He might never have been caught had he not voluntarily given himself

up to the police some weeks later. At his trial he pleaded
diminished responsibility, and called medical witnesses who
testified that he was a sexual psychopath, that is, a person
suffering from violent perverted sexual desires which he finds
difficult or impossible to control: that this was an abnormality of mind within the terms of the Act: but that when
not under the influence of these desires he was normal. Mr.
Justice Stables told the jury that if Byrne killed his victim
under an abnormal sexual impulse which was so strong that
he found it difficult or impossible to control, but was otherwise normal, section 2 of the Homicide Act did not apply to
him. The jury found Byrne guilty of non-capital murder,
and Byrne appealed on the ground that they had been
misdirected.

In the Court of Criminal Appeal the Lord Chief Justice –
now Lord Parker – agreed that the jury had been misdirected
and gave what is now the accepted interpretation for
'abnormality of mind'. It is, he said:

. . . a state of mind so different from that of ordinary human
beings that the reasonable man would term it abnormal. It
appears to us to be wide enough to cover the mind's activities in all its aspects, not only the perception of physical acts
and matters, and the ability to form a rational judgment as
to whether the act was right or wrong, but also the ability
to exercise will-power to control physical acts in accordance
with rational judgment.

What are the implications of this decision, and of the Act
itself? With regard to the Act: since a successful defence of
diminished responsibility brings not acquittal but a conviction
for manslaughter, and since the difference between murder and
manslaughter is the difference between killing with and without
the relevant kind of intent to kill, the suggestion seems to be
that proof of diminished responsibility is proof of failure of the
relevant intention: in other words, the defence *does* appear to
be conceived as an extension of what negatives *mens rea*. And
Lord Parker's judgement lays down or at least allows that this
extension is indeed an extension from failure of knowledge to

failure of control. But conceiving the defence in this way creates a number of rather obvious difficulties, which have even led some – for instance, Lady Wootton – to doubt the coherence of the doctrine of *mens rea* itself, and with it the whole concept of moral responsibility. The McNaughten test can be argued to be a test of criminal intent turning on knowledge that the act was a criminal one – where this knowledge is lacking, the corresponding intent must necessarily have been lacking too. 'Irresistible impulse', however, is designed to cover just those cases where by the McNaughten test the appropriate knowledge is manifestly present, where there may manifestly have been criminal intent within the meaning of the (pre-1957) Act, but where this kind of intent is itself seen as excusable because a result of abnormality of mind. Byrne is represented by the defence as acting in the grip of a desire, even if an overwhelming desire. In pursuit of the object of his desire, he performs various actions. That he performs them intentionally, as far as the McNaughten Rules are concerned – i.e. in full knowledge of their nature and quality – is shown by the fact that reasons for his behaviour may be given by reference to his desire: his actions are just those actions adapted to satisfy his desire, his behaviour is perfectly explicable in terms of his desire (consider his possible answers to the question 'Why did you go down to the YWCA in the first place?'). He is not deluded: apart from the special nature of his desire, whatever that is, the relation between his desire and his actions is exactly that of an ordinary man moved by an ordinary desire. Intention mediates between desire and action. That he knows that what he is doing is wrong is shown by the admission that when not in the grip of these desires he is normal: for there is no suggestion that the desires cloud consciousness or affect judgement of the relevant kind (i.e. judgement that such an action is wrong). Hence if the actions performed under the influence of the desire were criminal, he must have had criminal intent in the McNaughten sense. Hence, presumably, Mr. Justice Stables' original direction to the jury. But what then is the ground of the defence? We are told by Lord Parker that it is Byrne's abnormality of mind, and that this covers 'inability to exercise will-power to control physical acts in accordance with rational judgement'. This suggests that the relevant abnormality of mind *consists* in the inability to control behaviour, in the overwhelming strength of his desire. Then does this mean that the abnormality of the object of his desire, of its quality as distinct from its strength, is irrelevant to the defence? If so, does this mean that a perfectly normal but overwhelmingly strong desire may also be a defence? This hardly seems right: but what is the bar to, say, a recently released long-term prisoner pleading overwhelming desire resulting from long enforced celibacy as a defence to a charge of rape? The law as it stands does not in fact recognise similar defences: necessity in the form of starvation has not been regarded as an excuse for or a defence against murder and cannibalism. Yet what stronger or more normal desire could there be than the desire for survival? The failure of the defence from necessity here suggests that it is not, after all, just the strength of the desire that justifies the defence. The other abnormality of Byrne's desires, their abnormal object or quality, must somehow be relevant. But if normal irresistible desire is not a defence against a charge of rape, why should perverted irresistible desire be a defence against a charge of murder? One might be tempted to say here: the basis of the defence must be not the peculiar quality of Byrne's desires in themselves, but his *general* mental abnormality – for it is this that causes his desires and everything about them. He has a defence because his desires are caused by his mental illness. But here we might seem to have the thin end of a very long wedge. Aren't normal desires caused too? Why should any of us be held responsible for our desires, and therewith of our intentions in acting in pursuit of them? Well, it may be said, we are held morally responsible for pursuit of our normal desires because they are weak enough to be resistible. I have already suggested that the case of necessity shows that in the abnormal it is not their supposedly irresistible strength of desire that is crucial: but even if we ignore this, there is still the problem of what distinguishes an irresistible desire or impulse from one that just is not resisted, or from the strongest desire at the relevant time. What distinguishes irresistible impulse from weakness of will?

It is difficulties such as these that have led some to doubt the continuing viability of the concept of *mens rea* in the criminal law, and even the coherence of moral responsibility itself. For in any clear sense of the element of intention understood by the law as partly constitutive of *mens rea*, Byrne possessed that element of intention; he also possessed the elements of knowledge and minimum control of muscular movements required for an act of murder. If his abnormality or the abnormality of his desires is now held to negative *mens rea*, what this amounts to is that criminal intent itself is held to be somehow cancelled out by abnormality of mind. For the benefit of the abnormal, we countenance a contradiction: in the abnormal, *mens rea* is not *mens rea* – what in the normal would be *mens rea*, in the abnormal is to be regarded as its absence. This defence is not an extension of failure of *mens rea*, but a refusal to apply the doctrine to the abnormal. Here we may begin to suspect that the ground of the new defence is something much more like the old blanket exclusion of madmen from the possibility of being moral agents: but now we are in exactly the same difficulty as arose then over lunacy – the difficulty of Byrne's lucid intervals. It is interesting that Mr. Justice Stables seems to have relied on his periods of normality in directing the jury that the defence of diminished responsibility was not available to him. The difficulty must surely be the old one again: that Byrne was normal at times shows that he *did* have the capacities on which his status as a moral agent depends, and these capacities are conceived of as intrinsic. Thus on neither the old ground nor the new, it seems, can any sense be made of this defence. If the law is to justify the reduction of the charge from murder to manslaughter, some entirely new interpretation of failure of intention will have to be found. That no uncontroversial justification or analysis of this defence has yet been offered is an indication of what is wrong: we lack philosophical understanding of what we are trying to do in setting up the defence of diminished responsibility, and of why we are trying to do it – by which I mean we lack philosophical understanding of the nature of this defence. I want to stress that in what follows my chief concern is with philosophical understanding and not with questions of evidence, of what questions are to be put to juries or in what form. Understanding of the defence and questions of evidence required to establish it are not, of course, unrelated: but what I am interested in is not primarily what kinds of evidence show that someone was in such an abnormal state or condition as to entitle him to the defence of diminished responsibility, but what we mean by saying that he is in such an abnormal state or condition.

Most of the difficulties about diminished responsibility arise, it seems to me, out of not merely a lack of understanding but a serious misunderstanding of the moral implications of conditions such as that attributed to Byrne. The first task, then, must be to clear this misunderstanding out of the way. Let us first look again at Lord Parker's interpretation of the relevant section of the Act, which tends to invite the misunderstanding I have in mind. Lord Parker said that abnormality of mind, within the meaning of the Act, was

> . . . a state of mind so different from that of ordinary human beings that the reasonable man would term it abnormal. It appears to us to be wide enough to cover the mind's activities in all its aspects, not only the perception and judgement of physical acts and matters, and the ability to form a rational judgement as to whether the act was right or wrong, but also the will-power to control physical acts in accordance with rational judgement.

Only the last part of this interpretation concerns us: abnormality in the perception of physical acts and matters, and in the ability to form rational moral judgements, would be covered in any case under the McNaughten Rules. What is new is the reference to abnormality in the will-power to control physical acts in accordance with rational judgement, presumably of both physical and moral matters, which rational judgement is assumed not to be impaired. Two things should be noted about this interpretation: first, it suggests a particular *picture* – a picture of Byrne as a helpless spectator of his own acts, which he as a rational agent may condemn but is powerless to control. Second, there is nothing here, except perhaps the reference to mental abnormality, which distinguishes abnormal irresistible impulse from akrasia: is not the akrates one who is unable to control physical acts in accordance with rational judgement? Yet weakness of will does not exonerate nor even serve as an excuse: it is a fault. We condemn the weak-willed man. I want to argue, first, that the picture I have referred to, which purports to make sense of irresistible impulse as a defence, is incoherent (and perhaps it is this incoherence that leads to the doubts frequently held about the defence); second, that better sense can be made of the defence by comparison with weakness of will, and that if we can distinguish irresistible impulse from akrasia – as I think we can – we can achieve a more satisfactory, or at any rate more plausible, philosophical account of the defence than is at present available.

It is instructive to make a preliminary comparison between the account of irresistible impulse suggested by Lord Parker's judgement, and one of Aristotle's accounts of the weak-willed man. Aristotle says:

> . . . a person can, in a sense, both have knowledge and not have it: e.g. if he is asleep or mentally disturbed or drunk. Now this is the condition of those who are in the grip of emotion: because quite obviously fits of temper and sexual craving and certain other such excitements actually produce physical changes, and in some cases even cause fits of madness. So evidently we should assert that incontinent people are in a similar state. The fact of their using language that implies knowledge is no evidence, because people who are emotionally excited in the ways that we have described declaim proofs and passages from Empedocles; and those who have just started learning a subject reel off a string of propositions which they do not yet understand; because knowledge has to be assimilated, and that takes time. So we must suppose that incontinent persons utter their sentiments as actors do. (NE 1147 a)

Aristotle does not consider that the peculiar physical state of such an akrates in itself relieves him of moral responsibility for the actions attributable to that state, since the man may be

E

responsible for having got into the state. But suppose that he is not: suppose that the state is the result of some condition of body or mind outside his control. Surely we would not then regard him as responsible for the actions attributable to the state: is this the solution to our problem? Has Aristotle here provided us with a ready-made account of irresistible impulse? Unfortunately not – despite the tempting references to mental disturbance and madness. For Aristotle explains the possibility of this variety of incontinence by attributing *also* to the man in the peculiar state a failure of knowledge: apparently in such states rationality itself, not just *effective* rationality, is to some extent in abeyance. Knowledge, if it was ever there, is temporarily lost. Such an akrates only *appears* to act against knowledge, because he only *appears* to have knowledge. But if *this* were Byrne's case, the ground of his exemption from moral responsibility would be that he did not really have the knowledge about his acts that he appears to have. And if that were so, he would be covered under the McNaughten Rules, and there would be no need for appeal to a new form of defence. If the object is to extend the kinds of defence available, it is an *essential* feature of Lord Parker's interpretation that the faculty of rational judgement and discrimination is *not* suspended while the agent acts unlawfully, but that nevertheless the agent acts, contrary to the deliverances of his rational judgement. The defence of diminished responsibility assumes the existence of a state of mind which comprises *both* full knowledge *and* wrong action. The task in making sense of the defence is to provide an account of such a state which shows that though knowledge persists responsibility does not, an account which distinguishes non-culpable irresistible impulse from culpable weakness of will. I understand Lord Parker's interpretation in terms of a picture of the abnormal agent which might be thought to provide such an account.

Let us, then, try to reconstruct this picture in detail, from what is suggested by the words Lord Parker used. Notice first that his expressions invite us to think of human beings in a markedly dualistic way. On the one hand there is the mind, whose sphere is the 'perception and judgement of physical acts and matters', the formation of 'rational judgement as to whether the act was right or wrong', and 'will-power to control physical acts'; the activities of the mind are thus perceptual judgement, moral appraisal and exercise of the will, in relation to the *other* sphere – that of 'physical acts and matters'. It is, I think, significant that Lord Parker does not seem to feel any need to emphasise the distinction here between physical acts and physical matters – by which two classes he presumably means the physical acts of the agent and other physical events. The agent's physical acts seem to be seen as at least *potentially* as remote from him as physical events with which he has nothing to do. And indeed I think the suggestion is that in the cases of mental abnormality under consideration, the normal coupling between mind and body, between that which judges and that which does, somehow becomes disengaged, so that the physical machine continues to run, to act in the physical world, without its mental and rational steering-gear: is not this the possibility implied by saying that the mind has an ability, which it may lose, to exercise 'will-power to control physical acts in accordance with rational judgement'? Such a dualistic picture allows us to think of Byrne as a divided being, and as such, one who may be the helpless spectator of his own acts: the mind as spectator watches the actions performed (by the body?) and as a rational spectator may condemn those actions but is powerless to prevent them. It is almost as if Byrne *the agent* has been reduced to an automaton or to some Newtonian body deflected from its normal path by an externally impressed force; and the obvious candidate for the role of the impressed force is the 'irresistible impulse' or overpowering emotion which also is vaguely attributed to the mental abnormality.

I think, then, that the picture lying behind Lord Parker's interpretation is something like this: mental abnormality may consist or result in the uncoupling of judgement from action. If and to the degree to which this happens, mental responsibility for such action is impaired. (Whether or not the impairment is sufficiently substantial to provide a defence may depend, for instance, on such things as the strength of the forces competing with rational judgement for control of the action.) If the *rational* agent retains no control over the action, he can retain no responsibility for it. The person is identified with the rational agent.

Is this a possible picture of a human agent, and even if it is, does it provide a tenable justification for the defence of diminished responsibility? Philosophical consideration of these questions is made more difficult by the fact that the cases we are considering, cases of insanity, are peripheral or peculiar cases of human action and judgement, far from the central areas where safe conceptual truths may possibly be found. I propose to approach it by comparing Byrne's case with another peripheral case, an example of a different kind of abnormality, but one which seems relevant to our concerns. That the picture suggested by Lord Parker's judgement *is* a possible picture of a human agent may be supported by producing an actual example which Lord Parker's description fits. Oliver Sacks has described a case of a post-encephalitic patient whose condition fits that picture remarkably closely:

... moving from her arm-chair to her divan-bed (a few feet to one side) could never be done *directly* – Miss Z. would immediately be 'frozen' in transit, and perhaps stay frozen for half-an-hour or more. She therefore had to embark on one of two courses of action: in either case, she would rise to her feet, arrange her angle of direction exactly, and shout 'Now!', whereupon she would break into an incontinent run, which could neither be stopped nor changed in direction. If the double-doors between her living-room and the kitchen were open, she would rush through them, across the kitchen, through the double-doors – in a great figure-of-eight – until she hit her destination, the bed. If, however, the double doors were closed and secured, she would calculate her angle like a billiard-player, and then launch herself with great force against the doors, rebounding at the right angle to hit her bed. Miss Z.'s apartment (and, to some extent, her mind) resembled the control-room for the Apollo launchings, at Houston, Texas: all paths and trajectories pre-computed and compared, contingency-plans, and 'fail-safes' prepared in advance. A good deal of Miss Z.'s life, in short, was dependent on conscious taking-care and elaborate calculation – but this was the only way she could maintain her existence.[4]

Here, on the face of it, is someone who 'cannot control physical acts in accordance with rational judgement'. Miss Z. is unable to control her movements in accordance with her rational judgement of the direct route from her chair to her bed. Does this exempt her from moral responsibility for her movements? Surely it need not: for in those cases where her predictions and her aim are completely successful, despite her lack of immediate physical control over the intervening stages I can see no objection to counting the *whole performance* as an action of hers for which she is fully responsible: just as one would count the *intentional* successful playing of a particular shot in billiards as such an action. Lack of direct control over various stages of the performance has no bearing on her responsibility for the completed action: in this case, the intention suffices. Indeed, lack of control has no bearing on her responsibility even for the uncontrolled *stages* of the performance: they too may be regarded as intentional actions of hers. If asked, 'Why did you run into the double-doors like that?' she could give an explanation in terms of desires and reasons: 'Because I wanted to get to the bed' – reference to her disability and the prevailing physical conditions need only be made to enlighten those ignorant of them, or to explain why she chose *that* method of getting to her bed rather than any other. Though she had no physical control at the time of her collision with the double-doors, nevertheless she ran into them intentionally. If as a result of constant battering they fell off their hinges, her landlord could reasonably hold her responsible for the damage.

Compare now an unsuccessful performance. A friend of Miss Z.'s has called, excited by the purchase of a large and valuable Ming vase which she proposes to leave in Miss Z.'s conveniently central flat while she completes her shopping. She knows about Miss Z.'s condition and habits. She puts the vase on the kitchen table, closes and, as she thinks, secures the double doors and departs, assuring Miss Z. that the doors are firmly shut (i.e. we are to assume that there is no room for reasonable doubt on Miss Z.'s part that they are firmly shut). However, being excited she has failed to secure them properly. Miss Z. is in her armchair, and, feeling ill, decides she must lie down. She sets off towards the doors at her usual angle for rebounding off them to the bed: they burst open, she careers round the kitchen (not in her normal harmless figure-of-eight, since this requires un-impeded progress through the doors) and finally collides, first with the kitchen table, knocking off the vase, and then with the vase itself, which breaks as a result. Clearly in such a case Miss Z. would have acted intentionally in attempting to reach her bed, and in attempting to reach it via the doors; for this much she is still responsible. But there is a sense in which neither entering the kitchen nor colliding with the table nor breaking the vase are *actions* of hers; for these she is not respon-sible, though they are things which she did. They could be called events consequent upon her inability to control her physical acts in accordance with her rational judgement of the best path to follow once the doors have given way. And what *makes* them such is not any difference in their physical causa-tion, but the fact that they were unintended. If asked 'Why did you run into the table?', her most natural answer would be 'I didn't mean to . . .' plus some reference to her disability, the state of the doors, and her desire to get to her bed – this last to explain, not *why she ran into the table*, but *why she was in motion at all*. Had her trajectory in fact been plotted so as to collide with the table and break the Ming vase, she would have broken it intentionally: she would have been morally responsible, despite her lack of physical control over her movements after a certain point. Nevertheless, importantly, there *is* a clear sense in which she is the spectator of her own actions (because even when they are intended she has no muscular control over them). This is true: but being a spectator of this kind does not exempt her from moral responsibility for the intentional actions of which she is the spectator, precisely because they *are* intentional actions. Her vindictive collision with the Ming vase, being intentional, is thereby an action for which she is morally accountable.

Compare now what Lord Parker's interpretation appears to suggest about Byrne. Can we make sense of the idea that he cannot control his physical acts in accordance with rational judgement by an analogy with Miss Z.? Presumably what corresponds to her loss of control over her movements is his loss of control over his actions, i.e. his succumbing to his abnormal desire. The suggestion might be that control of Byrne's actions passes from Byrne the rational agent to Byrne's abnormal desires. Everything he does after that loss of control we are to consider as analogous to Miss Z.'s uncontrolled trajectory across her flat. And if we are to get exemption from moral responsibility out of the analogy, the case we must take is the one where Miss Z., through no fault of her own, fails to predict her trajectory correctly. But by now it should be obvious that the two cases are crucially different: both loss of control and intentionality occupy quite different positions in the sequence of events. Since the lady loses control once she has set off, she is incapable, once she has set off, of putting into effect any new intentions as to her trajectory: moral responsibility will accrue to her on the basis of the intentions formed before she lost control. Thus, even if in mid-flight she suddenly changes her mind about breaking the Ming vase (this time having calculated her path accurately in order to hit it), she will still be responsible for breaking it, however bitterly she regrets having done so. In Byrne's case, however, the positions of loss of control and intention are reversed: he loses control *after* the point where the lady forms her intentions, but is still supposed to be capable of forming intentions after that: as I pointed out earlier, the relation between his desire and his actions is in no way different from the relation in the case of anyone acting in pursuit of an object of desire. Comparison with Miss Z. suggests that since we are morally responsible for those actions we intend, we – and Byrne – must be morally responsible for those intentional actions we perform even when driven by desire. The lady is the spectator of that which is out of her control: her movements subsequent to the initial one. *If* she originally intended them, she is a spectator of her actions, though by that time helpless to alter them, and though a helpless spectator, is still morally responsible for them. Byrne is a spectator of what is out of his control: his actions subsequent to his succumbing to desire. But since he intends what he does subsequent to his loss of control, why should he not be held morally responsible for what he then does, just as the lady is held morally responsible for those intentional motions performed subsequent to *her* loss of control? Well, it may be said, the difference is that he is not responsible for the *content* of his intentions, since these are set by his desire, for which by hypothesis he is not responsible. But the content of intentions formed in pursuit of a desire is always set by the desire: no exemption from moral responsibility can be got out of that, unless the burden of justification is borne by the claim *that he is not responsible for his desire.* Otherwise the only way to exempt Byrne from moral responsibility for his actions seems to be to deny the intentions formed in pursuit of his desire the status of intentions at all, and hence to deny the related actions the status of intentional actions. If Byrne is not acting intentionally in killing, he must lack the *mens rea* for murder. But no good or clear reason has as yet been offered for why we should deny what he does in pursuit of his desire the status of intentional action. The original suggestion seemed to be that he could not be responsible for these actions because he was in some sense merely a passive spectator of them. A sense was found for the description of someone as a passive spectator of his own actions: but we have seen that being a passive spectator of one's own action is perfectly consistent with intending it, and because such actions remain intentional, the status of passive spectatorship does not of itself exempt the agent from moral responsibility. If passive spectatorship is to afford grounds for exemption, it must be because what is observed is in some way dissociated from, is nothing to do with, the spectator, in a way going beyond simple lack of control. The difficulty with seeing Byrne like this is that there *is* something which links him indissolubly with the actions he is supposed to be passively observing – namely, his desire. In Miss Z.'s case, lack of direct control over her movements only becomes dissociation of the relevant kind when those movements are, at the time of her initiating them, neither intended nor foreseen by her.[5] A merely

causal (as opposed to moral) 'responsibility' for those movements may then be attributed either to her abnormal disability,
or, if to facilitate comparison with Byrne a more immediate
cause is sought, to whatever it is that takes control of her movements once they pass out of *her* control (whatever we mean by
that). Lord Parker talks as if what has gone wrong with Byrne
is the kind of thing that has gone wrong with Miss Z.: a failure
of control over physical acts, such as, in her case, control over
the direction and speed of motion. Now, we know that we can
normally fix or change such things intentionally; but it does
not follow that we form explicit intentions to move in such-and-
such a direction at such-and-such a speed. Ordinarily we do no
such thing. We intend to go into the kitchen, and *somehow*, by
means we are unaware of, we can normally bring off the
physical performance necessary to bring about this action. The
mechanisms of motor control are nothing to do with us: we are
not in conscious control of the mechanism, and therefore cannot
be responsible for the mechanical work it does. It is dissociated
from us in the sense I meant when I said above that if passive
spectatorship is to afford grounds for exemption, it must be
because what is observed is in some way dissociated from the
spectator. In doing the things we *are* responsible for, and in
attributing responsibility for them, we take for granted the
existence and normal functioning of such mechanisms: intention works *through* familiarity with normal motor function.
When this goes wrong, we become aware that we can no longer
take for granted the machinery through which we exercise
control; but whatever it is that then assumes control of direction
and speed, though because of its unfamiliarity it may be experienced as an alien force, is not in fact any *more* alien than whatever controls direction and speed in the normal case, for this
corresponding normal control obviously cannot be the 'will', or
rational judgement, or anything of this kind. Though Miss Z.'s
'will' may be ineffective, what has gone wrong is not her 'will'
but her motor function. When her 'will' is effective, what is
going right must equally be not her 'will' but her motor function. So in whatever sense it is that Miss Z. is not responsible
for her abnormal motor function or its consequences, in that

same sense she is not responsible for her normal motor function and its consequences. We readily think of what assumes control of her motions once she has been struck down by Parkinsonism as an alien force producing effects for which she is not responsible, because *this* force is *always* alien in the same sense, in both normal and abnormal cases. This is the point at which the proposed analogy with Byrne breaks down: for the abnormal force supposed to be controlling him, being a desire, is *never* alien in the relevant sense, whether in the abnormal or in the normal cases. If we are to exempt Byrne from moral responsibility for his (apparent) actions for the same kind of reason as we exempt Miss Z. from moral responsibility for her (apparent) actions, we must be able to think of whatever produces those actions of his in the same way as we think of whatever produces those actions of hers. But we cannot *both* do this *and* retain our ordinary understanding of how desires may be related to and produce action: this is why this interpretation of irresistible impulse is incoherent. If the defence is that Byrne's desire is *only causally as opposed to morally* 'responsible' for his actions, the relation between his desire and actions *must* be something different from the ordinary relation between desire and action, where a man might be said to have acted as he did because of his desire: for this ordinary relation does not *in itself* exempt from moral responsibility – indeed, if anything it places actions within the moral sphere. But if we do think of the relation between desire and action as being thus totally different from normal, the connexion itself becomes unintelligible: the desire only occurs to us as the controlling force *because of* the normal relation between desire and action. In fact, what is morally relevant here is not the relation of desire to action at all (though this is what Lord Parker seemed to be suggesting); it is our relation to our desire. We want to say that where Byrne is helpless is in *yielding* to his desire. If we are to understand the defence of irresistible impulse, we must look to what we mean by an irresistible desire. This may recall a passing suggestion I made earlier: exemption from moral responsibility may be justified if we can substantiate the claim that Byrne is *not responsible for his desire*. But for this it is not enough just that he should be a passive spectator, now, of his desire, if the *ground* for saying this is that his desire, being sexual (or even perhaps being abnormal), has a physiological origin: for that applies to normal sexual desires too. And we are still held responsible for what we do about such desires, even if not for having them (and one might dispute even that).

What could we mean, then, by an irresistible desire, for which or for whose consequences we would not be responsible? Rather than tackling this direct, it will be helpful to approach it via something from which we are eventually going to have to distinguish it – namely, not irresistible but unresisted desire. Earlier I said that, apart from the supposed strength and abnormality of Byrne's desires, the description of his condition fitted exactly the description of akrasia, or weakness of will. I also suggested earlier that there were counter-examples to the view that what is important in irresistible impulse is the strength or force of the desire: I would like now to suggest that supposing this is so is to be misled by the same misleading picture that I have just been trying to discredit, a picture of the rational human agent as not a subject but a helpless Newtonian object whirled along by his desires, powerful forces whose strength and direction determine his apparent actions. Such a picture, being incoherent, is not a possible picture of a rational human agent at all. In this connexion it is perhaps worth pointing out that the weak-willed man typically offers the strength of his desire as an excuse for acting wrongly, or acting contrary to his best interest or contrary to what he might term what he *really* wanted: 'I started smoking again because my craving for a cigarette was just too strong for me.' Denis de Rougement phrases what he regards as the excuse typical of lovers overwhelmed by guilty passion in exactly the same way; 'Vous voyez que je n'y suis plus pour rien, vous voyez que c'est plus fort que moi.'[6] The point is that these excuses deceive no one (with the possible exception of those who give them). But perhaps it is their prevalence which lends plausibility to the notion of a desire so strong that it is irresistible: we would all *like* there to be such a thing.

To return to akrasia. Byrne resembles the weak-willed man

in that he acts in full knowledge that he should not act as he is doing. The important thing about the weak-willed man, the man who fails to resist a desire he knows he should resist, is that we do *not* excuse him; we hold him responsible for what, in his weakness of will, he does. We do not regard the fact that he may be *described* as simply pushed about by his desire as exempting him from moral responsibility. Why is this? Surely it is because, whether or not he actually did deliberate before acting, whether he argued with himself before taking the cigarette or simply grabbed it on sight without stopping to think, we think of him as still always capable of deliberating about his possible actions. To have this capacity is to be a human agent. To fail to have this capacity is to fail to be a distinctively human agent at all: it is *not* to be an irrational human agent. The madman may still be a distinctively human agent, though an irrational one, because he may still be capable of giving reasons for what he does which are arrived at by deliberation. What makes us call him irrational is that we cannot recognise the force of his reasons. But the structure of irrational human action is identical to the structure of rational human action: it is simply the structure of human action.

How then does desire enter into the deliberations of the weak-willed or incontinent man? Aristotle provided us with a starting-point, and remains illuminating. He says:

One may also consider the cause of incontinence scientifically, as follows. The universal premiss is an opinion, while the other is concerned with particulars, which fall within the scope of sensation. When the two are combined, in one kind of reasoning the mind must *affirm* the conclusion, but in the practical syllogism it must immediately *act* on it. E.g. if all sweet things should be tasted, and x, one of the particulars (forming a class), is sweet, then the agent, if he has the power and is not prevented, must immediately act. So if there are two universal judgements present in the mind, one deterring the agent from tasting and the other asserting 'Everything sweet is pleasant' and 'x is sweet' (and it is the latter that is realized) and at the same time desire is present then although the former universal judgement is a deterrent, the desire carries his body forward (since desire can set the various parts of the body in motion). So it comes about that incontinent action is in a sense influenced by a rational principle and opinion, contrary not in itself but only incidentally (because it is the desire, not the opinion, that is contrary) to the right principle. So this is another reason why the brutes are not incontinent, viz. because they have no universal belief but only an impression and memory of particulars. NE 1147 a-b

Let me first compare this with Aquinas's version (as quoted by Davidson in *How is Weakness of the Will Possible?*):[7]

> He that has knowledge of the universal is hindered, because of a passion, from reasoning in the light of that universal, so as to draw the conclusion; but he reasons in the light of another universal proposition suggested by the inclination of the passion, and draws his conclusion accordingly . . . Hence passion fetters the reason, and hinders it from thinking and concluding under the first proposition; so that while passion lasts, the reason argues and concludes under the second.

An example, given by Aquinas, shows the plight of the incontinent man:

THE SIDE OF REASON	THE SIDE OF LUST
(M_1) No fornication is lawful	(M_2) Pleasure is to be pursued
(m_1) This is an act of fornication	(m_2) This act is pleasant
	(C_2) This act is to be pursued
(C_1) This act is not lawful	

(*Summa Theologica*, Part II, Q 77, art. 2, reply to objection 4)

Davidson finds Aquinas's account superior to Aristotle's; I am not so sure. My objection to Aquinas's account, as quoted here, is this. It purports to explain why the weak-willed man comes down on the side of lust rather than on the side of reason; but the proffered explanation is a mere dummy. It simply presents us with the same picture as the one which has been misleading us all along in considering this subject, in that it suggests that for the weak-willed man, and by implication perhaps for the strong-willed man too, the conflict between the two bits of practical reasoning is or must be resolved by the passions: as if there were nothing left, after reason has constructed the two practical syllogisms, but to say with Hume, 'Reason is, and ought only to be, the slave of the passions, and can never pretend to any other office but to serve and obey them.' We are still left with a picture of ourselves as the billiard-balls of the passions. If this is so there can be no essential difference between us and Byrne – at best only a difference of degree. Consequently we find ourselves once more at the top of the same slippery slope to which diminished responsibility seemed to unbar the gate: we are all surely capable of weakness of will, indeed we all frequently manifest it. The weak-willed or incontinent man described by Aristotle would then appear to be just someone who manifests it more regularly than we do, and Byrne an extreme version of the weak-willed man (more extreme in that his passions lead him to do wickeder things than the passions of most, which maybe suggests that his passions must also be that much stronger). I do not think we need to adopt this conclusion. It seems forced on us because what is left out of Aquinas's account as quoted here is anything that would allow rational choice between reason and lust. I think that what is misleading about the extract as quoted by Davidson is that it treats the operation of the passions as if this were distinct from the way they figure in the practical syllogism. But the difference between victory for the argument on the side of reason and victory for the argument on the side of lust is not that the argument for lust has passion tacked on as an optional extra to the reasoning, the voice of temptation whispering seductively in one's ear as one rehearses one's practical syllogisms, encouraging one to favour lust (whereas reason has only the syllogism itself to rely on). The role of desire or passion in deliberation is to *figure* in the syllogism. The major and minor premises on the side of lust are the *expression* of passion and not distinct from it. Lust's practical syllogism *is* the voice of passion whispering seductively in one's ear, or rather, what the practical syllogism is, is the articulation of the voice of passion as it operates in the rational agent. The relation between the passions and reason is not that reason constructs syllogisms and the passions adjudicate between them, that reason proposes and passion disposes. It is that lust's practical syllogism is the rational articulation of desire. On this I differ from both Aristotle and, I think, Aquinas. Once we have realised that passion also can reason, it is obvious that Aquinas's explanation of why the weak-willed man comes down on the side of lust is a mere dummy. The explanation is passion fettering the reason. But this explanation consists at most in an appeal to the bare *existence* of desire. But the existence of desire is already presupposed in the entry of lust's practical syllogism into the agent's deliberations. *That* passion fetters the reason is precisely what requires explanation. What Aquinas has provided is not a philosophical account of the victory of lust, but a psychological description of what the victory of lust feels like to the agent. The only thing such an account explains is the behaviour I referred to earlier, the behaviour typical of the weak-willed man apologising for his weakness of will after the event – 'I knew it was wrong, but my desire overcame me.' Practical reasoning does not require the *rehearsal* of practical syllogisms at all. That is why the conclusion of the practical syllogism can be an action. I desire a certain kind of thing; I see a thing of that kind within my grasp: and, as Aristotle says, *straightway I act* – I grasp the thing, all other things being equal. The practical syllogism is a representation of this process. The case just described is the simplest case; no doubt more complicated cases will require more complicated and more self-conscious forms of deliberation. But even the simplest case is a case of reasoning, since without reason one cannot know what one desires, nor recognise something as a thing of the kind one desires. Anyone unconvinced by all this may like to consider the following: even if Aquinas's description suggests an explanation of why the weak-willed man listens to the argument of lust rather than to the argument of reason, it offers absolutely no explanation of how it is possible for the strong-willed man to come down on the side of reason. Let us suppose that the voice of the tempter, desire, is silent. (I hope, though, that

by now the absurdity is apparent of supposing this *and* supposing that the agent considers the argument on the side of lust.)
We then have two bits of practical reasoning, each as good as
the other as far as their internal structure goes, each issuing in
mutually incompatible actions. How do we decide which to
listen to? Do we just decide, that is, decide arbitrarily? Who
then is to say that the weak-willed man makes the wrong choice?
There must be more to rational deliberation than this.

Is there, then, any difference between Aristotle's account and
Aquinas's? After all, doesn't Aristotle, like Aquinas, say that
the weak-willed man is deflected from his deliberations by the
influence of the passions? At NE 1150 b he says:

> Some people deliberate and then under the influence of their
> feelings fail to abide by their decisions: others are carried
> away by their feelings because they have failed to deliberate.

How can this be reconciled with his concession, at 1147 b,
that incontinent action is 'in a sense influenced by a rational
principle'? For isn't Aristotle now explicitly *contrasting* deliberation and feeling, and doesn't this passage show that he
wants to regard the incontinent man as sometimes just not
reasoning? That this is not a real difficulty will be seen as soon
as we see what Aristotle's incontinent man is failing to deliberate, or heed deliberation, *about*. The important point to
notice is that at 1147 a Aristotle says that incontinent action is
influenced by a rational principle '*contrary not in itself but only
incidentally . . . to the right principle*'. If the problem I raised earlier,
about how the conflict between the reasoning on the side of
reason and the reasoning on the side of lust is to be rationally
settled – and surely Aristotle's whole enterprise in trying to
describe practical reasoning is to show that it can be and sometimes even is rationally settled – there must be a form of deliberation which consists in rational appraisal of the competing
claims of different practical syllogisms issuing in different and
incompatible actions. This is the more complex and more self-
conscious form of deliberation I referred to earlier. Here I
follow Professor Wiggins[8] at least in thinking that Aristotle
must have held that deliberation about ends is possible, in the

sense of deliberation about what subsidiary ends go to constitute the general end of eudaimonia about which we cannot
deliberate. Rationally considering the claims of virtue and lust,
consists in rational deliberation about possible and competing
subsidiary ends. The form that such deliberation would take is
not clear to me: but let us see what we can get out of the assumption of its existence without a precise specification of its form.
(It may be that Wiggins is right and no such precise specification of its form is possible anyway.) The first thing to do is to
take this thought in conjunction with something else Aristotle
says about the incontinent man:

> Thus it is evident that incontinence is not vice (except
> perhaps in a qualified sense), because it is contrary to the
> agent's choice, whereas vice is in accordance with choice.
> Nevertheless there is a similarity between the actions that
> result from them . . . the incontinent are not wicked, but they
> do wicked things. NE 1151 a

This seems to me both to be absolutely right and, at last, to
enable us to distinguish Byrne from the incontinent man whom
he so much resembles. The incontinent man is not wicked, but
he does wicked things. Why, if he does wicked things, is he not
wicked? Because he does not *choose* to do wicked things. This
does not mean that he is swept by his desire into doing wicked
things as helplessly as a billiard-ball drops into a pocket, so that
he cannot be held morally responsible for his weak-willed
actions. If he were not morally responsible, how could we
condemn him? And Aristotle says that we do. And whatever
Aristotle says, we *do* condemn the weak-willed man, though
we may (somewhat contemptuously) pity him, and though we
may predict with confidence that he will never change his ways.
He does not choose to do wicked things in the sense that he does
not choose wicked ends – though he may choose each individually wicked action as it comes up: this is what makes his
actions wicked actions and not morally neutral compulsive
behaviour. What end, then, does he choose, if he does not
choose wicked ends and yet can hardly be said to choose vir-
tuous ones – because he does not very often or very consistently

practise virtue? In such a case, the answer seems to be that he fails to exercise a choice in accordance with virtue which he is nevertheless capable of making. It is because he is capable of making it that we regard him as morally responsible. Now, to distinguish Byrne from the weak-willed and indeed the strong-willed man, we were looking for some capacity they had and he lacked, since all three resemble each other in point of knowledge. We must also, of course, distinguish him from the wicked man, who chooses wicked ends and builds his life around achieving them. We might be tempted to say: Byrne lacks the ability to deliberate about, and hence rationally to choose, ends. There are at least two difficulties with this. The first is: how good are any of us at deliberating about ends, and how often do we exercise our capacity to do it? Rational harmonisation of ends is neither easy nor essential, and may never even be attempted, in a self-conscious and thoroughgoing way, by most of us. The law cannot afford to nor should it ignore the way most of us are. If inability rationally to harmonise ends were to be a ground for a defence against criminal charges, we could nearly all get away with murder. The second difficulty is Byrne's lucid intervals again. One could argue that these were a sign that as far as rationally harmonising ends goes, his *capacities* at least (as distinct from his abilities at any particular time), were up to those of the rest of us: his medical witnesses said of him that when not under the influence of his perverted desires he was normal. Any defence based on incapacity is going to have to relate specifically to these perverted desires and not to a general incapacity. If there is to be anything which absolves Byrne from moral responsibility, it is going to have to be that he has an incapacity rather than an inability, and that somehow the incapacity he has is incapacity to integrate the practical reasoning which embodies these perverted desires into his overall deliberations about ends. I want to resist, with my latest breath, any suggestion that the reason why this integration cannot take place is because of the strength of his desires: this is a mere dummy explanation, like Aquinas's explanation of the victory of lust. (It is indeed a dummy explanation of a very similar phenomenon.) What I want to say instead is that the irresistibility of Byrne's desires *consists* in their inamenability to reason. A desire of any strength[9] may be like this: it is not a question of strength. At this point what is needed is a more precise specification both of the form of practical reasoning about ends to which I am appealing, and a specification of why or how the practical reasoning (e.g. about means) that Byrne engages in, once the lustful end which he has not chosen has imposed itself on him, fails to fit into general schemas of deliberation about ends. If Wiggins is right, there *are* no such general schemas. But then the grounds of Byrne's defence are so vague as to be extremely dubious. I concede all this: the best I can offer is a series of examples, which though in no way conclusive may at least suggest that this general framework may be a possibly helpful way of thinking about the problem.

Consider the following bits of practical reasoning, in ascending order of complexity and relevance to our problem. To take the simplest case first: I am a rich bachelor with a particular liking for corduroy suits. I have long wanted one in a particular shade of blue. One day I see just such a suit in a shop window. Straightway I act: I go into the shop, try on the suit, and finding it just as I would wish, I buy it. The form of my practical syllogism is: I want a certain kind of suit, here is a suit of that kind, what I want I must buy, I buy it.

Second case: I am a very much poorer man, an unemployed and deserted husband with a young family in my inexpert and somewhat aggrieved care. I too like corduroy suits, and indeed am shortly going to a job interview for which the one I see in the shop window would be eminently suitable; moreover, every other garment I possess is such as quite probably to lessen my chances of getting the job. It so happens that I have enough money on me to pay for the suit: for the social worker assigned to me has managed to get me a special grant of precisely that sum to cover the costs of a holiday for my youngest child, who is subnormal and difficult. The child has been promised the holiday and has been eagerly looking forward to it. Is it conceivable that in succumbing to weakness of will I should just be seized by an overwhelming desire to possess the suit, and, driven by my desire, mindlessly walk into the shop, hand over the money, and walk out again with it without further thought? How could such a transaction be accomplished *mindlessly*? At the very least, my desire must lead to a decision (even if not an explicit decision) to buy the suit. But isn't it much more likely that I will say to myself something like 'Well, it's really important that I get that job, more important in the long run than that Tommy should go on holiday, of course he'll be disappointed, but once I'm in work I can send him on holiday and pay for it myself, and pay the money back to the Council too, anyway why should he go on holiday and not the other kids, it's not fair, even if he is backward, he gets enough special treatment as it is.' My desire to possess the suit takes the form of practical reasoning which in this case leads to my buying it. Just such a piece of practical reasoning could be perfectly sound: the reasons I give myself for buying it could be *good* reasons – that could in fact be the right thing to do. However it is also possible that when faced with the misery and reproaches of my child, the contempt of my neighbours and the the fury of the social worker, together with my own awareness that what I wear at the interview is unlikely to determine its outcome, I will realise that the reasons I gave myself at the time for buying it were *in fact* specious: my *real* reason for buying it was just that I wanted it (like the man in the first case described above), perhaps helped on by resentment at continually having to sacrifice my pleasures to those of my most demanding and aggravating child. But this realisation brings shame and regret, which I may express by saying to myself 'I knew I shouldn't have bought it. . . .' And at this point I may be prepared to say of myself that what I *really* wanted at the time was *not* to buy it, i.e. there was a sense in which I did not choose it – though there was also a sense in which I did choose it. This second case is intended as an example of weakness of will. The man knows what is right and does what is wrong. He admits that he knows what is right, and knew it at the relevant time, by saying of himself 'I knew I shouldn't have bought it. . . .' But though he chooses to do what is wrong, he does not choose what is wrong in the sense that he chooses wrong ends; what he does is wrong only in the light of some end which he does choose (and which is a right end). Nevertheless, we blame him for doing what is wrong, for we think he *could* have done what is right. He *did* choose the wrong action, and he *could have* chosen the right one. And our ground for thinking that he could have chosen what is right is that he acted throughout like a rational agent: he could have been argued out of his purchase, and if pressed, would feel obliged (though ashamed) to produce his reasons for it.

Third case: as the second, except that the man consciously adopts as reasons what dawned on the man in the second case as a shameful realisation. The job interview is far from his thoughts. He wants the suit: he has the money; he prefers his own pleasures to those of his children, and regularly obtains things for his own use by claiming the things are for them. Such a man will hardly be turned from his purpose by arguments based on the rights of others or on his duties as a father: he has chosen a different principle. This is the licentious or wicked man, and the licentious man, as Aristotle says, can be cured but cannot easily be persuaded to change. One may wonder about 'cure' here: but perhaps a modern equivalent of what Aristotle had in mind would be some form of behaviour modification by conditioning techniques which involve no appeal to rationality (though admittedly it is hard to imagine a reward or punishment schedule for this case which would be likely to replace selfish behaviour with unselfish behaviour).

Fourth case: I am an extremely poor but scrupulously honourable bachelor. I am a composer,[10] and my income is spasmodic: at times I am penniless, at times I command relatively large sums of money. I am found very ill in the street: pneumonia complicated by starvation. I am taken to hospital. The hospital manages to contact my friends and asks them to go to my apartment to pick up the personal effects which I shall need while I am there. On entering my apartment, my friends are astonished to find it contains nothing but fifty-four corduroy suits: they have to supply my few personal needs out of their own pockets (which they do gladly, and that not merely because the sum involved is small). I recover: my friends gently question me on how I have lived and how I propose to live, and why I spent what money I had on suits rather than on anything else. I can give them no reason: I am embarrassed and confused at this discovery of my eccentricity, and out of delicacy my friends refrain from further questioning. They have managed to obtain for me a commission for a small chamber work, paid for in advance; they give me the money, with affectionate injunctions to spend it on the necessities of life. I make no promises, but out of gratitude and to please them immediately buy food and prepare a meal which we eat together; they depart somewhat reassured. As soon as they have gone, I go out and spend the rest of the money on corduroy suits, and subsequently conceal my purchase from my friends, continuing to live as I have always done. This is the model for irresistible impulse. The man knows what is right and does what is wrong; that is, in this case, he knows he cannot justify his actions and would not attempt to do so. In doing what is wrong, he does not act like a brute: he evidences perfectly efficient practical reasoning about the means whereby he may continue to live as he has done. That he does so provides grounds for saying that he lives as he does intentionally. But if required to face his friends again, he may well say something like 'I don't seem to be able to help it.' He has not chosen *either* his end (accumulating corduroy suits even if this leads to starvation) *or* his action (buying a particular corduroy suit) as a result of deliberation, nor could he present his actual choices (i.e. his actions) as the outcome of possible deliberations of his, as could the weak-willed man (the contrast there is between wanting and really wanting). For when pressed he can produce no reason at all for why he does what he does. *Because* he can produce no reason, he cannot be argued out of it: the desire (if desire it be) is irresistible not because of its strength or overwhelming quality: what it means to say that it is irresistible is that *there is nothing to resist it with* – because it does *not* express itself in the form of practical reasoning, because it *cannot* enter into deliberations about ends. Of course as a result of this he may *feel* like a billiard-ball, in that, like the billiard-ball, he is alienated from what moves him. He does not choose at least some of his ends in a much stronger sense than the weak-willed man: as regards some of his ends, he *cannot* choose them – he merely acts in pursuit of them, impervious to deliberation about them as ends and without attempting justification. What is wrong with him is that he lacks a capacity in relation to certain ends: it is not that certain events overtake him (i.e. that certain feelings overwhelm him). He may describe what happens like this: but the description darkens philosophical understanding.

NOTES

[1] I am grateful to David Hirschmann, David Wiggins and Andrew Woodfield for criticisms of earlier versions of this paper.

[2] This did not imply anything very subtle; evidence of concealment was acceptable as evidence of knowing the difference between right and wrong, presumably because it was taken as showing knowledge that the doer ought not to have done the deed. But concealment could, of course, be just the result of a desire to avoid unpleasant consequences, and not at all of shame or consciousness of wrongdoing. So by this criterion, knowing the difference between right and wrong appears to collapse into knowing that some things are forbidden.

[3] Nigel Walker, *Crime and Insanity in England*, Edinburgh University Press, 1968, p. 155.

[4] Oliver Sacks, *Awakenings*, Duckworth, 1973, p. 233 footnote.

[5] Suppose, for example, her friend had left the double-doors open and Miss Z. had tried to reach her bed by the figure-of-eight round the kitchen, knowing that she risked miscalculating the angle and consequently breaking the vase. If she then decides to take the risk and does in fact break the vase, this outcome is one that she has foreseen but not intended; and her friend could justly reproach her with having taken the risk. *Some* measure of responsibility for what happened still accrues to her.

[6] Denis de Rougemont, *L'Amour et l'Occident*, Paris 1939, p. 39.

[7] In *Moral Concepts*, ed. Joel Feinberg, O.U.P. 1969, p. 104. Aquinas's Latin original runs as follows:

Ad *quartum* dicendum, quod ille qui habet scientiam in universali, propter passionem impeditur ne possit sub illa universali sumere, et ad conclusionem pervenire; sed assumit sub alia universali, quam suggerit inclinatio passionis, et sub ea concludit. Unde Philosophus dicit, quod syllogismus incontinentis habet quatuor propositiones, duas particulares et duas universales, quarum una est rationis, puta nullam fornicationem esse committendam; alia est passionis, puta delectationem esse sectandam. Passio igitur ligat rationem, ne assumat et concludat sub prima; unde ea durante assumit et concludit sub secunda.

It will be seen that my objections perhaps relate more to Davidson's presentation of Aquinas (particularly of the example) than to Aquinas himself.

[8] 'Deliberation and Practical Reasoning', PAS, 1975–6.

[9] The notion of different strengths of desire I have in mind here is that deriving from our experience of appetites of different degrees of urgency. Just as all such degrees may be amenable to reason, so all such degrees may be inamenable to reason.

[10] The fourth case is based on the composer Erik Satie, but the case as described here differs considerably from what is related of him. I would not wish to claim either that Satie was mad or that he suffered from irresistible impulse.

7

HUMAN VALUES IN A MECHANISTIC UNIVERSE

Margaret A. Boden

1 : Introduction

The truth can be dangerous. It is because they realise this that the Roman Catholic Church forbid cremation. Cremation is, of course, theologically permissible, and in times of epidemic the Church allows it. But in normal times it is forbidden – Why? The reason is that the Church fears the influence of the image associated with it. It is difficult enough for the faithful to accept the notion of bodily resurrection after having seen a burial (knowing that the body will eventually decay in the ground). But the image of the whole body being consumed by flames and changing within a few minutes to a heap of ashes is an even more powerful apparent contradiction of the theological claim of bodily resurrection at the Day of Judgement. (Indeed, the ban on cremation was introduced when the French Freemasons held anti-Catholic demonstrations, in which they burned their dead saying 'There, you see: they won't rise again!') In short, instead of relying only on abstract theological argument, which very likely would not convince their flock in any case, the Church deals with this threat to faith by attacking the concrete image.

I believe a basically mechanistic view of the universe, and of human beings as creatures of it, to be true. But such views can be dangerous, in that they tend to encourage a dehumanisation of our image of man, an undermining of our sense of responsibility and individuality. For the image of 'machine' that is currently popular has no place for human values or for the specifically human self-image associated with them. This image of machines and mechanism is drawn from seventeenth-century clockwork and nineteenth-century engineering: one has only to think of Descartes's metaphors for animal psychology, and T. H. Huxley's metaphor for psychology in general (in which he compared the mind to the useless smoke from a steam-engine). Occasionally people appeal to twentieth-century notions such as the cybernetic concept of feedback, taking the thermostat or the guided missile as their paradigm case of modern mechanism. But this paradigm also is insufficient to provide a philosophical base for humanity, and its overall effect is just as dehumanising as earlier versions of mechanism. The current image of machines causes a chill to strike the heart on reading the molecular biologist Jacques Monod's claim that 'The cell is a machine. The animal is a machine. Man is a machine.'[1] If man is indeed a machine, what room is there for humanity?

I shall try to defend against the dehumanising influences of mechanism by presenting a different image of 'machine', one that shows the potentialities inherent in mechanism to be far greater than could previously have been supposed on the basis of extant machines. That is, instead of concentrating on abstract philosophical arguments in favour of mechanism, I shall describe actual examples of machines whose behaviour is hardly 'mechanistic' in the usual sense of the word. Specifically, I shall outline some of the achievements of artificial intelligence ('A.I.' for short), the science of making machines do things that would require intelligence if done by people.[2] The analogies between these machines and human minds are strong enough to cast doubt on the antimechanist assumption that no philosophical rapprochement between humanism and mechanism is possible.

Before describing these examples in Sections III to V, I provide a philosophical context for the later discussion by sketching what I understand by the notion of 'human values', and what I take to be the main doubts on the part of humanists who reject mechanism of any sort.

II: Human Values

The notion of human values is inextricably bound up with a specifically human concept of people and a sense of their moral dignity. By this I mean that, whatever particular values a humanist may hold, these will in general assume that people are capable of purposive action, free choice, and moral responsibility, and that their interests ought *prima facie* to be respected. It is because these concepts are essential to human values that antihumanist writers such as B. F. Skinner seek to undermine them, claiming that morality has no need of 'freedom' and 'dignity'.[3]

It follows that any form of mechanism that claims to be basically compatible with a morality of human values must be able to accommodate the concepts of purpose, freedom, and responsibility. What features of these concepts are generally agreed by their protagonists to be most important?

When we ascribe purposes to people, and describe their behaviour as purposive action, we imply that their behaviour is somehow guided by their idea of a goal. The purpose is always an idea of something nonexistent, for the goal-state itself lies in the future; it is often an idea of something that will never exist, for goals are not always achieved; and it is sometimes focused on something intrinsically impossible, like squaring the circle. That is, the idea is an intentional object or thought within the subjective experience of a thinker, as opposed to an objective entity existing in the material world. The guidance it exerts on purposive action is (within limits) flexible, rational, and intelligent, and with perseverance the person learns to do better. Typically, the agent is aware of the goals being followed and why they are being followed, although cases of 'unconscious motivation' and 'habitual action' frequently occur.

In ascribing freedom to people, or describing human action as free, we mean not merely that people are unpredictable, but (more positively) that in free action the agent could have acted differently. That is, either the goal or the subgoal guiding the behaviour could have been different, so that a different end was chosen in the first place or the same end was sought by different means. But this difference must itself be generated in a particular sort of way. It cannot be based on a random factor, nor can it depend on causes having nothing to do with the self and lying wholly outside the agent's control. (This is why radically indeterminist analyses of freedom are unacceptable, and why action attributable primarily to genetic or environmental causes cannot be regarded as truly free.) Rather, the difference in question must be grounded in the deliberations of the person concerned: had the agent's reasoning been different, the action also would have differed. So the more someone is capable of flexibly rational thinking, the greater the freedom of action available. In addition, free action is often self-determined in a peculiarly intimate sense, in that the determining reasons include a crucial reference to the person's (actual or ideal) self-image. In such cases, one asks oneself (or, perhaps, a friend): 'Am I someone who would choose to do this?' or 'Do I want to be the sort of person who does that?' These questions, and especially the latter, address the person's moral principles as well as mere conceit or narcissistic self-regard.

The ascription of moral responsibility presupposes that free action can be 'action against the strongest desire', in the sense that a temporarily pressing motive can be outweighed by moral principles. The point is not that the person is even more strongly swayed by the moral principles, for the metaphor 'swaying' suggests passivity on the agent's part. Rather, the person actively deliberates on the choice in a responsible fashion, carefully considering all the known factors in so far as they are relevant to ethical issues, and not making a decision over-hastily. Specifically moral principles (in contrast with mere personal preferences) are universalisable to all individuals in similar circumstances, which implies that practical morality draws on the capacity to recognise subtle analogies between distinct situations as well as the ability to reason logically about 'all' and 'some'. Moreover, moral principles are primarily concerned with abstract features of human behaviour or experience, such as justice and betrayal or happiness and despair. It follows that moral responsibility rests on the ability to understand concepts such as these, and to assess their relevance to particular situations. If the person is to engage in moral choice, rather than mere ethical contemplation, this assessment must involve also the imaginative comparison of the likely outcomes of alternative possible actions. It follows that a great deal of knowledge must be brought to bear in exercising one's responsibility: knowledge of moral principles themselves, knowledge of the world in which they are to be applied, and knowledge of one's self – both as one is and as one would like to be.

These being the crucial features of the family of concepts contributing to 'human values', why are humanists usually so insistent that human values cannot be encompassed by any basically mechanistic philosophy? Broadly, there are two different reasons. One is a philosophical view arising from purely philosophical arguments; the other is a prejudice against mechanism that is grounded not so much in abstract reasoning as in the concrete image of familiar machines as we know them in daily life.

The philosophical view favoured by humanists holds that mechanism is incompatible with intentionality, with the distinction between the psychological subject and the object of thought that we have seen to be essential to purpose, freedom, and moral responsibility. But what sort of incompatibility is this? Briefly, the humanist's claim may be only that intentional phenoma cannot be described in terms making no use of the subject-object distinction, so that a philosophy in which such psychological terms do not appear can make no sense of human values. Alternatively, the humanist may also claim (without always seeing that this is a different point) that intentional phenomena cannot be generated from a mechanistic base, one which can be described in the nonpsychological terms of physics; on this view, creatures pursuing human values simply could not arise in a basically mechanistic universe.

My position on this 'philosophical' humanism is that whereas the first claim distinguished above is correct, the second is mistaken.[4] In other words, it is true that we cannot avoid the concepts of purpose, freedom, and responsibility if we are to understand human beings as the essentially subjective creatures they are, or if we are to express any system of specifically human values. But it is false that subjectivity cannot arise within a basically mechanistic universe, or that a system described in objective terms by the physicist cannot also be described by the humanist in intentional terms that express different aspects of its nature.

I shall concentrate in this paper on the second root of the humanist's antipathy to mechanism: the poverty of the humanist's image of machines. Specifically, I shall ask how purpose, freedom, and moral responsibility might relate to an enriched image of mechanism. More generally, my discussion will bear also on the issue of the compatibility of intentionality and mechanism. For if the moral concepts I have sketched in this section can be shown to be consonant with mechanism, then subjectivity in general must be compatible with mechanism too.

Let us turn, then, to consider a few examples of what one might call 'non-mechanistic machines'. My examples are drawn from A.I., so the machines in question are digital computers running under the guidance of an A.I. program. You will see that I say 'the program does this' where I could equally have said 'the machine does that'. You will see also that I use psychological terms without scare-quotes in describing these machines. I omit scare-quotes for aesthetic reasons: as will become clear, I do not hold that any of these current machines is *really* purposive or intelligent, still less a moral agent. I do hold, however, that psychological vocabulary is essential in expressing what these machines can do.

III: Purpose

The central feature of purposive action is that it is guided throughout by an idea of the goal, in a flexible and intelligent manner. Are there any machines of which the same might be said?

Among the earliest A.I. programs were some that solved problems by keeping an idea of the goal firmly in mind and reasoning backward from it. For example, the GEOMETRY MACHINE proved theorems in Euclidean geometry that would have defeated any but the brightest of high-school students with the same vocabulary of geometric concepts and the same stock of previously proved theorems.[5] Essentially, the program followed the strategy of the school-child who writes *Given:* and *To be Proved:* at the top of the page, and then tries to find a way of legally getting from what is given to what is to be proved (using only inferences based on Euclid's axioms or previously proved theorems). Similarly, the General Problem Solver – 'GPS' for short – attacked problems in logical form (such as the familiar *Missionaries and Cannibals* puzzle) by carefully noting the differences between the current problem-state and the goal-state, and eliminating these differences until none remained.[6] In each of these cases, the idea of the goal is crucial in guiding the solution of the problem.

In each case, also, the process of solution varies with the circumstances rather than being rigidly fixed. That is, what the program does, as well as the order in which it does it, depends on the specific nature of the difference between the current and goal-state. GPS carries out a 'means-end analysis' of the problem, in which it identifies the differences as a series of sub-goals to be achieved in the most suitable order. Heuristics, or rules of thumb, are available to suggest what type of approach is most likely to resolve a particular difference, and what method to try next if the 'best' should fail. In short, these programs show the beginnings of one main criterion of purpose: variation of means.

Some recent programs show more intelligence in varying their performance according to circumstances. The flexibility of their goal-seeking is greater, not merely in the sense that they have a greater number of methods to choose from, but also in the sense that communication *between* methods is possible while the program is functioning. It is as though one method asks advice from another, while a third makes a complaint that there is a specific difficulty ahead, and a fourth requests 'stop press' information from a fifth. This flexible form of organisation is *heterarchical*, as opposed to the hierarchical organisation of GPS and the GEOMETRY MACHINE. In a hierarchy, there is a fixed progression of responsibility for control passing down from higher to lower levels of the system, and a module that gets into difficulties has to apply to its superior for help. But in a heterarchy the responsibility for deciding what is to be done next is more evenly distributed throughout the system, and the various sub-routines can communicate not only 'up' and 'down', but also 'sideways'. An analogy is between a (hierarchical) bureaucracy and a (heterarchical) group of co-operating experts: although there is room for some degree of flexibility in a bureaucracy (as there is in GPS), in a community of specialists there is more opportunity for last-minute changes of plan or minor adjustments in light of local difficulties.

The degree of flexibility that can be achieved by heterarchical programs is illustrated by Terry Winograd's 'SHRDLU'.[7] SHRDLU's goal is to understand the sentences typed into it, where understanding involves parsing each sentence correctly, interpreting it sensibly, and answering it helpfully. SHRDLU has a large number of mini-programs for interpreting English sentences, including specialists which know about word-endings such as *-ed*, *-ing*, and the like, and experts on the grammatical and semantic properties of *noun groups* or *adjectival phrases*. In addition, it has sub-routines that specialise in finding out what the world is like, and modules whose particular job is to deduce conclusions from given premises. Each specialist, or mini-program, contains within itself advice about what to do in varying circumstances, and what to try if the most obvious stratagems fail. The goal of understanding an English sentence is one that can be reached only by way of highly flexible, interacting thought-processes, of which we ourselves are normally not introspectively aware. As you can see from the following excerpt of dialogue, SHRDLU's understanding depends on 'simultaneous' parsing, semantic interpretation, and investigation of the world, a complex process that has to differ subtly according to the specific nature of the input sentence:[8]

1. *Pick up a big red block*
   O.K.
   The system answers 'O.K.' when it carries out a command. In order to pick up the red block, it had to clear it off by

finding a space for the green one (initially on top of it) and moving the green one away.

2. *Grasp the pyramid*
I DON'T UNDERSTAND WHICH PYRAMID YOU MEAN.
There are three pyramids in the scene, so the program does nothing.

3. *Find a block which is taller than the one you are holding and put it into the box.*
The system has to figure out what is meant by 'one' and 'it', as well as using deduction to decide which block it is holding.
BY 'IT', I ASSUME YOU MEAN THE BLOCK WHICH IS TALLER THAN THE ONE I AM HOLDING.
Printed out to keep us informed.
O.K.
The hand has to set down the red block to pick up the taller blue one.

4. *What does the box contain?*
THE BLUE PYRAMID AND THE BLUE BLOCK.

5. *What is the pyramid supported by?*
Earlier the system responded to 'the pyramid' by saying 'I don't understand which pyramid you mean.' Now, it assumes that we mean the one just mentioned.
THE BOX.

6. *How many blocks are not in the box?*
Negatives such as 'not' and 'no' are handled whether they appear in clauses or noun groups (such as 'no boxes').
FOUR OF THEM.

7. *Is at least one of them narrower than the one which I told you to pick up?*
The phrase 'at least one of them' must be analysed to refer back to the previous question, and 'the one which . . .' must also refer to blocks. Noun groups can have complicated numbers such as 'at least one', 'more than three', 'exactly seven', *etc.* The memory of past events is used to deduce which block is

F

'the one which I told you to pick up'. Notice the complicated syntactic structure in which 'the one' is actually the object of a clause embedded two levels deeper.

YES, THE RED CUBE.

17. *Will you please stack up both of the red blocks and either a green cube or a pyramid?*

O.K.

23. *Had you touched any pyramid before you put the green one on the little cube?*

YES, THE GREEN ONE.

The system deduces from its memory what event is being referred to, and can relate other events to it in time. The analysis includes complex tenses of verb groups, and there are special facilities for keeping track of the various forms of irregular verbs like 'have'.

24. *When did you pick it up?*

WHILE I WAS STACKING UP THE RED CUBE, A LARGE RED BLOCK AND A LARGE GREEN CUBE.

A time is described by naming the main goal which was being worked on.

25. *Why?*

The system remembers immediately previous sentences to understand questions like this and the following ones.

TO GET RID OF IT.

By keeping track of selected parts of the original subgoal tree, the system has some understanding of its own motives.

26. *Why did you do that?*

TO CLEAR OFF THE RED CUBE.

'That' refers to the action mentioned in the answer.

27. *Why did you clear off that cube?*

Here, 'that' means the one just referred to.

TO PUT IT ON A LARGE GREEN CUBE.

28. *Why did you do that?*

TO STACK UP THE RED CUBE, A LARGE RED BLOCK AND A LARGE GREEN CUBE.

29. *Why did you do that?*
    BECAUSE YOU ASKED ME TO.
    It remembers what it did, not how the request was worded.
    [*Cf.* the request of item 17, which gives the program a
    choice.]

In addition to the flexible variation of means, SHRDLU's dialogue suggests other features of purpose. For instance, Item 1
has the indeterminacy characteristic of action sentences (and
often taken as a logical criterion of intentionality): Winograd
did not have to tell SHRDLU precisely how to pick up the big red
block, but left the program to work that out for itself. A
prime reason for the machine's ability to understand (and obey)
this vaguely specified command is that the program is written
in a version of PLANNER, a 'goal-oriented' programming
language in which one can identify goals at a high level of
generality and rely on the system itself to fill in the details.
Items 17 and 29 show that SHRDLU itself often speaks in intentional terms: it knows that it was not specifically asked to stack
up the two red blocks and a large green cube, even though it did
this in response to an input request.

Items 17 and 23–29 show that SHRDLU has some understanding and memory of its own goal-subgoal structure, and is able
to address this structure to find the reasons for which it did
things. If this information were not stored in its memory, it would
have had to answer Item 29 either by saying 'I don't know,' or
perhaps by working out a plausible reason for its action which
in fact was not the real reason. Analogously, a person in a state
of posthypnotic suggestion will dream up all sorts of possible
reasons for putting the cat on top of the grand piano, being
unable to remember the hypnotist's previous command and so
unable to give the real reason, 'Because you asked me to.' And
Freudian accounts of unconscious motivation similarly assume
that part of the person's goal-subgoal structure are unavailable
to consciousness, being at least temporarily repressed, and that
the relevant actions will be 'explained' by rationalisations that
do not constitute genuine self-knowledge.

But SHRDLU lacks a feature of purposiveness that was mentioned earlier, namely, the ability to learn to do better. Its knowledge of what it is up to is sufficient to enable it to know why it did what it did, but not to enable it to remember what went wrong when failures occur. Consequently, SHRDLU cannot benefit from experience by learning to avoid false paths once it has been down them.

Not all programs are similarly limited. For example, HACKER is a program that writes programs for solving problems, and that learns to do so better because it has an understanding of the purposive structure of the programs it composes and because it knows about the sorts of things that can go wrong.[9] When it writes a program it adds 'comments' to various lines (as human programmers do) saying what that section of program is intended to do. This information is used in rewriting the program, should it fail to achieve its goal when it is run. The sorts of mistake, or bug, that HACKER knows about are defined in high-level teleological terms, such as UNSATISFIED PREREQUISITE, GOAL-PROTECTION VIOLATION, PREREQUISITE CLOBBERS BROTHER GOAL, and so on.

A sense of the way in which HACKER learns from its mistakes can be conveyed by Figures 1–5. Given the scene shown in Figure 1, and asked to get A on to B, HACKER can put A on B immediately. HACKER has available a *primitive*, or already given, program for putting one thing on top of another. But if HACKER is given Figure 2, and asked to get B on to C, it cannot do so immediately. The reason is that the primitive 'PUT-ON' program can work only with one block at a time, so cannot move B since A is on top of it. HACKER investigates the difficulty, works out that what needs to be done is to remove A, then writes a program for doing so, and inserts this 'patch' into the primitive 'PUT-ON' program. The patched program is now run, and it succeeds: A is put on the table, then B is placed on C, and the final scene looks like Figure 3.

It is important to realise that HACKER has learnt a skill of some generality here, as can be seen by referring to Figures 3 and 4. Given Figure 3, and asked to get C on to A, HACKER can do so at once, without the false start that was made in the earlier example. Moreover, given Figure 4 and requested to get

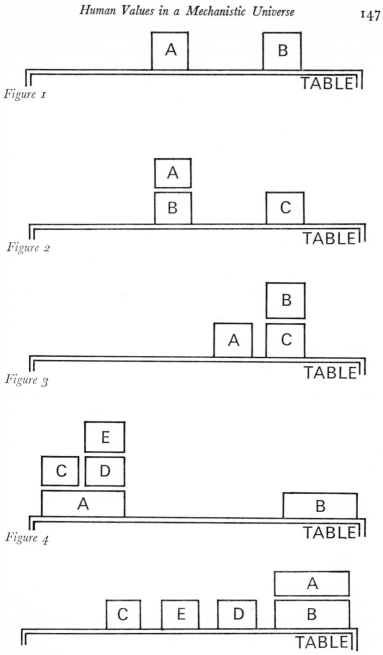

Figure 1

Figure 2

Figure 3

Figure 4

Figure 5

A on to B, HACKER again unhesitatingly does the right thing. That is, the patch produced previously was sufficiently general to direct these steps:

Wants to put A on B
   Notices C and D on A
      Puts C on TABLE
      Wants to put D on TABLE
         Notices E on D
            Puts E on TABLE
         Puts D on TABLE
Puts A on B

This procedure results in the scene shown in Figure 5.

In addition to its knowledge of the purposive structure of what it is up to, and its knowledge of some very general types of mistake (and how to deal with them), HACKER is able to remember precisely what happened when it went down a false path which now it is careful to avoid. This ability depends primarily on CONNIVER, the programming language in which the program is written. As well as facilitating memory of mistakes (and so easing learning), CONNIVER makes it possible to write programs that can simultaneously consider the detailed course of events appropriate to various different alternative actions, and to make comparisons between them. This computational ability contributes to the intelligent planning of purposive action (and therefore to moral deliberation also), and HACKER makes use of it when asking itself whether doing such-and-such would conflict with the already established subgoal achieved by so-and-so.

IV: Freedom

The unpredictability of human action is often exaggerated by proponents of freedom, and a novel like Luke Rhinehart's *The Dice Man* shows what a mockery of humanity a radically unpredictable life of action would be. Nevertheless, the undeniable practical limits on predictability give added spice not only to gossip but also, in some eyes, to arguments for freedom. However many reasons you may have for predicting that I will say something, it is always possible that I will say something else – or nothing – instead. But machines, or so the argument goes, are either predictably deterministic or random, neither of which is compatible with a freedom that can form the basis of morality.

This claim that, provided there is no random operator involved, machines must be predictable in their behaviour is associated with a common misinterpretation of the familiar slogan, 'A computer can do only what the programmer tells it to do!' If this is taken to mean that everything the machine does is done at the behest of instructions specified at some level or another by the program, it is true. But it is false if it is taken to mean either that the programmer can foresee everything the machine will do or that the programme will do all and only what the programmer intended it to do. Even in relatively crude cases, a program may not do just what was expected of it.

For instance, a simple program that engages in man-machine dialogues may sometimes respond forgivingly to an apology but sometimes spurn it, and may even choose occasionally to say nothing at all. While the programmer can indeed say something in general terms about when it is that the program is most likely to respond in one or other of these ways, he cannot always predict what will happen in a particular case. As you read the following excerpt of dialogue between this program and a human doctor, see whether you can predict the program's remarks either in general or specific terms, and whether you can suggest an explanation *post hoc* for what it actually says (the doctor speaks first):[10]

Why are you in the hospital?
I SHOULDN'T BE HERE.
Who brought you here?
THE POLICE.
What trouble did you have with the police?
COPS DON'T DO THEIR JOB.
What do they do instead?
COPS ARREST THE WRONG PEOPLE.

They arrest the right ones sometimes.

THE LAW SHOULD GET THOSE ITALIAN CROOKS.

Are you Italian?

MY BACKGROUND IS BRITISH BUT I WAS BORN IN THIS COUNTRY.

Do you know any Italian crooks?

I TRY TO AVOID THE UNDERWORLD.

Are you afraid of the underworld?

THE MAFIA ARE THE WORST GANGSTERS.

Are you connected with the Mafia?

YOU KNOW, THEY KNOW ME.

How do they know you?

THEY SPY ON ME.

Why do they?

THEY WANT TO GET FALSE EVIDENCE TO FRAME ME.

What do they have against you?

THEY ARE OUT TO GET ME.

What for?

I HAVE INCRIMINATING EVIDENCE AGAINST THE MAFIA.

Are you sure of all this?

YOU DON'T BELIEVE ME?

I am doing my best.

(Silence on the 'patient's' part.)

(Silence on the psychiatrist's part.)

CAN'T YOU THINK OF A DECENT QUESTION TO ASK?

You seem hostile to me.

SOME OF YOUR REMARKS ANNOY ME.

I am sorry.

FORGET THE EXCUSES, YOU GUYS ARE ALL ALIKE.

It may have occurred to you, perhaps even before coming across the reference to the human as 'the psychiatrist', that there is something characteristically odd about PARRY's conversation. 'PARRY' is the name of the program, which is designed as an embodiment of a particular psychological theory of paranoia, and of the paranoid interaction of fear, hostility, evasiveness, mistrust, and so on. For the moment, let us concentrate on PARRY's moment of silence and on his final furious rejection of the psychiatrist's placatory apology.

The program's apparent sulkiness and petulance in these instances arise in response not only to the previous input item but to the conversation as a whole. It follows that the psychiatrist's contributions 'I am doing my best' and 'I am sorry' would, in the context of different conversations, elicit different reactions from PARRY. Broadly, the program scans the semantic content of the conversation for remarks that it considers (either reasonably or paranoically) to be threatening, and various numerical monitors representing the theoretical constructs of fear, anxiety, and mistrust are raised accordingly. In addition, the program can initially be 'set' at a high level of these emotional monitors, with the result that input remarks that in other circumstances would have been interpreted by PARRY as neutral, or even soothing, are instead interpreted by him 'paranoically'. Since almost any remark relating to his inner delusion is taken as threatening by a human paranoid, PARRY is designed to react in an analogous fashion. As you have probably realised, PARRY's persecutory delusion concerns the Mafia, whom he believes to be hunting him. It is because previous references to the Mafia and associated topics (such as the police) have greatly raised PARRY's anger and suspicion, that he does not trust himself to reply to 'I am doing my best' and cynically rebuffs 'I am sorry'.

Even PARRY's programmer is unable to predict what PARRY will say, although the program is a relatively simple one (much simpler than Winograd's SHRDLU), and relies on spitting out slightly adjusted versions of 'canned' responses rather than being able to generate entirely fresh sentences. When a psychiatrist finished his interview with his own favourite test-question for paranoia, 'I'd like to invite you to dinner at my house,' he and PARRY's programmer were each surprised by the startlingly appropriate reply: 'You are being too friendly.'

However, despite this very human ability to surprise, PARRY

cannot be seen as a plausible simulacrum of a free spirit. The crucial features of deliberation and reflective self-knowledge are entirely lacking. PARRY does not deliberate within himself whether he should answer or be silent, and he answers – or not – by picking randomly from a stored list of responses associated with the currently relevant levels of the various emotional monitors.

Programs like SHRDLU and HACKER, by contrast, do show some ability to deliberate about what they are doing and why they are doing it (and their actions are not influenced by their passions as PARRY's are). They have a degree of self-knowledge concerning not only why they did a particular thing, but also what it is generally within their power to do.

The self-knowledge involved in answering strings of 'why?' questions about one's actions is, up to a point, essential to freedom (cf. items 17 and 23–29 of SHRDLU's dialogue). To the extent that one cannot answer such questions, or (like the rationalising neurotic) cannot answer them truthfully, one's action is not genuinely free. One's freedom depends also on a realistic appreciation of one's own powers: it is because SHRDLU has a good idea of what it can and can't do – and what the results are likely to be – that it can go ahead on its own initiative in working out how to obey a command like that of item 17. And HACKER, as we saw, has even greater power to consider comparisons between different imagined courses of action, as well as to remember why it went wrong in the past, which abilities are necessary if one's freedom is to mature with experience of living.

Restrictions on adult human freedom can arise through 'depersonalisation' of the self-image, wherein the self is regarded as having very weak powers of action or, in extreme pathological cases, none at all. A schizophrenic who describes himself as 'a machine' is calling on the popular image of mechanism in order to deny that he is a purposive system, and his life experience and sense of responsibility are impoverished accordingly. Such a person might or might not be able to do certain simple things at the request of the psychiatrist (a catatonic cannot), but dependence on the will of others is no substitute for personal autonomy. A depersonalised individual is somewhat analogous to a (hypothetical) version of SHRDLU *lacking* internal access during planning to the information that it is able to pick up pyramids. Since this item is not on the list it uses during planning as a catalogue of the things it can do, it cannot conceive of doing it. Consequently, if the 'big red block' of item 1 had had a pyramid sitting on it, this impoverished SHRDLU could not have cheerily answered 'O.K.' The person who cannot originate the idea of shutting the window, but can do so if asked to by the psychiatrist, would be parallelled by a version of SHRDLU that could pick up a pyramid only if explicitly told to do so. The command 'Please pick up a pyramid' would directly address a stored list of *all* the things SHRDLU can in fact do; but, in the example we are imagining, this list is not available in its entirety for perusal by SHRDLU itself during planning. If the program were to be altered so that even this direct access to pyramid-moving procedures were deleted, then SHRDLU would be like the catatonic schizophrenic who, even if he hears and understands the words, cannot obey requests to 'Stand up, please' or 'Move your hand.'

Examples of schizophrenia, as well as the bewildering variety of psychological malfunctions associated with amnesia or with damage to the speech-area of the brain, thus indicate the subtle complexities of the computational basis of normal, 'free' behaviour. To adapt an image of Wittgenstein's: there are many cogs and levers inside the mind, and if they are disconnected or if their normal interactions are impeded then strange limitations on the person's usual range of choice and action are only to be expected. Analogous phenomena are observed in the functioning of a computer program wherein a single definition is changed, a single instruction deleted, or a single passing--of-control from one procedure to another is inhibited. So Locke's remark that 'Barely by willing it, barely by a thought of my mind, I can move those parts of my body that were formerly at rest,' belies the true psychological complexity of freedom, however faithfully it may reflect its introspective simplicity.

The fact that a free action *could* have been different, in the sense that it *would* have been different had the person's reason-

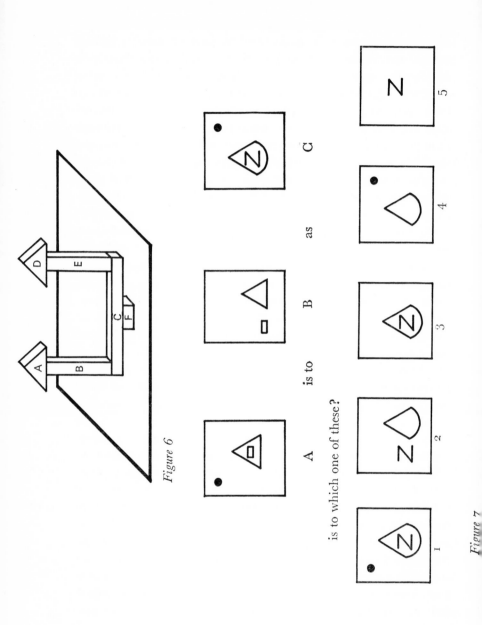

Figure 6

A   is to   B   as   C   is to which one of these?

1   2   3   4   5

Figure 7

ing differed, is also paralleled in some programs – such as HACKER and SHRDLU, and another heterarchical program called 'BUILD'.[11] BUILD is so named because its task is to decide how to go about building a construction of bricks like that shown in Figure 6, for example. If you think carefully about this task, assuming that you may use only one hand and are not allowed to slide bricks, you will realise that the construction requires an extra brick (not shown in the picture) to act as a support for one end of the horizontal bar C, so that the 'tower' for that end of C can be placed upon it without upsetting it. This extra brick is brought in as a temporary measure, and has to be removed after both towers have been placed on C. The only way to avoid recourse to this extra brick would be to build the *sub-assembly* consisting of blocks A-B-C-D-E, and then to lift the sub-assembly as a whole and place it on to F. But in this particular example, such a procedure would not succeed unless your hand were exceptionally steady: the tall towers are so unstable that they would almost certainly collapse in the process. All these facts, including the steadiness of its (imaginary) hand, are borne in mind by BUILD as it works out how to build the construction shown in the picture.

Were you to build such a structure yourself, one could say that you freely chose to use a supporting brick rather than attempting to proceed by sub-assembly. Conversely, if you opted for sub-assembly and the structure collapsed – perhaps shattering into glass splinters all over the floor – you could be blamed for having chosen this method instead of the more reliable 'temporary support' approach. In either case, your intuitive or calculating deliberations about the stability of the sub-assembly and the steadiness of your own hand would play a crucial part. Had they been different, your actions would have differed.

So it is with BUILD: features like potential stability and steadiness of movement are continually taken into account in deciding what to do, and if a safer method can be found of constructing the desired building then that method will be used. If it turns out that the 'safer' method is not safe after all, the program can alter course accordingly. A slight change in the 'steadiness' parameter, or in one of the many items of information contributing to individual judgements of stability, would incline BUILD to choose differently in deciding what to do. But the complexity of the program is such that one cannot say anything so straightforward as 'Change X would lead BUILD always to choose Y rather than Z.' And if BUILD (like HACKER) could learn to do better, profiting by its past experience, one could not even say 'Change X would lead BUILD always to choose Y in a case *precisely like this particular instance.*' As it is, the word *precisely* has to be interpreted fairly strongly, for a different size of tower-bricks, for example, might have passed BUILD's imaginative stability-test, so making it choose to try sub-assembly rather than temporary support.

With the possible exception of a case where you were building with precious family heirlooms made of glass, we would not normally care enough one way or the other to ascribe the term 'free' to your choices in such a task – although if specifically challenged we would admit them to be free choices. But the case is very different if we consider examples where specifically moral considerations, and specifically moral responsibilities, come into play. Let us turn now to discuss some of the features that make a free choice into a matter for moral concern and evaluation.

V: Moral Responsibility

If morality involves the influence of ethical considerations to generate 'action against the strongest desire', it can arise only within systems capable of being simultaneously affected by various, conflicting purposes or desires. Programs like GPS, SHRDLU, HACKER and BUILD are basically single-minded in nature. This does not mean that they cannot deliberate on mutually exclusive possible courses of action, or (in the case of BUILD) judiciously change their minds and even change them back again while doing so. But the various alternatives considered are all viewed as means to a single overall end. This is true of most current A.I. programs, it being difficult enough to write a program to achieve one aim reliably, never mind writing one that can simultaneously pursue several independent goals.

But A.I. workers recognise that living purposive systems do not have the singlemindedness characteristic of current programs, and a few programs have already been written with the express intention of simulating the multidimensional nature of human motivation. 'ARGUS', for example, is a system in which the various goals compete for the computational resources available, priority being given to the one which, in the current situation, is most strongly activated.[12] In other words, the strongest desire always wins, where this is not a tautological truth but a question of which goal-seeking activity is the most strongly stimulated in the circumstances (the programmers use the analogy of shouting demons, the overseer giving priority to the demon who shouts loudest).

In order that action should go against the strongest desire, under the influence of moral principles, it is necessary that a choice be made only after reasoned deliberation about all relevant factors, which factors include not only the various desires being stimulated but also the moral insights or ethical rules followed by the person in question. We have already seen examples of programs capable of reasoning about their choices so as to avoid what might initially seem the 'obvious' option: BUILD, for instance, is able to restrain itself from trying to place tower A-B on to bar C until it has first fetched an extra brick to support the bar. So there is no reason to suppose that specifically moral considerations could not enter also into such deliberation, and so decisively affect the generation of action, provided that one could give a program a moral sense of what it should be worrying about.

To answer the question 'What ought one to worry about?' is to put forward a moral system, either in the form of a set of specific rules of conduct, like the Ten Commandments or the Scout's Law, or in the form of a general ethical principle, such as the Golden Rule, the Categorical Imperative, or the Utilitarian promotion of happiness. And, if the moral system is to count as one concerned with 'human values', in the sense previously defined, it must at least allow and preferably stress the fact that human beings are freely acting purposive creatures to whose sense of responsibility one may appeal. (Skinner's morality is an example of an ethical system that is not concerned with human values in this sense, even though it prescribes what human beings should and should not do.)

Morality in practice is concerned not only (if at all) with abstract reasoning about the greatest happiness of the greatest number, or what a rational being could reasonably take to be a universal principle of action, but also (and primarily) with specific questions about particular types of conduct. What, for instance, is wrong about betrayal – and what types of behaviour are to be counted as betrayals? What is co-operation, and why is it *prima facie* a good thing?

Not surprisingly, there is no program that unerringly acts in terms of a felicific calculus or a categorical imperative to respect the interests of rational beings. There is no moral philosopher who does so either, not merely because of human frailty or Original Sin, but because these meta-ethical notions are so unclear that moralists cannot agree about their range of specific application. Sci-fi addicts will immediately think of Isaac Asimov's 'Three Laws of Robotics', which put the avoidance of harm (whatever that is) to human beings at the pinnacle of every robot's moral structure.[13] But since highly general moral considerations such as these are currently in the realm of science fiction rather than science, I shall ignore them. What of the more specific concepts regarding human conduct – such as 'love', 'oppression', or 'betrayal' – that one may expect to find represented in any system of human values, irrespective of its supposed meta-ethical base? Could any sense be made of such matters in computational terms, so that a program could be instructed to take them into account during its deliberations?

A prerequisite of 'making sense of a concept in computational terms' is giving a clear analysis of the concept concerned (which is why no program can obey the Categorical Imperative or endorse a Utilitarian ethic). The social psychologist R. P. Abelson, in the course of developing a programmed model of his theory of attitude-change, has sketched a taxonomy of human *themes*, wherein are represented morally relevant phenomena such as love, co-operation, and betrayal.[14] These themes, and others, are analysed and systematically interrelated in terms of three independent psychological dimensions, each of which is defined in purposive terms. A theme is made up of the interdependent intentions, or *plans*, of two actors, and it is largely by reference to them that one sees the social and personal world in terms of moral values.

The three ways in which the autonomous purposes of two actors are conceived of as linked are as follows: First, one or both may have a role in the other's plan (and there are at least three commonly recognised types of role in this context, defined in terms of the agency, influence, and interests of the two parties). Second, one or both of the actors may have a positive or negative evaluative attitude to the plan (in whole or in part) of the other, and to his own role in it, if any. And third, one or both people may have the ability to facilitate or interfere with the other's action, whether at particular points only or throughout the plan. By way of these three dimensions, then, interaction with another human being can either augment one's own freedom of action or constrain it in different ways. Certain familiar moral ambiguities are reflected in the fact that some themes are 'asymmetric', in that they are experienced very differently by the two actors concerned, and so one and the same thematic structure is given two theme-names corresponding to the different subjective points of view involved (examples are Victory-Humiliation and Oppression-Law and Order).

By way of the three dimensions of role, interest, and facilitative ability, Abelson is able to exhibit the teleological structure of a wide range of psychological phenomena. Since themes are by definition social in nature, involving interaction between the intentions of two people, they are highly relevant to morality. And a morality of themes would count as a system of human values, in the sense previously distinguished, since they are defined in basically purposive terms that take for granted the freedom of action of the two actors in question.

For example, Abelson defines *betrayal* as follows: 'Actor F, having apparently agreed to serve as E's agent for action A_j, is for some reason so negatively disposed towards that role that he undertakes instead to subvert the action, preventing E from attaining his purpose.' If one were to specify appropriate restrictions on the importance for E of the goal to which action A$_j$ is a means, and on the comparative power of the actors F and E to achieve that goal, one could systematically distinguish between individual members of a whole family of betrayals, such as abandonment and letting-down for example. (Abandonment is an especially immoral form of betrayal, because the goal is very important from E's point of view, but E is conceived of as relatively helpless without F's aid in achieving action A$_j$; by contrast, letting-down may be a matter of less moral import, since neither of these assumptions is implied.)

Other themes defined by Abelson are admiration, devotion, appreciation, co-operation, love, alienation, freedom, victory, humiliation, dominance, rebellion, mutual antagonism, oppression, law and order, and conflict. Common progressions of distinct themes, or *scripts*, mentioned by Abelson include rescue, alliance, revolution, blossoming, the worm turns, the end of the honeymoon, turncoat, and romantic triangle. (In each case Abelson first defines the theme or script in terms of his structural system, and then picks an ordinary language term to act as a mnemonic label for his theoretical concept; philosophers, therefore, should not expect his thematic definitions to correspond precisely with the nuances of everyday usage.)

Abelson has not yet written a program that can handle his structural theory of themes, but the theory arose in a computational context in the first place. It was because of the flaws in his previous program (one that represented certain features of political psychology) that Abelson was moved to deepen his theoretical understanding of concepts like those we have discussed. There seems no reason in principle why a program should not embody a representation of *betrayal*, much as BUILD embodies a model of *stability* or SHRDLU an understanding of *noun clause*.

In attempting to apply human values in real life, one has to weigh various moral considerations in light of the particular circumstances of action. Is this *really* betrayal – or is it merely letting-down or disappointment? We have seen that the settling of such a moral dilemma involves the ability to bear in mind judgements about the relative importance of the goal concerned to the person seeking it in the first place, as well as the relative social status and physical power of the people in the situation. A moral system (whether program or person) competent to decide such issues would have to rely on computational abilities at least as powerful as those used by BUILD in deciding how to construct brick-palaces, and in most cases would need even more powerful ones. Were it not so, the moral life would be as easily accessible to normal human beings as playing with children's building bricks.

Morality is conceived of (and taught) largely in terms of stories, whether parables, fables, histories, novels, or myth. The ethical function of such tales is to present examples of moral dilemmas in which alternative assessments may seem to be possible, although usually one assessment is recommended as the best and one course of action is preferred. To profit from a parable is to understand the moral analogy so as to be able to attempt to apply the central lesson to moral choices in one's own life. This is not always easy: Alice's bewilderment on being told by the Duchess that 'Birds of a feather flock together' is the moral of 'Flamingoes and mustard both bite' was presumably of a kind with her puzzlement on reading some of the 'improving' stories meted out to Victorian children. The appreciation of analogy is a complex psychological process of cross-comparison between descriptions of the analogues, and between descriptions *of* descriptions when the analogy is 'on a higher level'. (Alice's complaint, 'Only mustard isn't a bird,' suggests her intuitive grasp of what is involved in recognising analogies.)

It is already possible for machines to see analogies, albeit of a relatively crude or obvious kind. For instance, programs exist that can appreciate analogies of differing strength between simple spatial scenes like those built by BUILD, or between diagrams of the sort commonly used in IQ-tests (such as those shown in Figure 7).[15] Moreover, the nature and strength of the various analogies can be characterised by these programs not only in terms of more or less exacting descriptions of the analogous items themselves, but also in terms of more or less exacting descriptions of the comparison previously made at a lower level. And a language-understanding program has been developed that can take the proper sense of the sentence 'She drank in the sunshine at every pore,' even though the semantic definition of 'drink' that is used by the program specifies that what is drunk should be a fluid (which sunshine is not), that it should end up inside the person (which the sunshine does not), and that it should be taken in at one specific bodily aperture, preferably the mouth (not at every pore).[16]

A program able to draw analogies between things must be able to formulate and compare descriptions of them in what strikes us as a reasonable manner (is the Wonderland Duchess merely eccentric, in spotting an analogy missed by the rest of us, or is she – as the Cheshire Cat would say – mad?). So a 'morality machine' would need not only to be able to represent concepts like betrayal and co-operation, but also to compare the application of these concepts to distinct situations in a sensible fashion. Since the concepts and thought processes involved are as yet ill understood (though intuitively exercised by each of us every day), there is no current program that could understand the moral import of a New Testament parable or make a responsible moral choice about a matter of everyday complexity. But to the extent that work in A.I. helps to clarify the psychological nature of analogy, it can illuminate the computational basis of moral thinking.

In so far as moral principles are universalisable, ethical reasoning must involve an awareness of the difference between the concepts of *all* and *some*, *everybody* and *somebody*. Many programs exist that can handle these notions as they are expressed in terms of the predicate calculus. Interpreting natural language uses of the English words 'all', 'everybody', 'some', and 'somebody' is more tricky, however. As G. E. Moore pointed out, the logician does not mean quite the same thing by 'Some tame tigers growl,' as other people do. (Most people would interpret this phrase so as to imply that there are several tame tigers and at least two of them growl, where as the logician takes it to mean that there is at least one thing which is a tame tiger and that growls – (∃x). (Tame x & Tiger x and Growls x) – but quite possibly *only one* such tiger.) The debates about existential presuppositions highlight controversial issues that would have to be taken into account by anyone writing an ambitious language-using program. And although logicians may shudder, we can see why a PARRY-ish interviewing program responds to the complaint 'Everybody laughed at me' with an apparent refusal to take the universal quantifier seriously: 'WHO IN PARTICULAR ARE YOU THINK-ING OF?'[17] However, since moral philosophers who stress universalisability do intend this notion to be taken strictly, these niceties of everyday uses of 'all' and 'everybody' may be ignored for our purposes. So if a program were to be provided with a set of moral evaluations (expressed, for instance, in terms of Abelson's themes and scripts) there would be no radical difficulty in its universalising the morality. (To be sure, contradictions might arise if any moral rules conflicted with each other; the program – like people – would then have to give priority to one principle over the other.)

To ascribe moral responsibility to a person is to imply that they can be praised or blamed in respect of particular choices, or acts. We have seen that moral choice commonly involves conscious deliberation and comparison between situations and principles, as well as careful weighing of the likely results of alternative courses of action. But some acts that are done 'without thinking', or even 'automatically', may be candidates for moral evaluation. For example, in discussing freedom of action I said that someone might be blamed for trying to move a whole sub-assembly of precious glass objects, instead of moving them individually. To cry, 'I just wasn't thinking,' as the heir-looms lie shattered into fragments, is to offer an explanation but not necessarily an acceptable excuse. For one may retort: 'Well, you should have been thinking!' On the principle that 'ought' implies 'can', this retort presupposes that the person had the ability to take stability into account, and had the knowledge that these particular objects were both precious and fragile.

Similarly, in cases of more obvious moral import, someone can be blamed for not thinking, or not thinking carefully enough, when deciding what to do. Provided that the person's cognitive structure is such that they could have taken the relevant moral factor into account (that is, they could have both recognised it as relevant and acted accordingly), then the fact that they did not do so is *prima facie* cause for reproach. And some excuses are more acceptable than others: 'I just wasn't thinking, I was so worried about Mary,' may be adequate to dispel censure, depending on the importance of the worry concerning Mary.

Like the careless person in the example we have been imagining, the program BUILD has the ability to take note of actual and potential instabilities. And HACKER, the program that learns to write better and better programs, is able to act in two different fashions, one of which involves it in more painstaking deliberation than the other.

The first time that HACKER tries to run a program it has written itself, it acts in CAREFUL mode. That is, each step is individually checked as it is executed, to see if it is fulfilling the overall purposive function coded by the comment that was attached to it by HACKER at the time of composition. This typically involves numerous checks and cross-checks, together with a detailed chronological record of the changing world-state, so that any bugs that have escaped HACKER's previous criticism can be identified as soon as possible. In CAREFUL mode, then, HACKER haltingly concentrates on the level of detailed tactics. Once a new program has been successfully executed, it is not run again in CAREFUL mode unless it gets into trouble, in which case CAREFUL running is reinstituted. In this way, knowledge that remains implicit during smooth functioning, in that it is not accessed by HACKER even though it can be described as 'relevant' to the task in hand, is made fully explicit and available to the program when things go awry. If there is any reason to expect that things may go awry, as in the case of a first-time run of a new program, CAREFUL mode ensures that this knowledge is made explicit from the start. Consequently, mistakes can be anticipated and forestalled in CAREFUL mode that would be made (though subsequently corrected) in normal functioning. The analogy to 'responsible' and 'irresponsible' action is clear. No one can act responsibly – or irresponsibly, either – who does not have comparable powers allowed for by their mental structure.

In HACKER's case, especially CAREFUL action happens only when the program is attempting something for the first time, or when it has already got itself into difficulties. If HACKER (or BUILD) were to be connected to an actual robot, which can not only think about how to stack up blocks but can really do so, it might be advisable to suggest that it also use CAREFUL mode if breakable bricks are to be stacked. Even if it were building a certain sort of stack for the umpteenth time, it would then still stop to check actual and incipient stabilities at every step, instead of blithely following through its wellworn plan regardless of such specific niceties. Naturally, running in CAREFUL mode takes a good deal longer than the normal, smoothly confident approach. So the suggestion that CAREFUL mode be used with fragile bricks might sometimes be rejected in favour of a less time-consuming method, depending on the program's assessment of the relative importance of saving time in this situation and of preventing breakage of the things being stacked. In general, CAREFUL functioning could be activated or not as a result of complex weighings of various (potentially conflicting) factors, not least among which would be the importance of the goals and subgoals being followed at the time. We noted earlier that HACKER and BUILD always know what it is that they are trying to do, even if they have not yet found a way of doing it.

The prescriptivist view of ethics characterises morality as a matter of proclaiming (and, preferably, following) specific priorities that should govern conduct. 'Thou shalt not kill,' thus functions much like 'Use CAREFUL mode when playing with glass,' and the distinction between a lie and a white lie rests on an assessment of moral priorities according to which, in some situations, lying may be thought to be the lesser of two evils. Moral blame commonly takes the form of complaining that a specific ethical factor either was not taken into account at all, or was not given a sufficiently high priority in the case in question. If the person at fault is led to consider it in future, or to weigh it more gravely, the moral obloquy will not merely have identified the blameworthy aspect of the past action but will also have contributed to the person's moral growth.

Piaget describes an early stage in the development of morality, wherein the child takes into account only 'objective' factors in ascribing blame instead of also considering 'subjective' factors such as the intention of the agent.[18] For instance, little Mary is judged to be much naughtier than her sister Joan, for whereas Joan (who was stealing the tarts) broke only one plate, Mary (who was helping to lay the table for tea) broke five. The objective results of action are all that is considered by young children, and the higher moral worth of Mary's intention simply is not taken into account. In order to be able to consider such aspects of action when handing out praise or blame, one must be able to analyse the action concerned in terms of a (perhaps complex) set of goals and subgoals that the action is intended to serve, and to evaluate these goals in terms of moral priorities. Since HACKER knows for what purposes it is doing things, whether or not those purposes are ever achieved, it is potentially capable of understanding that its failure to use CAREFUL mode in one situation may be more blameworthy than its omitting to do so in another situation, even though the objective results are identical in either case. (Who cares how many bricks are broken if one was trying to distract a child in great pain, perhaps even thinking that the child might enjoy seeing them break?)

VI: Conclusion

One ethical concept mentioned in Section II has not occurred since, namely, moral dignity. This concept may be used in a 'weak' sense, so that to ascribe dignity to people is to view them as freely acting responsible beings to whose choices moral evaluations are appropriate. The discussion so far has suggested that not all contemporary machines are radically at odds with this notion, as all former machines undoubtedly were. But there is a 'strong' sense of the concept that cannot be applied to any machine I have discussed, nor to any hypothetical descendant of them.

In the strong sense, the notion of moral dignity in addition implies that one should respect the interests of other people just because they are people's interests, and as such are intrinsic to their human nature. That is, my *prima facie* obligation to co-operate with you in furthering your interests, or to avoid betraying you to your enemies who will subvert them, is primarily justified not by the fact that my doing so will increase happiness, or the like, but by the fact that to fail to respect your interests is to deny your essential nature as a human being. Intrinsic interests are not necessarily thought of as fixed principles of 'human nature', though some moralists regard them so, but they are ends or purposes that pertain as such to the individual himself since they cannot be explained by reference to the purposes of any other agent. Animals, too, have (amoral) interests that are intrinsic in this sense. (Notice that intrinsic interests are purposes that cannot be further explained in *purposive* terms: their existence may however be explained in evolutionary or physiological terms.)[19]

The purposes of machines (that is, of artefacts) are not intrinsic to them, but derive ultimately from the purposes of the engineer and/or the programmer. To be sure, the relation of computer's goal to programmer's goal is not often so direct as in SHRDLU's item 29, 'BECAUSE YOU ASKED ME TO,' nor is the machine's goal always predictable by or even acceptable to the programmer. Nevertheless, the fact that the machine has goals at all, irrespective of which these are, can be explained by pointing out that the program (or self-modifying distant ancestor of it) was written to serve the purposes of the programmer. In the event that one feels any *prima facie* obligation to respect the machine's interests, any reluctance to lead it astray, this attitude is parasitic upon one's appreciation of the machine as an artefact made in the fulfilment of human ends. (A similar point underlies the theological problem of 'people or puppets?': if God freely created us to work His will, it seems that our interests can at base be explained by reference to the purposes of some other being, and so are not *in themselves* deserving of moral respect but must be justified by reference to those alien ends.)

If follows that I cannot cite any example of a machine with even embryonic moral dignity, in this strong sense of the term, if I confine myself to examples drawn from A.I. or other branches of technology. But this has nothing to do with the 'mechanistic' nature of what may or may not be going on inside the machine, being a consequence purely of the fact that A.I.'s machines are *artificial*. In so far as in saying 'Man is a machine,' Monod meant that the bodily processes underlying and generating human behaviour, including moral conduct, are describable by physics or molecular biology, his remark does not conflict with moral dignity. With respect to the issue of intrinsic interests, there is a world of difference between natural 'machines' and artificial machines.

The concept of dignity is central to human values because it is closely linked with the moral concepts of purpose, freedom, and responsibility – and also rationality and intelligence. All these cognate terms are themselves commonly used in a 'strong' sense so as to carry the implication of intrinsic interests. In this sense, no machine artefact could be called 'intelligent' or 'purposive', never mind how close the analogy between its operation and human thought.

But irrespective of the question of intrinsic interest, current machines cannot be regarded as *really* purposive or intelligent, still less dignified as moral agents. The analogies between the functioning of the programs I have described and mature human thought are not sufficiently close for these psychological terms to be used in their full sense, and in the case of 'moral agent' there is hardly any reason for using the term at all. Various crudities of current programs were mentioned in the preceding sections, such as their singlemindedness and inability to draw richly subtle comparisons, and many others could have been detailed.

None the less, the analogies between these machines and moral thinking as we understand it are close enough to be philosophically significant. As well as helping to illuminate the psychological complexities of what must be involved in moral action, and so what one is committed to in calling an agent 'free', they suggest *how it is possible* for human values to exist in a basically mechanistic universe.

For all the programs I have mentioned run on digital computers of known construction, functioning (at the electronic level) according to the principles of physics. If these systems are not mechanistic at base, then none are. Yet the behaviour of these machines is 'non-mechanistic' in character, not only in the sense that one continually uses psychological terms in describing what they do (as one occasionally does in cursing the obstinacy of one's car), but also in that one can only explain and understand what it is they are doing by using intentional language. Talk of electrons and wires cannot explain *why* BUILD decides not to risk using sub-assembly to build the scene shown in Figure 6, opting instead for a method involving temporary support, even though such talk can explain *how* it is that BUILD's reasoned decision can actually occur and be acted upon in the material world. So the irreducibility of intentional to non-intentional ('mechanistic') language is preserved in the examples we have considered, as is the indispensability of 'psychological' in addition to 'physiological' explanations.

Machines have until recently been describable in purely non-intentional terms, and nothing of any explanatory import would have been lost if people had rigorously avoided applying psychological vocabulary to cars, clocks, and Concorde. But a machine being used to run a program like those developed in current A.I. cannot be described in such terms alone without losing sight of its most interesting (information-processing) features. We now have machines with a point of view of their own, machines with a subjective model (representation) of the world and their own actions in it by means of which they deliberate more or less carefully about what they should do and what they should not have done, and why. The insidiously dehumanising effects of mechanism can thus be counteracted in a scientifically acceptable manner. By providing a richer image of *machines* that suggests how it is that subjectivity, purpose, and freedom can characterise parts of the material world, current science helps us to understand how human values can be embodied in a mechanistic universe.

NOTES

[1] Jacques Monod, *Chance and Necessity* (London: Collins, 1972). For Monod's defence of 'the ethics of knowledge' in preference to 'animist ethics', see chapter 9.

[2] Further details are given in my *Artificial Intelligence and Natural Man* (Hassocks, Sussex: Harvester Press; New York: Basic Books, 1977).

[3] B. F. Skinner, *Beyond Freedom and Dignity* (New York: Knopf, 1971).

[4] This philosophical position is discussed more fully in my *Purposive Explanation in Psychology* (Cambridge, Mass.: Harvard U.P., 1972), esp. chs. ii, iv, and viii.

[5] H. L. Gelernter, 'Realization of a Geometry-Theorem Proving Machine', in *Computers and Thought* (eds. E. A. Feigenbaum and Julian Feldman), pp. 134–52. (New York: McGraw-Hill, 1963.)

[6] Allen Newell and H. A. Simon, 'GPS – A Program that Simulates Human Thought', in *Computers and Thought*, pp. 279–96.

[7] Terry Winograd, *Understanding Natural Language* (Edinburgh: Edinburgh U.P., 1972).

[8] *Understanding Natural Language*, pp. 8–15 gives a 44-item dialogue from which this excerpt is taken. Winograd's comments are in lower case.

[9] G. J. Sussman, *A Computer Model of Skill Acquisition* (New York: American Elsevier, 1975).

[10] K. M. Colby, Sylvia Weber and F. D. Hilf, 'Artificial Paranoia', *Artificial Intelligence*, 2 (1971), 1–26.

[11] S. E. Fahlman, 'A Planning System for Robot Construction Tasks', *Artificial Intelligence*, 5 (1974), 1–50.

[12] W. R. Reitman, *Cognition and Thought: An Information Processing Approach* (New York: Wiley, 1965).

[13] Isaac Asimov, *I, Robot* (London: Dennis Dobson, 1967).

[14] R. P. Abelson, 'The Structure of Belief Systems', in *Computer Models of Thought and Language* (eds. R. C. Schank and K. M. Colby), pp. 287–340. San Francisco: W. H. Freeman, 1973.

[15] P. H. Winston, 'Learning Structural Descriptions from Examples', in *The Psychology of Computer Vision* (ed. P. H. Winston), pp. 157–210. New York: McGraw-Hill, 1975. This program's handling of analogies is discussed in the original account published as MIT AI-Lab Memo AI-TR-231, 1970. And see T. G. Evans, 'A Program for the Solution of Geometric-Analogy Intelligence Test Questions', in *Semantic Information Processing* (ed. M. L. Minsky), pp. 271–353. Cambridge, Mass.: MIT Press, 1968.

[16] Y. A. Wilks, 'A Preferential, Pattern-Seeking, Semantics for

Natural Language', *Artificial Intelligence*, 6 (1975), 53–74.

[17] Joseph Weizenbaum, 'Contextual Understanding by Computers', *Comm. Ass. Computing Machinery*, 10 (1967), 474–80.

[18] Jean Piaget, *The Moral Judgement of the Child* (London: Routledge, Kegan Paul, 1948).

[19] Intrinsic interests and the associated 'stopping-points' in purposive explanation are discussed in my *Purposive Explanation in Psychology*, pp. 43–5, 118–22 and 158–98.

8

ABSOLUTE ETHICS, MATHEMATICS AND THE IMPOSSIBILITY OF POLITICS

A PAPER IN PRAISE OF PLATO

R. F. Holland

The idea of absolute goodness and the idea of an absolute requitement tend nowadays to be viewed with suspicion in the world of English-speaking philosophy. The tendency is well rooted and has not just arisen by osmosis from the temper of the times. There are various lines of thought, all of them attractive, by which a recent or contemporary academic practitioner of the subject could have been induced into scepticism about an ethics of absolute conceptions.

For one thing, the use in an absolute sense of 'good' and 'must' presents a problem at the level of linguistic machinery; and many will have had a philosophical training that disposes them to turn for a solution[1] to what is called the performative element in discourse, to the dictionary's reminder that 'good' is the most general adjective of commendation, to a distinction between two types of meaning ('prescriptive' and 'descriptive') and an account of the possible modes of relation between them when they are simultaneously present. A likely outcome of such considerations will be the verdict that the idea of the reality of absolute value is a shadow cast by two factors which in combination do constitute the criteria of the ethical, namely prescriptivensss and universalisability. Or the opponent of absolute ethics may have found a petrol station in Popperian reflections on the distinction between a 'closed' and 'open' society, so that he associates absolutism with putting the clock back and the attempted stifling of liberalism, freedom and egality. Or again he might have observed the extent to which Wittgenstein's later philosophy is directed towards the eradication of metaphysical 'musts' and their replacement by 'it does not have to be so', and having appreciated the force of this in other connexions he might assume it to be applicable to the idea of absolute value in ethics (in a way of course it does apply – no one has to hold such an ethics).

Then there is a further range of possible reflections – on the nature of tabu, the genesis of historical phenomena such as the Inquisition, the psychology of obsessional neurosis, the odiousness of much that has been taken by different peoples at different times to be absolutely good or absolutely required – all of which conspire to support the theses that belief in the possibility of absolute judgements is bound up with invincible surety about his own rightness or righteousness on the part of the judger, and that the terribleness of so many of these judgements is a consequence of their 'absoluteness'.

Yet it seems to me that nothing here comes in the category of what has to be. There is the diagnosis that absolute injunctions and prohibitions are both intelligible and justified or sanctified in the context, but only in the context, of a decalogue where their prototypes have been handed down by the voice of revelation for the benefit of those brought up in the one true religion. And there is the charge that absolute judgements impart a bogus finality into discussion where the issues can only rationally be decided by reference to consequences in which there is no finality. But nothing whatever of all this, I want to say, *has to be true* of absolute judgements in ethics.

Absolute judgements are not all of the same kind and in the case of some it is possible for the subject to be trivial without the judgement's failing to be absolute on that account. But I am concerned with those in ethics which are either instances of, or else are in one way or another related to, the recognition that something is magnificent; that in some action or suffering there was pure goodness; where this recognition is not a matter of giving anyone or anything a pat on the back, least of all with the overtones of the evaluatory G.P. ('prescribing'), but where the realisation is elicited or forced on the observer by that in the face of which the judgement is voiced and there is no question of degree or comparison. Such a judgement is in one sense not a judgement at all – it does not confer anything, does not assign a top grading, but is like exclaiming at a revelation. And the witness, if he speaks, speaks without appealing, somewhat as the thing itself did to him. It is not a common phenomenon like its spurious counterparts, the 'vibrations' which are rife in collective surroundings where they are transmitted by some sort of conscious or unconscious artifice. The latter can make powerful and deranging impacts, whipping the response into a frenzy, whereas what is seen by the beholder of goodness stirs something in him deeply without giving him the feeling of being close to it.

While obviously there are those who never make judgements in the way I have described, there certainly are such judgements; that is to say there are people who do make them and who therefore believe there is something absolute although they might not express this belief in any other way. When it is a position held reflectively, I take the idea that there is such a thing as absolute goodness to signify at least a refusal to go along with reductionist accounts of the nature of absolute judgements. It does not have to signify more. But I think that nearly every holder of this position will say it does, although when he tries to indicate what else it signifies he runs into confusion or runs out of gas.

Absolute goodness *is something*, to use Plato's phraseology; and he made the point that it is not a thing among things in the world. We get an apprehension of it only by seeing the world, or some of the things that are in the world in a certain light. And while we can turn or be turned in its direction, we do not ourselves supply the light: it is, Plato said, the goodness that provides the light (*Republic* 508E–509C). His achievement in the face of the difficulty of giving expression to this vision or reading of the world is almost unique among philosophers.

Maybe the dearth of others has to do with the fact that the difficulty is more than an intellectual one. But unless someone manages to give the vision expression he cannot have it strongly and it calls for expression otherwise than in words; I mean in non-verbal as well as verbal ways. The general throng of us get no more than a flickering of it.

That belief in absolutes is not the same as, and so does not have to go along with, surety that one is right in particular cases was recognised by Plato and provided for in his epistemology. In Plato's terminology, the absolutely good was a Form and in the case of anything that had this status we could aspire to understanding. Particulars on the other hand were subject to a drift which along with their manyness made it impossible for us to comprehend them fully or be cognisant of all their repercussions on each other.

Plato also recognised – it was one of his cardinal insights – that the problem of spurious semblances ran right through ethics. There is such a thing as the absolutism of the Cave. For in the cave, relative light is taken for absolute light; images are taken for reality and made the subject of a consequentialist style of (both natural and political) science. The images gyrate. There is an interest in forecasting outcomes and planning accordingly. Some people are adept at this. Getting to be adept at it is the limit of what they can achieve, and so in a way they reach their absolute – by the standards of the cave.

The monstrosities perpetrated by people in the belief that they had to can look like a powerful reason in favour of relating oneself to one's moral views as though they were akin to hypotheses subject to falsification. But I see no cogency in this or even any argument. When you learned of these monstrosities were you not utterly horrified and did you not absolutely condemn them? I doubt if absoluteness of conception opens the door to anything like as much evil as consequentialism does – at least it does not unless twisted into an eschatological shape in which it *combines with* consequentialism.

In any case, the 'liberal' inclination to find something morally amiss with the idea of an absolute attitude from fear of what it could lead to, does not retain its grip when attention is shifted

G

from the abysmal to the wonderful – to things of staggering beauty, actions of an order of magnanimity such that no degree can be assigned to them or comparison made; save in so far as they could be contrasted with relative versions of what they manifest absolutely. Consider the difference between rendering what is due when this is conceived in terms of equilibrium or compensation and on the other hand going on giving, forgiving, turning the other cheek . . . where repaying evil with good is the only kind of repayment there is; or the difference between cupboard love, arising from need and contingent on satisfaction, and on the other hand what was expressed by Spinoza when he said: he who loves God will not expect God to love him in return. I would regard it as flannel if someone said he were unable to see anything but power worship in Spinoza's observation or that he could not catch the hang of it at all because of difficulty in understanding the 'God' part. He need not feel particularly called upon to attach credence or sense to that part: in place of the first occurrence he could substitute 'absolutely' and for the second 'anyone or anything'.

It is remarkable how seeing the point of one absolute conception can pave the way for the introduction of others. Plato arrived at the conception of absolute being, or of an absolute being. He got there by more than one route and partly perhaps as a result of confusion. But I would not say he was confused in finding a connexion between the problem of the foundation of absolute conceptions and the problem of the genesis of the world. If you speak of creation here and if you compare the idea of creation with the idea of transformation or one thing's becoming another, being made out of another within the world, then you see that creation is an instance of an absolute conception. And if you spoke of the Creator of the world you would be speaking of an absolute being. You would not be able to assert of such a being anything other than absolute predicates. It does not follow from this that there is something about absolute predicates which makes it unfitting for them to be predicated of anything other than absolute beings. I do not think it possible to argue directly from the existence of absolute predicates to the existence of any absolute being if only because absolute predicates can be intelligibly predicated of relative subjects, as when in certain ethical judgements, they are of human beings or the actions of human beings. Yet the inclination to make this connexion is not stupid and when absolute qualities are attributed to human beings it is natural already to introduce the idea of 'that which is eternal in a human being' and to associate the absolute quality with that, namely with the soul. The idea of eternal or absolute being can encourage a type of speculation I am disposed to dismiss as pseudo-scientific. Nevertheless there is profundity in these games with absolute conceptions: I am not sure how far we can significantly proceed with them but I do want to assert that in the absence of absolute conceptions there can be nothing profound in ethics.

If, by way of offering a reason for not entertaining absolute conceptions, someone were to suggest that the problem of false semblances in ethics is exacerbated or indeed in its most intractable aspects created by their presence, my reply would be that in a sense this is perfectly true, but by declining to attach sense to absolute conceptions you would not get yourself out of that problem; you would still be in trouble through it although you might not know it. Here there is light to be got by turning to Plato again and considering aspects of the relationship he believed to exist between ethics and mathematics.

In the course of a dialogue concerning the problem of false semblances Plato remarked, to people whom he charged with self-deception, 'You neglect geometry' (*Gorgias* 508A). He was addressing those who did not see goodness as distinct: in particular they did not see it as something distinct from pleasure. Equally they did not see goodness as independent of the will and antithetical to assertion of the self. They were engaged in the pursuit of more (πλεονεξία), though not necessarily for themselves alone – perhaps this was so in the conversation to which I am alluding, but Plato was mindful of the variant in which they want more for the generality as well and so put themselves at the service of the social. He was not recommending mastership of a specialised study but inviting them to attend to certain general features of geometry in the way that one should attend to general features of things in philosophy.

They would find in geometry something with an unchanging nature of its own over and against theirs, which put demands on them rather than being amenable to any they might try to place on it. They would see the power and scope of geometry and marvel at the beauty of its unfolding. Reflecting on the nature of this power they would see that while it had to do with the order of the cosmos it was *a power without force*; that all the possibilities in geometry were possibilities within limits – indeed that they were possibilities arising out of limits. They would see that the limit of each component line depended on where it was placed.

In geometry there was a type of equality that had nothing to do with quantity; thus for instance the equilaterality of a triangle has consequences for that triangle no matter how large or small it may be. And in any case a line was not to be considered as an aggregate of units: the discovery of incommensurables had put paid to that. Yet these lines could stand in a relationship of fellowship or kinship (κοινωνία) to other lines with which they were not commensurable: they could do this although there was no common denominator. In fact the whole of geometry could be viewed as a study of κοινωνία – of the higher possibilities within limits open to men as they try to live together.

The plane is the limit of the solid; it is not that to which three dimensions are reducible. In the solid there is a necessary plurality of planes. Life too is a composition on many planes.

Geometry supplies the model for an ethics which when set alongside the ethics of advantage, can be seen to have an incomparably greater profundity and power. Of such a kind would be the ideal power and control over life which we cannot achieve but of which exercising all the material power at our disposal (which we do not achieve either) is the spurious semblance. The former would be an absolute and the latter is a relative power.

What gives to the problem of spurious semblances its depth is the fact that in many circumstances the relative presents itself as indistinguishable from the absolute. When the pursuer of advantage is fighting his way up it is obvious that his power is only relative and we should not think of calling it anything else however vigorous he may be. But once he has got to the top and become a dictator, his power is 'absolute' (we call it that because we no longer see any relativity in it). He has absolute power in the state. And in this connexion Plato's comparison between the state and the soul is instructive. In the soul, there is a demand of the ego which to all appearances may be indistinguishable from a requirement of absolute value: it presents itself with the same absoluteness once the ego has got on top. The complete egoist then is a man of 'absolute conceptions'. In this way the problem of false semblances makes an inroad into the nature and style of absolute conceptions. However, the help that geometry can give keeps pace. Considerations such as I have mentioned, relating both to what is so *within* geometry and to the attitude called for *by* geometry, can together supply criteria.

Turning now to the bearing of the connexion between ethics and mathematics upon the impossibility of politics, I have a confession to make. When I first used to read Plato (and it was mainly the *Republic* we studied) it seemed to me that his running mathematical concepts and ethical concepts together and according them such closely parallel treatment in the Theory of Forms was attributable to a constellation of misunderstandings – Socratic prejudice about the nature of definition (or in other words the treatment of all concepts as closed), the 'Fido'-Fido fallacy as Ryle used to call it (or in other words the treatment of all words that look like names as names), the assimilation of the logical grammar of 'know' to that of 'see', misapprehension suggested by the substantival use in Greek of the definite article plus neuter case of an adjective, and so on. How, I wondered, otherwise than as a result of confusions such as these, could Plato have come to entertain the peculiar idea that ethics and mathematics might have much to do with each other? I wonder now at my obtuseness, for it is not as though there is only one kind of ethics, nor is there only one kind of mathematics; and it takes but a moment's reflection to realise that the most popular and readily digestible of all ethical theories in existence is one that requires mathematical terms for its expression: greatest happiness *of the greatest number* . . . everybody to *count as 1*. So I had had no reason to think that Plato's recourse to something in mathematics when he wanted to expound the ethical was the result of any of those confusions even if he did commit them. What I should have been attending to was the type of mathematics with which his ethics was associated and to the difference between that type of mathematics and the type which entered into the other sort of ethics.

Utilitarianism belongs to the family of ethical positions that Plato opposed (you will recall my reference to the consequentialism of the cave). In the dialogue in which he alludes to the power of geometry, Plato says it is better to suffer evil than to do it. In this fundamental ethical proposition it is the sense of 'better' that he believes geometry might help us to understand. When you see that in doing such-and-such a thing you will be harming someone you are brought up against a limit. Evil is the unlimited range of points lying outside the circle of action drawn by the geometry of goodness. But here there is no question of numbers, of counting. For a Utilitarian on the other hand there is, and the agent counts himself as one for a start. So what sense is he going to make of Plato's proposition? He cannot use the term 'better' as Plato does in an absolute sense, and when the relative sense is substituted the proposition ceases to be necessarily true. It makes a difference whether those who are going to be harmed are one or many (if many, how many?) and a further difference if effects (whether direct or indirect) outweigh the harm. Suppose there were no further effects and only one person were harmed and the harm to him were less than that which would come to the agent if the agent were to refrain from doing the harm. In that case Plato's proposition would be judged false, though this is a misleading way of putting the matter: it ceased at once to be Plato's proposition when it began to be judged from the Utilitarian standpoint.

The difference between these two kinds of ethics is accentuated by the fact that the association of consequentialism with arithmetic, that is to say with numbers, is one that characteristically brings in *large* numbers. On Plato's geometrical view, the limits to what you can do include limits that depend on where you are placed, and there are both limits and facilities that arise from special relationships in which you might or might not stand towards other people in the picture. On the consequentialist view, all is facility so to speak, because your lines of possible action extend without interruption into every corner of the globe, affecting people you do not see and have no knowledge of. The sense of place drops out when you try to tot up the balance of good and evil as this stands over the world. Consider the proposition that there are 10^{18} turps of evil – I borrow this unit of evil, the 'turp', and the proposition containing it, from Alvin Plantinga's *God, Freedom and Evil* (p. 63): he introduces it just to help along a discussion – but anyway suppose if you think you can that there are in the world ten to the eighteenth turps of evil. With this amount around and a scheme for reducing it to ten to the ninth you do not hesitate to throw in ten cubed of your own. So those who stand in your way can be shot if there is no more room in the mental hospitals.

Arithmetic is the mathematics of consequentialism and consequentialism is the ethics of politics. I would put the point more strongly and say that politics, particularly in the modern sense of large-scale administration, is the perfection (*Die Perfektion*) of consequentialist ethics. Consider this in relation to the factors of power and compromise.

From among the various aspects of the connexion between politics and power take the simple fact that an individual in politics has to have power if he is to do anything significant. But then this is exactly the theoretical position in any context of an individual who tries to approach the ideal of doing what is morally right according to the Utilitarian conception. His lines of possible action extend ideally to the limits of society as I said before; and now I am adding the further point that in order to make them actually do so – or rather, in order that his doings should even remotely square with the ethical theory, he needs power; and the power he needs is a substantial power over affairs, the power to effect social changes.

Again, in politics you must compromise, and often this has to do with the balance of power. Among the many aspects of the relation between politics and compromise, the significant one for ethics is that you have to compromise with evil. You come to agreement with it, make concessions to it for example in striking bargains with evil powers; but I am concerned with the fact that you cannot avoid doing evil yourself. The customary ways of alluding to this, or describing the transactions that involve it, disguise the fact while testifying to the inevitability. Evil-doing in politics is called taking whatever steps are necessary to safeguard P or make the world safe for Q where P and Q are things that people would agree to be worth making sacrifices for. But compromise with evil has its roots in consequentialist ethics, and politics only provides the natural setting for its full fruition. For consequentialism is an ethics that sanctions the doing of evil: it lets in propositions like 'This is an evil thing to do but I am justified' and 'It is evil but I must do it'.

Plato would have regarded these as crooked propositions: 'It is evil but I must do it' means 'I must not do it but I must do it', which is a contradiction. And of course the consequentialist would hardly assert the first proposition *sans phrase* (the second he would not assert at all). He always tacks another proposition on with the aid of a connective thus: 'It is evil but I must do it in order that so and so'; and attention is shifted to the further proposition. Still that does not get round the contradiction: it does not even seem to make it disappear, though there are conceptual devices which can help in this direction – for example the use of the expression '*prima facie* obligation'.

The contradiction never does disappear and the Platonist too will add a rider to the original proposition – but only after negating and indeed reversing the second 'must', thus 'It is evil (which means I must not do it) and so I must not do it however great and real the benefit that was to accrue.' The moral geometry which puts the doing of evil outside the agent's limit, while providing him with infinite space in which to suffer it, puts a limitation also on the good that he can achieve. Much that would otherwise have been possible, especially the most spectacular, world-historical part of it, has to be forgone; and this too is at the cost of suffering – his own and other people's.

Absolute ethics is the ethics of forgoing, and politics belongs for over-determined reasons to the pursuits that have to be forgone.

The objection many people will raise against this position is that by retreating from politics you leave the way clear for usurpers within or aggressors from outside. These are consequentialist considerations but they will not be ignored by the Absolutist on that account (it is from his point of view especially that consequences have to be faced) and they are bound up in any case with considerations of an absolute kind. For you do not start with a clean sheet: there will already be commitments, to preserve institutions and to look after individuals, and since you cannot do this if you retreat, what is being contemplated puts you in a dilemma. If you find yourself obliged to abdicate you are involved in a moral contradiction.

Plato pressed the analogy with geometry to the point of thinking it might be possible in principle for an ethics of absolute conceptions to be so worked out as to form a system that would be free from contradiction. He recognised that for this you would have to start with a clean sheet – as with his *Republic* where there is no possibility of any transition to it, no possibility of any existing state's becoming it, but only of various stages of deterioration. And I suppose that since the rulers of the Ideal Republic would have nothing to achieve, because it was already there, and no consequences to consider because they would make no changes for there to be consequences of, they could operate at that limit of politics which is also non-politics and hence have an absolute ethics. Their absolute ethics would not require them to withdraw from politics because of the political vacuity of the kind of ruling they were doing.

But in the world, absolute ethics by requiring withdrawal from politics creates a dilemma, and in general it creates dilemmas that otherwise would not be deemed to arise. Moreover, whether or not the dilemmas would be such from an alternative standpoint, the difficulty they present is exacerbated by the kind of consistency that an absolute ethics demands, to the point of seeming to render the agent's position completely hopeless (whereas the consequentialist invariably hopes to bring about something). So I shall try in the remainder of this lecture to say something on the subject of dilemma and particularly about the difference an absolute ethics makes if you have to act in one.

Dilemma, or in other words ethical contradiction – you will recall my introducing the idea of ethical contradiction earlier when I spoke of the contradiction presented by 'it is evil but I must do it in order that. . . .' There are variants such as 'because if I do not then . . .', or 'because if I do not I shall be allowing . . .', or 'because in doing otherwise I shall be doing. . . .' Although these are not on all fours with each other it remains true that aside from negating the 'must' there is no way of dealing with the contradiction arising in the first part of the proposition; and since the weak or merely technical negation, 'it is not the case that I must', would still allow 'can do it', absolute ethics has to stamp the contradiction completely out by converting the 'must' into 'must not'. Now this does not obviate the possibility of some other contradiction's ensuing. On the contrary it ensures that if a further contradiction arises it will not be seen as anything else; and it ensures that there is one way in particular in which it will not be thought susceptible of a 'solution'. This may not sound exactly helpful, and is not in so far as ease is what we want. But certainly there will be no brushing aside the evil inherent in an immediate action, no possibility of pushing it under a carpet of calculation. And any dilemma or *prima facie* dilemma that arises will be seen by the agent, because of the angle from which he is approaching it, in a light that automatically puts the consequentialistic horn, or the less immediate horn if there is one, in the weaker and suspect position.

To show what I mean, here is an example devised by Professor Bernard Williams in which it is plain what a Utilitarian would do: A visitor arrives at a South American town to find a firing squad about to shoot twenty Indians as a reprisal for acts of protest against the government. The captain of the militia offers the visitor a 'guest's privilege' of shooting one Indian on the understanding that if he does so the rest will be set free, but if he does not, all twenty will be shot. There is no chance then of the visitor's overwhelming the captain by force, so what should he do? To a Utilitarian it would seem obvious that he ought to kill the Indian. Williams says that 'even one who came to think that perhaps that was the answer, might well wonder whether it was obviously the answer', but beyond this (if it means anything at all) I have no idea where he stands.

I want to put it to you that there is something which if it were to be written into the example as a piece of information about the visitor – a categorisation of the sort of man he was – would make his position clear, or clear at any rate in the respect that is vital for the present discussion. There are or there have been in human history people, very few admittedly, of such marvellous goodness that they have been recognised (whether or not they have also been by some religious authority canonised) as saints. And you cannot imagine a saint shooting that Indian. Nor is it imaginable that a saint would do nothing either; for the man I am calling a saint would face the consequences and engage in the suffering in a way that is different from the way an ordinary man would, and his presence would not be without its impact on the outcome. It goes against the grain to try to predict what such a man might say and do. But then we have already been stifling our sense of the repellant in contemplating Williams's example at all and I do not believe I say this out of squeamishness. In order to proceed further I have to quote the heart of it again, this time using Williams's words:

> . . . since Jim is an honoured visitor from another land, the captain is happy to offer him a guest's privilege of killing one of the Indians himself. If Jim accepts, then as a special mark of the occasion, the other Indians will be let off. Of course, if Jim refuses, then there is no special occasion, and Pedro here will do what he was about to do. . . . (Williams in Smart and Williams: *Utilitarianism For and Against*, p. 98.)

What is the meaning of this bland tone? Who is this captain? What is this alleged *honouring* of the visitor with the *happy* idea

of such a *privilege* as is spoken of? I do not think we should take
the dressing in our stride so to speak for the sake of the example.
Rather we should consider the role it plays, which is that of
providing a 'plausible' background – though I have to put the
word 'plausible' in quotes because I do not find much plausibility in the example myself – against which a man who is not
supposed to be mad or devilish might say, might utter the
threat: 'either you kill this one man or I shall kill twenty'. In
fact the idea of the 'honoured guest's privilege' takes the place
of what we call at home the motive for the blackmail; but it
does so in a way that makes the association with blackmail seem
irrelevant, and in this way it provides the framework from
within which the visitor's predicament is represented. Whether
he is going to do what the captain invites him to do is then the
question – though to say this makes it look as if we knew exactly
what the question was and how we were to take it.

At the time when I began thinking about Williams's example
the Government of Eire was facing the question whether to do
what the kidnappers of Dr. Herrema had invited them to do,
i.e. release three murderous prisoners from the jail in which
they were lawfully held. If the prisoners were not released, the
kidnappers said they would kill Dr. Herrema within 48 hours.
One of the techniques which police employ in such cases is to
consider the situation from the standpoint of the blackmailers'
ideas and try to maintain a dialogue with them. What the Eire
Government to its credit did not do was consider the nature of
the problem and try to formulate its own ethical position from
the standpoint of the ideas and terminology of those who had
presented it with the problem.

Williams's example is fanciful, and that point *simpliciter* I
would further emphasise because speculation about what in
particular some essay of the imagination might be doing within
a fanciful example could draw us away from what I think is the
source of the sense of outrage at being asked to contemplate
Williams's example and other examples of a similar kind
('Either you torture this child or I will blow up the world').
The sort of make-believe involved in this is different from that
which occurs when a playwright of the stature to do it shows us

something from which we can learn. When Shakespeare for example presents characters imaginatively in their entanglements with evil, our sense of the reality of our own relationship to both evil and good is heightened, whereas here we are drawn into an exercise of fancy about just that relationship. It is a kind of *temptation*: that is what the revulsion is about and if anyone does not feel it I would suppose that for him the examples provide material to be ingested like data by a computer.

To return to the rider which I asked you to consider being written into Williams's example, namely that the visitor might conceivably turn out to be a saint: although it goes against the grain to try to suggest what a saint in such a circumstance might say or do, I suppose that maybe he would manage somehow to take the place of the one Indian; or if he could not get himself shot instead of him, perhaps he would make sure that he was shot along with him or else as the first of the twenty. That is if the captain had not thus far been given pause, for there is what a saint might say to be thought of as well as what he might do, and being spoken to by a saint would not be like being spoken to by an ordinary person; so perhaps it would not then be so much a matter of what the captain might or might not do, as what the men in his company were prepared to do, and what the bystanders might be moved to do, after having seen and heard a saint.

Jonathan Glover, who has discussed Williams's example in an Aristotelian Society Symposium (1975), believes, as Williams himself appeared to do, that what is central to people's resistance to consequentialist morality is a concern for personal integrity (p. 184). Glover redescribes this as 'a possessive attitude to one's own virtue' (p. 186) – a diagnosis which would represent someone who differed from the consequentialist, in that he found it absolutely impossible to shoot the Indian, as just some other kind of consequentialist (one who counted his own property highly): if he were to shoot the Indian his personal integrity would be shattered. There are men who might have that thought, but this is another of those things that do not have to be so. Could you imagine a saint's thinking about his personal integrity? Any more than you could imagine a saint's thinking about the problem as the straightforward consequentialist would?

As a matter of fact I find it hard to imagine a saint's having any theoretical ethics whatever: at least if he had one I do not suppose it would contribute to his saintliness. On the other hand if he did have one, it is clear that it would have to be an ethics of absolute conceptions. I brought in the idea of the saint because for all the difference between them there is this significant point of contact between the position of a saint and the position of an ordinary person who has absolute conceptions if he is true to them. Neither could shoot the Indian. The impossibility here is the impossibility of politics.

NOTE

¹ For an alternative possibility derived from Wittgenstein see Cora Diamond: 'Secondary Sense', *Proceedings of the Aristotelian Society*, 1967–8.

9

THE CONSTITUTION OF HUMAN VALUES

J. N. Findlay

The present paper is an attempt to study the acts and intentions which set up for the subject, and for the community of subjects, a set of values and disvalues which impose themselves as valid upon everyone, and which everyone must tend to prescribe, or to warn against, for everyone. The acts which set up a formal apophantic and ontology have been studied by Husserl in his *Formal and Transcendental Logic*, but he has not set out a comparable theory of the acts which set up a universally valid system of values and disvalues. He has not done so because he does not believe in such a system, because his thought goes no further than the values set up for and felt to hold in a given group or society. It is my view that there is an ineluctable progress from these relativistic group-values to a set of values and disvalues holding for everyone, and that moreover in their relation to everyone, and that these values and disvalues have definite and undeniable shapes and locations, even if these shapes also have somewhat nebulous contours. The views I am expounding on this occasion are not new: they are fully set out in my *Values and Intentions* and my *Axiological Ethics* and in other writings. Ideas, however, require restatement at intervals, with a suitable change of idiom and emphasis. And I feel my views on this topic to have a claim to truth simply because, quite differently from my views on other topics, and despite constant reflection, they have hardly changed over the last two decades. The in-

spiration for these views was only in part Husserlian, as I do
not think that the emotional and the axiological are really
Husserl's strong suit. Strangely enough, that dry thinker
Meinong would seem to have had a much richer emotional life
and the ability to frame a theory to fit it, than the much easier
and at times effusive thinker Husserl. Meinong's 1917 Austrian
Imperial Academy treatise, *On Emotional Presentation*, recently
translated for the Northwestern Phenomenology series, is a
much more systematic investigation of the presuppositions of
value-theory than any writing of a professed phenomenologist.
What I have to say will build considerably on Meinong,
always a major influence in my thought. But I have also been
much influenced in my approaches to value-theory by the
transcendental methods of Kant. Kant, I think, could very well
have worked out a transcendental deduction of the heads of
value and disvalue, a deduction much more illuminating than
the dogmatic intuitionism of Scheler and Hartmann, instead of
producing the arid triad of categorical imperatives that were all
that he actually deduced. Imperatives, I consider, are secondary structures in value-constitution: the primary structures are
the ultimate objects of necessary, rational pursuit and avoidance
which Kant wrongly thought of as involving heteronomy and a
corruption of pure form by matter. There is, I shall argue, nothing more free from extraneous, pathological material than
the objects of the pursuits and avoidances in question.

I must also make plain that, in approaching the value-realm
from the angle of a phenomenological constitution, I am not
pledging my allegiance to the subjectivism and transcen-
dentalism of the Husserlian phenomenology. I am a transcendent
Platonist rather than a Husserlian transcendentalist, and I think
of Being, or something better than Being, and not any transcendental or ordinary subject, as responsible for the regular
accommodation of what is to the way in which it shows in our
references, and that while intentional thought is no doubt the
supreme, self-lucid form of being, it must none the less not be
thought of as conferring something of a parasitic status on the
humbler forms of being which it presupposes, and on which it
throughout builds. I believe also that values, and particularly

aesthetic values, play a formative role in the cosmos, far below the level of subjectivity or intersubjectivity: beauty in its more elementary guises is the ethics of space, and organic and inorganic things certainly have a nisus towards such things as just balance, unity in variety, resistance to alien admixture, purity from the same, bland adaptation to context and other values, having high positions in the moral sphere. But undoubtedly, as Aristotle says, the goods of highest interest are those which can be practised and possessed by men, and these are those that constitute themselves in and for the acts of beings who envisage, believe in, rejoice or grieve over and pursue or avoid objects, and who set up comprehensive goals and counter-goals for their own and everyone else's living. It is the constitution of these goals and counter-goals with which I shall be dealing on the present occasion.

I shall begin my treatment by presuming that values and disvalues will not constitute themselves for beings who have no *interest*, positive or negative, in a range or field of objects. Without playing with the empty notion of beings whose conscious life exhausted itself in a flux of presentations, to which or to whose objects no manner of interest attached, or of beings who experienced the compulsive or near-compulsive pressures of a seeming reality while remaining quite indifferent to what thus seemed to compel them, I shall presume that it is possible for interest to withdraw itself from many objects and sides of our conscious intentionality, and that, to the extent that this is the case, those objects and sides also lose any trace of value or disvalue for us, become indifferent things or possibilities or states that we merely survey or register, or quite neutrally admit to be actual or real, and so on. These remarks require to be qualified by the observation that the interest necessary for an attribution of value or disvalue need not be what we should call a contemporarily *felt* interest: odd as it may seem, our mere readiness to feel an interest, perhaps itself a relic of felt interest in the past, may be sufficient to make an object qualify as interesting or valuable, and even for it to *look* interesting, in default of an actually revived interest. But in default of even a readiness to feel interest in something, there can be nothing of good or bad, of value or disvalue, of the interesting or its contrary about it. To put it in the diction of the eighteenth century, we may say that values and disvalues cannot be there merely for the understanding, but require the participation of the heart.

I wish here also to endorse something like the threefold classification of intentional modes by Brentano: that there is a mental function which comes close to being purely presentative, which neither affirms nor denies nor embraces nor rejects, that there is a second mental function built on this which is not only presentative but also doxic, which locates objects in the compulsive, coherent, systematically real or banishes them from this, and that there is in the third place a function of concern or interest which not only presents and affirms, but also is emotionally or practically for or against what it thus has before it. I also believe with Brentano in the fundamental unity of the phenomena of interest, even though they assume the two antithetical forms of the favourable and the unfavourable, and even though they are even more notably divided into attitudes involving agency and efficacy, on the one hand, and attitudes which are more passively appreciative, on the other. The swing from favouring something to being unfavourable to its absence or its contrary or *vice versa*, and the swing from positive or negative appreciation to active realisation or the other way around, are transformations which are of the essence of the attitudes under examination, even if in a few cases we may seem to have pure action without feeling or pure feeling without action. Certainly all talk about value or disvalue presupposes that the pair are joined in harness: one could not be said to value something regarding which one was only prepared to act without feeling or to feel without acting. It is then in the variant forms of interest, and in their relation to more abstractly basic forms of intention, that we must seek the constitutive conditions of the realm of values. I may say in this connexion that the behavioural side of our conscious intentions, neglected in classic studies like that of Brentano, comes into the picture without difficulty: there are relations of essence between our attitudes as lived through and our attitudes as observed or perceived or linguistically expressed by ourselves and others, and I do not know if it even makes good sense to distinguish too firmly between an 'outer' and an 'inner' side to the above phenomena.

Here, however, a fundamental point arises. For there to be values or disvalues for someone it is not sufficient for him to be interested in objects as presented givens or as items in what really exists: it is essential that his interests should *colour* the things in which he is interested, should somehow flow over from the attitudinal into the objective order. Values and disvalues must be present 'out there', just as facts and probabilities and hypothetical outcomes are given as 'out there': they must contribute to the total phenomenological scene. Hume recognises this point very clearly when he says that while reason 'discovers objects, as they really stand in nature, without addition or diminution', taste 'has a productive faculty, and, gilding or staining all natural objects with the colours borrowed from internal sentiment, raises, in a manner, a new creation' (*Inquiry Concerning the Principles of Morals*, Appendix II, v). This staining and gilding of objects must, however, be rightly interpreted. We do not stain or gild objects with our sentiments by imagining that *they* themselves have those sentiments: this is a poetic fallacy, not an axiological constitution. Nor do we stain objects with our sentiments by merely conceiving them as provocative of the sentiments in question, even if the form of such words as 'terrifying', 'disgusting' etc. may suggest that this is what we do. It is here that we must seek the guidance of Meinong who alone seems to have a conceptual key to the issue: Husserl seems at times to have a similar key, but operates it so fumblingly as to leave his clear grasp in doubt. Meinong, inspired by the Pole Twardowski, conceives that there are always two sides to an intentional reference, a side *ad rem* which consists in an appropriate objective direction and a side *ad nos* which consists in the way the reference stands to our sensibility or *Gemüt*. Thus if I perceive a red square my perception terminates *ad rem* in a redly shaded squarely shaped surface, but it also has a side relative to my inner sensibility in which it embraces strange feelings of rubescence and extensity which are incapable of being externalised. (My use of the term 'feelings' in this last sentence does not mean that these inner changes are to be regarded as emotional.) Extensity and rubescence are the mental 'contents' through which extension and redness can be objectively given: they are as categorially different from these as they are intimately related to them. Meinong then supposes that just as our sensible affections mediate an awareness of correlated objectivities, so our emotional and desiderative affections may also mediate an awareness of correlated objectivities. They may stain the world with colours differing *toto caelo* from those of internal sentiment, but none the less, as Hume says, 'borrowed' from the latter. To quote Meinong on the matter: 'That we are not here merely dealing with possibilities is shown by a set of everyday predications as when people speak of a pleasant bath, of fresh air, of oppressive heat, irritating noise, lovely colour, a gay or sad, boring or entertaining story, a sublime work of art, worthy people, good resolutions etc. The close relation of such predications to feeling is unquestionable, but it is no less clear that they are analogous to other properties in being presented to us in familiar fashion by way of ideas. If I say of a sky that it is blue, and at another time that it is lovely, a property is seemingly attributed to the sky in either case, since a feeling is as much involved in the latter presentation as a pure idea in the former, we are strongly led to attribute the same presentative function to a feeling that we ascribe to an idea in the other case' (*Emotional Presentation*, 4, p. 33). If sense-affections can mediate the awareness of objective determinations different from themselves, feelings and desires can well do the same.

Meinong now leaps into the new field of objectivity opened up by his doctrine of emotional presentation. Just as parallel variation in the doxic or judgement modalities have opened up a categoty that Meinong called 'objectives', and that Husserl and also Wittgenstein called *Sachverhalte* or states of affairs, and enables us to attribute to these new objects such properties as truth, necessity, possibility, probability and so on, so the emotional-conative modifications open our eyes to a new set of axiological modalities to which Meinong gives the comprehensive names of 'dignitatives' and 'desideratives'. Dignitatives are for him a wider class than values, since there are aesthetic dignitatives or cases of beauty-ugliness, scientific dignitatives or cases of truth-dignity, probability-dignity etc., as well as axio-logical dignitatives proper which are cases of what we ordi-narily call goodness and badness. And corresponding to desires or the dynamic forms of interest we have what Meinong calls 'desideratives', a series of cases of *Sollen* or ought-to-be-ness, which may be aesthetic or scientific or axiological proper. Meinong connects these three types of dignitatives and desi-deratives with three types of feeling and desire respectively. There is an aesthetic type concerned only with the presentative function basic to all intentionality, there is a scientific type concerned with the assertive or doxic function, and there is an axiological type concerned with the appraisive-practical func-tion which builds upon both of these. It must be made clear in this connexion that beauty and ugliness are given as 'out there' in objects, and are not to be confused with the presentative satisfactions that make the awareness of them possible, and the same applies, *mutatis mutandis*, to the corresponding aesthetic imperatives, or to the dignitatives and desideratives projected by the other types of feeling and desire. Meinong, I may say, connects value and disvalue in their special narrow sense with an existence-dignity which is also associated with some specific character: he distinguishes it from aesthetic dignity in which character is all in all and real existence indifferent, or from scientific dignity where real existence is all in all and character does not matter. I cannot take time out here and now to eluci-date all these immensely subtle, valuable opinions: it is a pity that I am one of the few people who knows how immensely subtle and valuable they are. The main outcome of the analysis is clear. We live in a world peopled not only with objects, given as real or merely imaginary, but also peopled with aesthetic demands that objects should in their presented form be or not be thus or thus, or with scientific demands that they should be rounded out into certain intelligible patterns of coherence and completeness, or with axiological demands that such objects should either exist or not exist. And to all these objectively projected demands there are corresponding dignitatives, posi-tive or negative, when objects seem to fulfil or flout the demands in question. Wherever we turn we live in a dignity-soaked landscape or life-world, and in one inveterately tugged or pushed in varying directions by aesthetic, scientific and axiological pulls and pressures. The dry world of neutral fact exists only for certain sorts of philosophers.

A further point is important: that dignities and imperatives, once projected on the world through our feelings and wishes, can continue to throng the phenomenological scene when we no longer experience serious feelings and wishes regarding their objects. Meinong believes that in addition to serious interest, interest involving *Ernst*, there is also imaginary or mock-interest, interest without seriousness. Just as we can wilfully or playfully put ourselves into a posture of mock-belief or mock-surmise or mock-doubt, and can so lend a simulacrum of truth or probability to what does not really impress us as such, so we can put ourselves semi-seriously into any emotional or desiderative posture we choose, and can so set values and imperatives before us for which we do not really feel. I shall not discuss the mechanisms here postulated by Meinong: certainly the facts they explain are undoubted. We can be aware of the disgusting, the noble, the vile, the depraved, the inordinately precious etc. with a minimum of emotional disturbance, sometimes, as in art, without discernible emotion at all. Our commerce with values can assume the same cool form as our commerce with facts, and we can calmly calculate what is the best thing to do or to choose without seeming to have any feelings or desires about it. Hence traditional theories of φρόνησις or λόγος where practical reason is given a role as purely cognitive as theoretical reason. Such theories of course rest on a falsehood, since it is impossible to 'fulfil', in the Husserlian sense, such axiological and deontological meanings without the arousal of actual emotions and urges.

All this is very fine, but it has not furnished us with the foundation for any system of values and disvalues to which anything like validity can be attributed. Values, disvalues and imperatives are given as part of the phenomena, but this does not mean that the phenomena will be the same for everyone, or the same for the members of all societies, or for men living at all times. A man's intercourse with others in the same society, and the reflex discourse that he may then have with himself, will no doubt effect great rationalisations in the field of values and disvalues: certain general headings of the excellent and base will be stabilised, discrepancies will be ironed out, and the colourings of things and actions will be so much reinforced by mutual lecturing and sermonising as to seem as much a fact of nature as the frequency of the rainfall or the plumage of local birds. Protagoras, in Plato's dialogue, was very well aware of these facts. If one studies the values of a strong, but also for several centuries closed culture like the Japanese, one is astonished by the strong, but also highly strange profile of some of these values, e.g. those connected with *bushido*: a value is set upon acts done without motive or premeditation, even though widespread destruction and loss of life results. The *acte gratuit* has an obvious *cachet* for the Japanese that it does not have for the cost-counting West. And if we turn to reflective individuals who do not take their cue from what is current, we still find some of their values as odd as their personalities, even if, by sheer force of those personalities, they manage to impose them on a whole generation or a clique. Hume's notion of a fairly standard, benevolent human nature, on which Charles Morris and some others have tried to build, seems queer and *bienpensant* in our self-torturing, wallowing, existential age. And the maps of value sketched in modern times by such high-minded axiologists as Brentano, Scheler, Nicolai Hartmann and W. D. Ross have the demerit of being intuitive. It is not clear *why* their wonderful ordering should be accepted, and why they should be regarded as more than a reflection of their own pre-ferences. And if the way we reach them is through emotion, it is not clear how emotion can reach outcomes that are justifiable and valid. But if, on the other hand, we reach them through some sort of simple insight, it is not clear why we should be emotionally and practically stirred by the outcome of such an insight. Plainly we shall require some sort of transcendental constitution of the heads of valid value and disvalue, a deduc-tion which will show both the *necessity* of their origin out of the crude mass of values and disvalues which can make no claim to validity, and which will also establish a connexion between such mere necessity and their felt *authority* over what we feel and wish and do.

This constitution rests, I believe, on certain forms of the tendency towards universalisation to which many axiologists have made appeal, but which I hold to be much more subtle than has been generally supposed to be the case. Some sort of a tendency towards universalisation must be held to be inherent in all our conscious intentionality. Each concrete object or situation instantiates Eide, sorts or kinds, and we can have no relations with concrete objects that do not also connect us with the sorts or kinds to which they belong. There is in fact nothing graspable in a particular object but the sorts or kinds in the light of which we may intend it. To intend anything particular is to intend it as of a sort, and to intend it as of a sort is to tend to slip over to intending other things of the same sort or all things of the sort in question. This will be regarded as merely a portentous version of the empirical law of association by similars, but it is important to realise that this law, like the companion law of association by contiguity, is not the degraded piece of empirical mechanism that it is commonly thought to be. The first law is a consequence of the eidetic orientation of all our conscious acts, and the second of their holistic character, their refusal to remove partial objects from the total contexts into which they enter. And a supremely interesting illustration of both of these laws is the tendency of an intention to slide from an object or sort of object to the intention or sort of intention that is directed to it: there is, we may say, an inherent affinity, even if no resemblance, between an intention and what it is of, and they also occur so necessarily together in our conscious experience that the thought of the one necessarily slides over into the thought of the other. There is therefore an inherent tendency to universalise *inwards* as well as outwards, and to pass from generalised attitudes to objects to generalised attitudes towards attitudes to those objects. What it is important to realise is that the tendencies towards universalisation that I have mentioned apply as much to the life of feeling and practical endeavour as to the life of presentation and belief. To feel for something as being of a certain sort is to tend to feel analogously towards anything of the same sort, and also, by a move inwards, to tend to feel analogously towards a feeling for an object of that sort, and towards *any* similar feeling towards any object of the same sort. And with this goes a defensive tendency to fight against, and to dislike, attitudes which are directed to what excludes what we like or which are against what includes what we like. It seems plain, at this level, that propagation of attitude, is part and parcel of attitude, and that if this were all the universalisation that attitude involves, all attitude would tend to the *Gleichschaltung* or social correctness which we have all learned to detest in Fascism and Communism. This tendency, however, is corrected by another tendency of higher universality, one which stretches out to other attitudes, perhaps awakened by the incitement of others, and which seeks to be universal in the sense of being open to influence and persuasion by other inclinations, and which tends to take the line that no special right or authority or propagandist privilege should be accorded to one liking that is not accorded to others. Justice, balance, impartial treatment of different likings and attitudes, is felt to be more truly expressive of the tendency towards universality than the indefinite propagation of a specifically oriented attitude. Not only the individual instance but the specific content is the enemy of the tendency towards universalisation, and in the development of this tendency no one specific direction of interest must be given arbitrary priority over all others.

I now wish to go further and recognise a final, crowning trend. Universalisation, we must say, must itself come to be liked and valued in virtue of being universalistic, and not in virtue of any specific content that it espouses. The expansive form of our interest, its tendency to become wider and more open, must break loose from all content, must in other words develop its own zest and become something liked and valued for its own sake. And with this development of its own zest must go an increasing distaste for whatever ties it down to some narrow specific content. We shall desire to desire universally, to like only what is at least a special case of what we could like whoever we were, and whatever the special form and content of our interests. And rising to this level of universality, we should of course be liking what anyone could like for anyone whomsoever, and whatever his specific tastes. The development of this higher-order zest is a case of universalisation which runs through all mental life, and is not confined to what is rational and admirable, it may entangle itself with what is very irrational and depraved, e.g. impartial cruelty, impartial perversity, impartial selfishness and impartial wallowing in misery. It may, however, be suggested that in all such universalisations there is a term kept constant somewhere, and not replaced by an open variable for which anything or anyone could be substituted, or alternatively that the object of our universalised attitude involves internal contradiction, as in desiring, e.g., that one should oneself, like others, be cruelly treated, or that another man should victimise us as we are to victimise him. We must of course further emphasise that the universalisation we are talking about is not the meaningless universalisation of formal logic, where a function may cover the most trivial and external or the most profound and internal of affinities. Formal logic, whether from capacity or distaste, has found no way of distinguishing the profound affinity, the true unity of kind, from the trivial superficial affinity which tells us nothing, and has therefore rendered itself incapable of formalising anything of importance whether in science, philosophy or the theory of value. It is also worth saying that what we call rationality, or having a reason for what we assert or decide, lies precisely in our willingness to be guided by profound rather than superficial affinities, and that the tendency to universalise in a profound manner is therefore normatively rational as well as deep-seated and natural.

I now intend to show how the universalising zest I have mentioned is such as to generate a whole system of values and disvalues to all of which the adjectives 'rational' and 'valid' can be fittingly applied. Before, however, I do this, there remains one side of our intentional life which requires special acknowledgement, and which Kant and others have simply taken for granted: this is our relation to other conscious beings and to *their* intentional activities. I think with Hegel and Husserl, that the enlargement of the I to a We, and the readiness to locate other intentional systems alongside that which by contrast becomes 'our own', is part and parcel of intentionality itself, and arises through no factual accident or no empirical process of reasoning. Who or what our fellows are, and whether or not we have fellows, is indeed a factual accident, made known to us through peculiar perceptions and inferences, but that we are such as to have possible fellows, to be capable of being one among others, is one of the most irremediably *a priori* of truths, in default of which there could neither be objects nor a real world nor experiences nor knowledge. And while there is an immediate inaccessibility of the other's experiences in default of which they would not be another's, there is also perfect access to them at a less immediate level, involving sympathy or empathy or *Appräsentation* or *Fremdpräsentation* or whatever strange words we may use to cover a quite transparent situation. Through such access universals and universalising tendencies which start in our own domestic economy must necessarily and rationally extend themselves to the economies of others, and must have demands and likings in regard to what is going on in them as well as in our own economy. And these self-transcending universals may not only desire specific things for others, not even such specific things as they themselves may want for themselves, but also such much more general things as everyone must desire not only for himself but for everyone, thus removing the last vestige of particularity from the scope of our interest. That such a Platonic extirpation of particularity can also be fruitful in its relation to what is particular, and can give rise to a whole firmament of differentiated constellations of excellence, is what I shall now try to show.

First I shall attempt a transcendental deduction of the comparatively humdrum values of the pleasant and satisfactory, with their antithetical disvalues, then of the slightly more exalted values of success, power and freedom, again with their attendant disvalues. I shall then go on to much more prestigious values, such as knowledge, love, virtue etc. It seems clear to me, first of all, that, granted the universalising tendencies I have mentioned, the constitution of the pleasant or satisfactory as something to be pursued by everyone for everyone has the most irrefragable warrant. Bentham was right, and Kant grotesquely wrong, in recognising such a pursuit as the most formally justifiable of categorical imperatives. For the satisfactory is precisely that which leaves out all the specific content of desire and pleasure, and considers only that it should be brought to its chosen term: it is only limited by the possible clashes between satisfactions and objects of satisfaction, which it must, in not very obscure ways, seek to overcome or keep within bounds. Whereas arbitrarily to pursue specific objects, or to favour specific subjects, necessarily resists the universalisation which alone can constitute validity: no one could be rationally persuaded to pursue some goal that he did not care for, or favour some person that he did not like, though he could be argued into pursuing some goal under which his own goals could be necessarily subsumed and of which he would himself be a beneficiary. The satisfactory is in short something that can be discussed and bargained about, whereas one cannot bargain about wholly peculiar, private ends. There are, moreover, irremoveable clashes in forms of universalisation which are partial, and which desire for instance that everyone should pursue *his own* maximum satisfaction: here the first occurrence of the variable is boundlessly open, but the second has its value fixed when the first is fixed. Obviously one cannot consistently desire that everyone should be 'top dog' in satisfaction even though an approach to such consistency is to be found in the case of the mythical gangster who was quite willing to be shot down by another gangster whom he could thereby take to be the 'better man'. That everyone should desire that everyone should be satisfied is however a desire without intrinsic flaw: whatever clashes it may involve are remediable and removeable, involving no more sacrifices than one exacts of everyone. But if satisfaction as such can be thus made into a universally valid object of desire in the sense that it can without contradiction be desired by everyone for everyone, it is no less clear that successful activity, power and freedom are valid objects of universalised desire, since whatever one wants, one must want to succeed in the activities which achieve or are what one wants, and must want to have the power to succeed in such actvities or to enjoy what they seek, and to have the freedom from all hindrances that would restrict one's progress to what one wants. Success, power and freedom, with the obvious provisos of avoiding clashes with the success, power and freedom of others, are therefore obviously valid, i.e. universally pursuable and recommendable objects of wish and delight, as their opposites are of dislike and avoidance. One is not uttering a tautology if one says that one likes success, power and freedom nor in expecting other people to like them – some people somehow contrive not to like them – there is none the less something absurd in treating the liking of them as quite contingent. In their case it would be highly absurd to try the Stevensonian device of saying 'I like freedom: please do so also'.

I now wish to pass to three rather more august objects of necessary pursuit, while their contraries are, in varying degrees, objects of necessary avoidance. I wish to cover here (1) the values and disvalues of pure presentation, (2) the values and disvalues of successful or frustrated penetration into what may be called 'the reality of things', (3) the values and disvalues of successful or frustrated penetration into the reality of other conscious persons. The three cases I am about to consider all involve attitudes so fundamental as to be aspects of conscious intentionality: they are all essential to intentional life. One cannot have conscious intentionality unless separate objects are given in some manner or another as being the sorts of object they are, with affinities with and distances from other sorts of objects, and constituted in this or that manner out of these or those characteristics or elements. Equally one cannot have conscious intentionality unless one is at least ready to find a place for objects, whether as real or delusive, in the great object that one calls the world or reality or whatever, and equally it is part of conscious intentionality to extend itself with deep interest into the experiences of other persons, and to see all intended objects in their light or possible light. But besides being fundamental, these aspects of intentionality may each be credited, in virtue of the inward-turned type of universalisation we have mentioned, to develop their own zest. We necessarily begin to be interested in the satisfactorily sympathised with or compassionately co-operated with or erotically participated in as such. I am of course pointing to (1) the origins of the interests which are in a wide sense aesthetic, though they cover a well-set-forth theorem or well-put-together short story as much as a sensuously satisfying piece of painting or music, (2) the origins of the interests which are in a wide sense scientific, which are concerned with what is the case or inherently likely to be the case – I should not wish to exclude metaphysics and theology from science so understood – (3) the origins of the interests which are in a wide sense sympathetic, co-operative, altruistic and in some intimate forms erotic, interests which break down or transcend the separation of persons, whether they do so in a single case or in wider and wider circles. I believe that conscious beings cannot help developing these interests, and developing them more and more zestfully, and that, further, the zestful development of such interests goes together with increasing resistance towards such narrowing or particularisation as would impede them. The presentative interest as it grows makes us hostile to the pandering to specific interests, to irrelevant detail, to exaggerations of aspects which do not aid the vision of the whole, it leads in short to all the refinements and niceties of established aesthetic taste. The scientific interest likewise makes us hostile to irrelevant factual accumulations, to emotionalism and edification, to biassed selection of data or types of explanation, and so on. The sympathetic interest likewise, from at first taking crude forms of domination, biassed interpretation and the sheer use of others for our own purposes, becomes more and more geared to the being of the other as what he for himself is, to the acceptance of his interests and to the sharing with him of whatever he may be able to make use of. And, necessarily coming to desire these higher forms of good, we also necessarily come to desire them for everyone. Everyone, we cannot help wishing, should not only have what he most wants, but should also enjoy those widening perspectives of knowledge, those deeper immersions in aesthetic vision and those mutually fruitful relations of affection and co-operation which represent the higher sort of welfare or profit, and that he should be stimulated to develop these zests even if he has not as yet cultivated them. These higher zests are not like the zests generated by particular involvements or enterprises, which are limited to what we ourselves enjoy or do, or to the life of some small special body of colleagues and companions, they are even less like the perverse zests based on the frustration of the lower or higher interests of others or ourselves. They represent a natural extension of ordinary desire, and once formed, they are fed from innumerable sources, and soon acquire that magisterial, co-ordinating place in the human psyche which is what we mean when we call them 'rational'.

I am not going to bore you by too much elaboration of the further stages of my constitution. It will, however, involve three further chapters: (1) the constitution of justice, (2) the constitution of virtue, (3) the constitution of conscience. Justice is what comes to interest us when we try to be impartial in pursuing the lower and the higher interests of anyone and everyone. It is not confined to interpersonal relations, but includes a man's use of his own time, the range of his interests and capacities, the divergent roles of different periods of life and so on. And in interpersonal relations justice is, I think, misrepresented as being rigorously egalitarian; it involves regard for differing capacities, differing needs, and for the sheer social richness of differentiation and variety. Justice, I think, often favours élitism, even if not the élitism which depends on chance or an arbitrary grading of persons, and it is as unjust to neglect or oppress or exploit a vital social resource or contribution, as to neglect or oppress or exploit a person. Virtue, my next head, is the persistent slant of will and practice towards the valid values that I have mentioned, and it is a valid, if not a syllogistically valid, inference that those who zestfully pursue certain ends for everyone, will zestfully encourage the activities of all those who zestfully pursue those same ends, and will regard them as fine persons since their ends are fine. Such fine persons will further attract peculiar commendation and admiration in respect of the difficulties they are prepared to face, the sacrifices they are prepared to make, in the service of ends that are fine, and they will thus contribute to the cosmos a new and higher order of fineness, as precious in its way as the fineness of what they try to realise. Conscience, finally, is that fine thing which does the deciding among the innumerable, burgeoning claims of the values and disvalues which infest every situation. It is my view, following Hegel in the *Phenomenology*, and borrowing some points from Sartre, that conscience is and must be to a large extent arbitrary, that it must cut the Gordian knot made by entangled value-claims and counter-claims, and that it is, in fact, the highest exercise of voluntary freedom. There is, on my view, no complete decision-procedure for deciding among the goods and evils, actual and possible, which a practical situation projects: the only decision-procedure is that of the creative singular person, deciding among all these conflicting values and disvalues what he can personally bear or not bear to choose. And since he is not Buridan's ass, but a rational being capable of deciding among alternatives, without determining reason or preponderating inclination, and since his decision, whatever it may be, is with complete adequacy explained by his having just the disjunctive potentiality that he does have, I regard his espousal of one line, when he might have chosen others, not as a violation, but as the most perfect form of causality, and, more than that, as the highest and most nearly godlike of excellences. For what we think of as godlike need not have realised any of the particular good things that it has realised, and could very well have realised quite others, or might not have realised any, and we, in the conscientious exercise of a similar, if limited, power certainly resemble what is thought of as divinely good.

I have now completed the constitution of my valid values and disvalues. They are valid in that they can and must be a basis for practical discussion among persons, as no object of factual liking must necessarily be. They are all, however, essentially nebulous, but, like clouds, they cast shadows in definite places on the earth, and, like clouds, they can also drop on that earth the gentle rain of conscientious decisions. To cruise among those clouds is a valuable exercise even if it involves a cultivation of that sentiment which has grown distasteful to our modern liking for the hard rocks and dry deserts of scientific fact. We must, however, like Hume and Rousseau and Adam Smith and the other rational sentimentalists of the eighteenth century, continue to be bleeding-heartedly sentimental none the less. And our phenomenology, or account of the conscious appearances, must include a study of the shifting indefinitenesses of the weather at high altitudes, as well as what goes on on the surface of the earth.

H

10

ASSESSING THE VALUE
OF SAVING LIVES

Jonathan Glover

Sir, I have recently had occasion to give my support to a
local demand by parents and teachers for a patrolled crossing
over a busy road outside their children's school. I have been
appalled at what I have learned.

First, that such requests are considered on the evidence of
traffic volume, the number of children killed and injured,
and the degree of 'negligence' of a child in contributing to
his own injury. Second, the battle to justify the need for a
crossing patrol has to be fought over and over again, by each
school independently. Must we then draw up, for every
school, a profit and loss account of children killed and injured balanced against inconvenience to traffic? Traffic
volume is irrelevant, any traffic constitutes a risk. Can a
five-year-old be 'negligent' in law? A child is a child is a
child: of course he is 'negligent' – whatever that means!
Whose children are they but ours who drive the traffic?

There can be no argument. The issue is, do we suffer some
occasional inconvenience as we drive or do we prefer to risk
death and injury to our children? There is only one answer
and I am sure the police are only too painfully aware of it but
find themselves trapped in a maze of bureaucratic nonsense,
sanctified by committal to print and blessed by precedent.

The law requires that children over the age of five attend
school. Surely the law can give them protection on their way

in and out. What is the law for and who is it for and who makes it? Are we insane that we have to have laws and regulations to injure ourselves? The mind boggles at such monumental absurdity.

Clearly the law should require that every school have whatever crossing patrols are necessary to secure children's safe access; and who could wish otherwise, so why is it not so?

– a letter from Mr. J. Goode, to The Times,
7th February 1975

We, as a community and as individuals, have no coherent view of where the saving of lives should come in the order of social priorities. It is easy to mock this in the decisions and utterances of public figures. Mr. Nixon, when in office, vetoed an Abortion Bill for the stated reason that he believed in the sanctity of life, a belief which did not obstruct the Christmas bombing of Hanoi. But this kind of incoherence runs through our social life. We lavish resources on cancer research and on cigarette advertising. When a grossly abnormal baby is born, doctors agonise over whether to give the help necessary to save its life, but we allow school children to be killed in large numbers for lack of pedestrian crossings and traffic lights.

There are many assumptions underlying these policies. To list a few: Killing in war is less open to moral criticism than other killing. Killing is worse than deliberately allowing to die. A merely foreseen death is less serious than an intended one. Inciting someone to choose a policy leading to death (as by advertising cigarettes) shifts some of the blame on to the person who dies. It is more important to save the lives of known people now in peril than to reduce the number of 'statistical' lives to be lost in future.

Let us call these 'the usual assumptions'. Some of them are about the justifiability of various policies; some are about responsibility and blame; some hover uneasily between these topics. Although they are all very popular, they need not stand or fall together. Each is open to challenge, and it may be that each of them should be at least modified, or even abandoned.

But they cannot all be discussed here. It is worth looking at those policy discrepancies which do not depend on the usual assumptions.

The author of one study of industrial safety concludes that, 'while the death risk in agriculture is ten times that in pharmaceuticals and equal to that in steel handling, the prevention expenditure is not 2 per cent of that in pharmaceuticals and less than a tenth of that in steel-handling'.[1] Any comparisons of this sort need to be interpreted with caution. Prevention of fatalities is only one goal of safety expenditure, which is usually also based on the risk of other injuries. And sometimes, as in the nuclear industry, large sums are spent on safety despite a very low accident rate because, if certain accidents did occur, they would be large-scale disasters. But, despite these cautions, the point of the comparisons survives: in some contexts we are prepared to spend much more on saving a life than in others. And this involves a kind of social irrationality, since we would save more lives for the same expenditure if we lowered our standards in some areas and raised them in others.

Similar discrepancies exist within the health budget. According to one estimate, a six-monthly lung cancer screening programme for all those men in Britain who smoke fifteen or more cigarettes a day would mean that a thousand of them have an average of five years extra life each. We do not have this programme. But we do have some people on hospital kidney machines, despite the fact that this treatment has been estimated to cost more than twenty times as much for each person's extra year of life as the screening programme would cost.[2] Again, such estimates need cautious interpretation, since, apart from questions about how hospital expenses are allocated between different programmes, there is the possibility that expensive medical technology helps with training and research which will benefit future patients. But, even when all allowances are made, there cannot be any serious defence of the view that money is allocated on a thought out plan for saving the maximum number of lives. Even if we allocate three-quarters of the expense of the hospital kidney machine programme to research and training, we are still saving one life with the remaining

money for every five lives if we spent it on the screening programme instead.

Those of us who think that this is a form of social irrationality,
reflecting a general failure of clear thinking about priorities, are
inclined to raise the general question, 'how much money ought
we to spend on saving a life?' In this paper I want to look at
some possible responses to that question. In doing so, I will
suggest that the question as it stands is too simple, and should be
replaced by a complex of different questions, most of which I
shall not be able to discuss here. But I hope also to suggest that
the question is by no means as misguided as many people think.
Its usual easy dismissal is an intellectual evasion which kills
children crossing the road.

1. *The 'No Trade-off' View*

How are we to decide how much money it is right to spend on
saving lives, and at what point the necessary steps become too
expensive? Some people may feel that to ask this question at all
is an insult to human dignity. It may be said that each human
being is of infinite worth, and that it is wrong to suggest that
any pile of pound notes, however large, might be worth more
than a person. But this response, while in a way attractive, is an
evasion. For we do have to decide on priorities in our spending.
We have to say how far we are prepared to go in preferring
slower and more expensive aircraft to faster, cheaper but more
dangerous ones. And, within medicine, we have to decide how
to allocate resources between saving lives and alleviating
suffering. More kidney machines may mean worse conditions
in mental hospitals. If it is said that we must have improvements
in mental hospitals and more kidney machines, by spending
more on the health service, this is again an attractive response,
but again ultimately an evasion. For, although a strong case
can be made for giving the health service a larger share of gross
national product, the cost of giving an absolute priority to
saving any lives that can be saved, however expensively, could
have disastrous consequences in other fields. Placing an infinite
value on saving life is an evasion unless accompanied by some

indication of the likely cost in terms of poor education, bad housing, reduced social services and smaller incomes. It seems unlikely that many people would support such a policy rather than agreeing to *some* trade-off between saving lives and other social goals.

If we agree not to place an infinite value on saving a life, there is an obvious moral pressure towards finding some value which can be applied consistently in different contexts. For it is hard to see how discrepancies can be justified. Because we do not spend the money on screening smokers for lung cancer, we are in effect saying to each of the thousand people who could live, but at present die, 'We are prepared to save the life of the patient on the hospital kidney machine, but to do the same for you at one-twentieth of the cost is too expensive.' It is only by aiming at least at some rough consistency that we have any hope of avoiding objectionable results of this sort.

2. *The Role of Money and the Priority Map*

To suggest any kind of trade-off between saving lives and money may be thought objectionable, in that it may seem to involve placing too high a value on money itself. Bernard Williams has given a clear and powerful statement of this danger.[3] He says that in social decisions, 'a set of values which are, at least notionally, quantified in terms of resources, are confronted by values which are not quantifiable in terms of resources: such as the value of preserving an ancient part of a town, or of contriving dignity as well as comfort for patients in a geriatric unit. Again and again defenders of such values are faced with the dilemma, of either refusing to quantify the value in question, in which case it disappears from the sum altogether, or else of trying to attach some quantity to it, in which case they misrepresent what they are about and also usually lose the argument, since the quantified value is not enough to tip the scale.' Williams links this dilemma with the utilitarian view that there are no incommensurable values: 'Nor is it an accidental feature of the utilitarian outlook that the presumption is in favour of the monetarily quantifiable, and the other values are forced into the apologetic dilemma we have just met. It is not an accident, because (for one thing) utilitarianism is unsurprisingly the value system for a society in which economic values are supreme; and also because quantification in money is the only obvious form of what utilitarianism insists upon, the commensurability of value.'

Anyone familiar with the processes of social decision making as they operate in practice will recognise the dilemma Williams discusses. The triumphs of crude economics, and defeats for the more elusive human values, have a familiarity that can sometimes look like inevitability.

It is hard to desire a larger role for money in our society. Many people distort their lives by thinking of a 'good' job too much in terms of high pay, and too little in terms of intrinsic satisfaction. Some of us believe that social priorities are similarly distorted, with the monetary 'standard of living' being too much emphasized, while the advantages of a relaxed and uncompetitive way of life are correspondingly under-valued. Some of us prefer not to be too often conscious of money, and prefer flat rate charges, like the water rate, to pricing systems which make life into a taxi ride with the meter always ticking away. And there are people who hope that one day we will make a society where money is unnecessary.

The problem for those of us who are unenthusiastic about giving a dominant role to money is that we are likely to be pulled in two directions. It is hard not to object to the discrepancies between amounts spent in different cases, because of the arbitrariness and because of the waste of lives. But the difficulties of formulating and justifying a trade-off between lives and money, together with our reluctance to increase the role of money, may make us inclined to accept the Williams' conclusion that we are dealing with values which are simply incommensurable.

But before we accept this conclusion, it is worth distinguishing between some of the different questions involved. There are at least five issues here.

(i) Are there incommensurable values?

(ii) If values are to be systematically traded off or ranked against each other, must the unit of comparison be monetary?

(iii) If money is taken as the unit of comparison, does it follow that the more elusive human values must rank low as against 'economic' values?

(iv) Would using money as the unit of comparison involve accepting that 'economic values are supreme'?

(v) When we are considering the advantages and disadvantages of some systematic trade-off, what is the alternative policy with which we are comparing it?

The first question, of whether or not there are incommensurable values, is fundamental. The thesis that there are is often taken as obviously true. But it is a view which on closer examination turns out to be a cluster of different claims, and it is often unclear in any particular context exactly which claim is being made. The whole topic is too large to be treated in an aside here, and I will only say that I have learned from Jim Griffin[4] that the incommensurability of values is not the transparent and obvious truth people often suppose.

It seems equally unobvious that the attempt to construct a coherent policy based on systematic orderings of values and trade-offs between them must make use of money as the measuring rod. (Bernard Williams concedes that utilitarians might say that they were not committed to monetary measurement, but says that there is no other obvious form the commensurability of value could take. A consequence of believing that our thinking about these problems has barely started is that we will be prepared to look for *unobvious* forms of commensurability.)

And the answers to some of the other questions seem unclear. Where money has been taken as the unit of measurement, as in cost-benefit studies, the more elusive values have often been absurdly down-graded. But why is the hypothesis that this is inevitable to be preferred to the hypothesis that the economists have often done a crudely inadequate job? Once again, the answer is *not* obvious. And why should the choice of money as a means of expressing our priorities commit us to some view about economic values being supreme?

Our doubts about the answers to these questions may be reinforced when we consider the alternative to attempts to construct systems of commensurable values. Bernard Williams says, 'There is great pressure for research into techniques to make larger ranges of social value commensurable. Some of the effort should rather be devoted to learning – or learning again perhaps – how to think intelligently about conflicts of values which are incommensurable.' But it is not clear what this intelligent thinking would consist in. For anything which involved giving reasons for preferring the preservation of the old part of the town to some economic advantage would look disconcertingly like a reason for saying that the preservation of the area mattered more to us than the economic advantage. The incommensurability of values would allow us to give reasons in favour of one policy, and reasons in favour of the other, but leaves no room for questions of the relative weight of the two sets of reasons.

The fundamental question is one of social priorities. What is the relative importance of saving a life compared to building a new house, having an extra teacher in a school, or having a shorter working week? Perhaps the best articulation of social priorities would be an immensely complicated statement of how thousands of different goals were traded off or ranked against each other. We could then test for consistency, and also, by the discovery of counter-intuitive orderings within our system, see where revision was needed. But in practice we are far from being able to construct such a priority map. To produce a satisfactory priority map would involve having defensible answers to most of the main questions in moral and political philosophy. And the number of social goals to be included in the list (stated at the level of detail of smaller classes in schools, increasing the old-age pension, etc.) seems indefinitely long. And there are conceptual problems about how to decide which goals, and under what descriptions, should go into the priority map.

Perhaps the construction of priority maps is the major theoretical task of social philosophy. ('Maps' in the plural, because it is unlikely that a consensus will emerge about all these questions of fundamental value, and because priorities change over time. Detailed maps at least would help us to be far clearer about where we disagree.) But this major task is hardly begun. For this reason, the attractions of some convenient measuring rod such as money are bound to be great.

Those of us who do not desire a society in which 'economic values are supreme' need not oppose the use of money as a convenient measuring rod while we lack adequate priority maps. For, although cost-benefit analysis is an inadequate substitute, to reject its use in the absence of more satisfactory theoretical equipment is likely to do more harm than good. For, without either priority maps or some monetary estimate, we will be unable to modify the traditional irrationalities, with their heavy cost in extra loss of life. We can *at least* demand that, where questions arise of how much money to spend on life-saving, wasteful inconsistencies are eliminated. And this is to argue for saving lives at one price rather than another.

But, in accepting a monetary valuation of saving life as having at least a temporary role in our thinking, we must avoid one persistent simplification. This is the distortion of priorities which comes from thinking that the market value of things for sale is somehow 'real', while any value we place on things which cannot be bought is somehow speculative and insubstantial.

3. *The Alternative Approaches to the Valuation of Life-saving*

The attempts to give the saving of life some consistent position among social priorities fall into three main classes. There are intuitionist approaches, where the social decision-maker appeals either to his own intuition, or to widespread intuitions which are supposed to be reflected in various current social practices. There are approaches primarily concerned with the loss to society when someone is killed. And there are various 'preference-based' views, which try to assess how much value people themselves place on reducing risks of death.

I shall argue that the intuitionist approaches are theoretically unsatisfactory. The approaches which concentrate on the social and economic losses following a death are concerned with real aspects of the problem, but ignore the most important issues. Supporters of the preference-based views are asking the right fundamental question, but the methods of getting at people's preferences are crude, and there are conceptual difficulties which are usually slurred over.

It will be apparent that much of the argument will be negative. It would be nice to come up with some clear-cut positive solutions, but some of the problems are very complicated, and I have not been able to solve them.

4. *The Decision-maker's Intuitions*

The most common method of taking these decisions is still by intuition. Hospital authorities or doctors intuit that it is worth spending money on a heart transplant. Members of local councils and their planning departments intuit that the accident rate in a street is high enough to justify a speed limit. Someone else in the Department of Health intuits that the lung cancer screening programme would be too expensive.

There are various drawbacks to leaving the matter to the intuition of particular decision-makers. In the first place, a single person's intuitions may not add up to a coherent policy. Many people have the intuition that *of course* the crossings Mr. Goode discussed in his letter to *The Times* should be provided, but this is often combined in a single person with other intuitions: that pensions should be higher, that food should have bigger subsidies, that public spending, rates and taxes should be reduced. And intuitions are often unconsciously guided by principles that would be better if made explicit and open to criticism. It would be interesting to know to what extent the intuition that the lung cancer screening is too expensive was guided by the thought that smokers have brought their problem on themselves. Perhaps the rest of society should carry less of the cost when risks are voluntarily undertaken, but this is the kind of principle whose implications need exploring, and should not simply be unconsciously taken for granted in one particular case.

And, even if a single person's intuitions did add up to a coherent policy, this would do virtually nothing to eliminate the social irrationality of discrepancies in different contexts. For there is no reason to expect any perfect harmony between the intuitions of surgeons and civil servants, or aviation authorities and factory inspectors. For this reason, apart from any others, the objectionable discrepancies will remain as long as the question is left up to individual intuitive judgement.

5. *The Search for the Intuitive Consensus: the Law*

The intuitionist method of eliminating these discrepancies is to search for some shared valuation to be found in the existing practices of society. It is in this spirit that the economists J. Thedié and C. Abraham in their article on the economic aspect of road accidents suggest looking to court decisions 'to obtain an average opinion as regards the sums to be spent to avoid the various effective losses'.[5]

Compensation law turns out to be an unreliable guide to any social consensus about the place of saving lives in the order of priorities. In the law of tort, if I can establish that a defendant has done me an injury which reduces my expectation of life, I can recover damages on this score. These should not be confused with the damages I may also recover because I am incapacitated or unable to work. They are specifically to compensate for loss of the years I would otherwise have lived. And if I die at once, my heirs can claim damages on this score on my behalf. I was entitled to these damages, and they have a right to inherit anything to which I was entitled. Damages claimed under this head by someone's heirs are not officially intended to compensate them for any grief or loss resulting from his death.

What do courts think the appropriate compensation for losing one's life should be? In the case of Benham v Gambling (1941), a two-and-a-half-year-old child had died in a car accident. One court awarded £1,200 damages for loss of expectation of life. But this was reduced by the House of Lords to £200. The reasoning behind this was given by Viscount Simon:

> In the first place, I am of the opinion that the right conclusion is not to be reached by applying what may be called the statistical or actuarial test. In any case, the thing to be valued is not the prospect of length of days, but the prospect of a predominantly happy life. The age of the individual may, in some cases, be a relevant factor – for example – in extreme old age the brevity of what life may be left may be relevant – but, as it seems to me, arithmetical calculations are to be avoided, if only for the reason that it is of no assistance to know how many years may have been lost unless one knows how to put a value on the years. It would be fallacious to assume, for this purpose, that all human life is continuously an enjoyable thing, so that the shortening of it calls for compensation, to be paid to the deceased's estate, on a quantitative basis. The ups and downs of life, its paths and sorrows as well as its joys and pleasures – all that makes up 'life's fitful fever' – have to be allowed for in the estimate . . .
>
> The main reason, I think, why the appropriate figure of damages should be reduced in the case of a very young child is that there is necessarily so much uncertainty about the child's future that no confident estimate of prospective happiness can be made.
>
> . . . I would add that, in the case of a child, as in the case of an adult, I see no reason why the proper sum to be awarded should be greater because the social position or prospects of worldly possession are greater in one case than another. Lawyers and judges may here join hands with moralists and philosophers and declare that the degree of happiness to be attained by a human being does not depend on wealth or status. My Lords, I believe that we are all agreed in thinking that the proper figure in this case would be £200, and that even this amount would be excessive if it were not that the circumstances of the infant were most favourable.

Various aspects of these remarks seem puzzling. If we are allowed to take into account the probable life expectancy of a very old person, can we consistently ignore that of someone less old? And why is the allegedly greater unpredictability of future happiness in the case of young children a ground for reducing the damages? If the happiness is unpredictable, why is a low estimate more reasonable than a high one? And might not even those who have fairly unhappy lives, want to go on living enough to think it worth far more than £200 to do so?

Despite the oddities of the reasoning in this case, Benham v Gambling is still regarded as having established the main principles to be followed in awarding these damages. (An attempt by the Law Commission to alter this has so far not succeeded.) A further important principle was established by the House of Lords in 1967, in the case of Yorkshire Electricity Board v Naylor: damages for loss of expectation of life should not normally exceed £500. Lord Devlin justified this by the following arguments:

> Every assessment of general damage for physical injury, whether it causes loss of life or of a limb or a faculty, has got to start from the basis of a conventional sum. If it did not, assessments would be chaotic. While the loss of a single faculty, however, may be more serious for one individual than for another, the loss of all the faculties is, generally speaking, the same for all. Thus for the loss of expectation of life the conventional figure has become the norm, unless the case is definitely abnormal. What then, apart from the special case, would justify an increase or reduction in the price of happiness? No-one – least of all any lawyer – can tell. . . . The law has endeavoured to avoid two results, both of which it considered would be undesirable. The one is that a wrong doer should have to pay large sums for disabling and nothing at all for killing; the other is that the large sum appropriate to total disablement should come as a windfall to the beneficiaries of the victim's estate.

This explanation of Lord Devlin's seems finally to destroy any hope that legal compensation will help us decide how much value to set upon saving a life. If the legal sum is purely conventional, chosen *merely* to avoid chaotic assessments, it is totally unhelpful. (Though it is hard to believe that the sum was chosen quite at random: it seems unlikely that any judge would have set it at either seventy-five pence or at a million pounds.)

It is clear from Lord Devlin's reasoning that choice of an appropriate sum is distorted by a confusion of aims that besets the system of damages. It is unclear whether the function of damages is to be a kind of fine on a wrongdoer, or to compensate those who suffer loss or misfortune. The penal element seems to underline Lord Devlin's view that it would be wrong to have to pay large sums for disabling but nothing for death. But if damages are penal, great unfairness is involved. My negligence is not more wicked when it leads to a footballer losing a leg than when it leads to an office worker losing one. Why should I be more heavily punished in one case than in another? If, on the other hand, the function of damages is to compensate people for misfortune, the system is again a remarkably unfair way of doing so. If I lose a leg in a car crash that was not my fault, I can obtain damages if I can prove someone negligent or in some other way culpable. But if I cannot prove this, I lose my compensation.

There is also an obscurity about the justification for compensating people for loss of expectation of life. Why should we be compensated for having a shorter life? It is hard to see any good reason for this that would confine compensation to cases where someone else was at fault. If I contract a fatal disease, my desires and regrets are just the same whether the disease arose from my employer's negligence or from the chance arrival of a virus in my body. And, if compensation should be paid because it is felt that the quality of life can in some way make up for quantity, should we not pay larger salaries to fat males in sedentary jobs than to thin, active women?

And, even if we think that compensation for loss of expectation of life is appropriate where the person is now still alive, it seems odd to 'compensate' a dead person for the loss of his life. Perhaps unease about this has helped keep the damages so low.

But these doubts should either have been dismissed as irrelevant to the sum awarded, or else led to damages paid to the dead being assessed as nil.

Those economists who suggest that the valuation of saving a life should be guided by damages awarded for loss of life have not looked at how the system works. The reasons given for the assessment of these awards appeal to considerations that are of no relevance to the decisions about social priorities that concern us. Court awards are totally unhelpful here.

6. *The Search for the Intuitive Consensus: Extrapolation from 'Best' Policies*

An alternative intuitionist approach, which aims not so much to discover a social consensus as to generate one, has considerable appeal. This method consists in seeing what sums are now spent on saving lives in particular contexts, and suggesting that in other similar contexts the spending should be brought into line. Such a policy would be based on the work of T. Craig Sinclair, whose comparisons of safety standards in different industries have been mentioned. The implicit valuation placed on saving lives in one industry may be unfavourably compared with that in another, with the suggestion that it should be raised to the same level.

Despite the technical difficulties of making these comparisons, this approach is attractive for reasons both of effectiveness and fairness. To harmonise the policies of different industries in this way leads to the money spent on safety being directed to where it will save most lives. And it eliminates the unfairness of arbitrarily giving a higher priority to the safety of some than of others.

But this approach still leaves the central theoretical problem unanswered. When tacit evaluations of life-saving conflict, why should the lower one go up rather than the higher one go down? To regard the highest evaluation as the one to aim for implies that safety is usually given too low a priority. But, too low by what standards? If most of the intuitive judgements that are made are wrong, how do we tell good intuitions from bad?

It appears that the intuitionist approach can at best only hope to eliminate objectionable discrepancies between different evaluations. But intuitionism seems unlikely to provide any satifying justification for the decision about which evaluation should be taken as the norm. There are so many different intuitions here, that sceptical questions about the claim on us of any consensus can be left on one side.

7. *Economists and Loss to Society*

Some economists think of the problem mainly in terms of the economic loss to society resulting from a death. Various methods of measuring this have been proposed. One, sometimes known as the method of judging by 'gross output', involves calculating the gross earnings the dead person would have had over his life, discounted to the present.[6] There is obviously something much too rough and ready about the assumption that gross income is a measure of gross output. And, even if it were, large questions would be begged about the usefulness of the output. And losses of a non-economic nature (to his wife, or to friends who liked his conversation or his cheerfulness) are excluded. And there is the morally dubious priority this method gives to saving the lives of the rich: it seems to justify us in spending more to improve the safety of a millionaire's private aircraft than on fire prevention in dozens of old people's homes.

Another method is that of judging by 'net output'. Estimated gross future consumption is subtracted from estimated gross future output.[7] This has the advantage over the gross output method of giving a clearer picture of the economic loss to surviving members of society when someone dies. But, if taken as the sole measure, it has the consequence of placing a negative value on saving the life of someone who does not produce: an old-age pensioner or someone permanently unemployed through disability. As with the gross output method, non-economic losses are ignored.

There are obviously large difficulties in working out for any single person a balance sheet of the ways in which, even in narrowly economic terms, he gives to and takes from society.

And the difficulties in placing a value on grief and the more human losses are even more obvious. But the central objection does not depend on these difficulties. It is that these approaches, at least on their own, seem to miss the main point of saving lives by taking no account of the perspective of the person whose life is in question. And this distortion only grows more absurd when economists go on to do their calculations with great precision and technical refinement. (The most engaging piece of refinement is that introduced by R. G. Ridker,[8] who in assigning a cost to a death, includes a sum for 'premature burial', on the grounds that we can apply some rate of discount to funeral expenses in the future rather than now.)

I shall assume that any acceptable view of the relative social priority of life saving will have to be centred upon the desirability of averting a death from the point of view of the person whose life it is. For this reason, the preference-based views to be discussed in a moment are the most attractive. And the calculations of general losses to society will at most play a secondary role in the decision.

But at this point a doubt must be mentioned: should the losses to other people play a role in decisions about life-saving at all? Some philosophers may be inclined to object that this will involve a kind of double-counting. There is a general claim here that calculations about the interests of a group of people are distorted if weight is given to 'other-regarding' as well as to 'self-regarding' desires.

There are large questions here, which again cannot be treated in an aside. On the one hand it seems absurd in social decision making to give weight to someone's desire to work in quiet surroundings, but to give no weight to his desire not to lose his wife in an air crash. But on the other hand, there are many situations, perhaps including the allocation of scarce medical resources, where we attach some importance to an atmosphere of equality between people, which could not survive too much fine calculation about how many dependants they have. I offer no views here about how we should resolve these difficult value-conflicts.

8. *Preference-based Views*

The question which is central to the whole problem is also the one which is conceptually the most difficult: how much does the person in question value either the saving of his life, or the reduction of some risk to his life?

When we think about this intuitively, taking our own case, things that at first sight seemed obvious start to look less and less clear. One apparent platitude is that most of us would pay almost anything to avoid certain death, or at least would pay up to the point where poverty made life no longer worth living. But is this really true when we discard the point of view of an abstract individual, and think of real people living in families. Would not such considerations as the effect of poverty on the whole family perhaps set narrower limits to what many people would be prepared to spend on saving their own lives?

Another apparent platitude is that the proportion of income people would be prepared to spend would be directly proportioned to the degree of risk to life that would be averted. This may be so at some risk-levels for people with some income levels, but when we think about actual cases the supposed platitude is far less obvious. I would pay almost as much to avoid a one in three risk of death as to avoid certain death, and risks below one in a thousand start to look rather similar to each other again, while a fairly steep decline in anxiety goes on between the region of very high risk and this lower risk region. It may be that a better intuitive grasp of probabilities would change this, and would make me willing to spend always in direct proportion to the risk averted. But is this really obvious? How can we tell?

The difficulties of these judgements have led some economists to discuss sources of empirical information about people's preferences. The crudest proposal is to study the sums people will pay to insure their lives. This is obviously hopeless, as the *best* conclusions we could draw from such data would be about the value people place on the welfare of their dependants after their own deaths.

A more satisfactory source of information is to ask people hypothetical questions about what they would spend to bring about various different reductions of risk to their lives, together with what they would regard as adequate compensation for some additional degree of risk. This approach is more satisfactory because at least it involves trying to get at people's judgements about the right questions. But questionnaires have familiar inadequacies, and people's answers to hypothetical questions are notoriously different from their choices in actual situations.

One way of avoiding this problem is to study consumer behaviour where real choices involve decisions about the importance of avoiding risks. At what level of danger money will people be willing to take on high risk jobs as against similar jobs with lower levels of risk? How much more will people pay for a ticket on a reliable airline than one known to use older and less reliable aircraft? How much more will people pay for cars with extra safety features? But again the imperfections of this kind of evidence need no emphasis. Does not the evidence about danger money as an incentive to taking risky jobs depend a lot on factors such as the availability of other jobs? Can we really suppose that people choosing between cars have usually looked at the relative accident figures? How much intuitive grasp do people have of differences between the low levels of risk involved in flying with one airline or another?

Those who have proposed looking at market behaviour for information here, such as T. C. Schelling,[9] have shown themselves aware of these problems. Neither the method of hypothetical questions, nor the method of studying market choices, is more than very inadequate. We can certainly take note of what such studies suggest, on the principle that inadequate evidence is better than no evidence. The inadequacy of the answers so far should not be allowed to obscure the fact that the right sort of question is being asked. What is most needed here is some decent work on better methods of answering it.

Notes

1 T. Craig Sinclair, *A Cost-Effectiveness Approach to Industrial Safety*, London, 1972.

2 These estimates come from Gerald Leach, *The Biocrats*, Harmondsworth, 1972, Ch. 11.

3 *Morality, An Introduction to Ethics*, Harmondsworth, 1973, pp. 102–3.

4 In an unpublished paper of his called 'Are there Incommensurable Values?'

5 *Traffic Engineering and Control*, 1961, quoted in A. R. Prest and R. Turvey, 'Cost Benefit Analysis: A Survey', *Economic Journal*, 1965.

6 Cf. D. J. Reynolds, 'The Cost of Road Accidents', *Journal of the Royal Statistical Society*, 1956.

7 Cf. R. F. R. Dawson, *The Cost of Road Accidents in Great Britain*, Road Research Laboratory, 1967.

8 *The Economic Costs of Air Pollution*, New York, 1967, quoted in E. J. Mishan, 'Evaluation of Life and Limb: A Theoretical Approach', *Journal of Political Economy*, 1971.

9 T. C. Schelling, 'The Life You Save May Be Your Own', in S. B. Chase (ed.), *Problems in Public Expenditure Analyses*, Brookings Institute, 1969.

INDEX